Make it Happen!

Bob Duffy *with* Natalie June Reilly

A Bob Duffy Book
Published by Bob Duffy
P.O. Box 5647
Carefree, AZ 85377

All rights reserved under International and Pan-American Copyright Conventions.
Published/Manufactured in the United States of America
Cover design by Sean Reilly
Cover photo by Brad Reed
Edited by Lilia Ortiz

For Mom and Dad

"Your ability to bounce back continuously, to force and control the situation despite overwhelming odds is what really counts. That is greatness."

~Robert M. Waldbillig, Captain, USAF

*St. Louis Hawks, Bob Duffy (#24), takes a jump shot
at Kiel Auditorium against the Syracuse Nats in 1962.*

TESTIMONIALS

SPORTS

When I was a high school player in Lyons, New York, Bob Duffy was a nearby legendary player. Later in my life I see why he was so successful in many ways (academic, coaching, business, and, most importantly, philanthropy.) A great instructional read ... Make it Happen.

—**Jim Boeheim**, selected to Basketball Hall of Fame, head coach of the men's basketball team at Syracuse University

I first knew Bob Duffy as a collegiate opponent coach. It is interesting that we, at different times, played for the Detroit Pistons. I am aware of Bob's respected reputation and broadcasting business success and, more importantly, his philanthropic achievements.

—**Dave Bing**, selected to Basketball Hall of Fame, Founder of Bing Steel Company, former Mayor of Detroit

Bob set the standard of excellence for those of us who played basketball for Colgate in the years following his outstanding career. He is the inspirational example of how to convert the pursuit of excellence into business success, and then, through his charitable gifts of time, talent and financial treasure, how to convert that success into benefits to others.

—**Robert L. Tyburski**, Vice President and Sr. Advisor Secretary Board of Trustees, Colgate University

BUSINESS

I have been in the investment world for over thirty years. It is a people business and I was so fortunate to work with Bob Duffy very early on in my career. Bob taught me a lot about inspiring and motivating people, management of dynamic organizations and leadership. For that experience, I will be forever grateful.

—**Paul J Finnegan**, Co-CEO, Madison Dearborn Partners

Bob Duffy's life is a true American success story. From the vantage point of friend, colleague and client I have observed the many skills that have allowed him to excel as an athlete, broadcaster, entrepreneur, and community leader. His ability to attract outstanding people who share his competitive spirit and vision led to a track record of enviable achievement.

—**William Clark**, CEO and Chairman of Shamrock Broadcasting owned by the Roy Disney family.

PHILANTHROPY

Working with Bob Duffy as the chair of Scottsdale Healthcare Foundation was the highlight of my career. His innate leadership ability lifted our Trustees to new heights and his interpersonal skills were invaluable in working with donors and with our staff. Bob brought a positive, "can-do" attitude to every aspect of his chairmanship and it was all borne out in the new Trustees he attracted and in the philanthropy he solicited.

—**John Ferree**, President of Honor Health Foundation

Whatever Bob Duffy sets out to do, you can be assured that it will be done well. As a Trustee of the Heard Museum, he worked effectively to promote the museum, especially in his leadership of a highly successful annual charity golf tournament that supported the Museum's educational programs. The keys to Bob's success are always the same--- he pays attention to every detail, he inspires others to follow his example of hard work and he treats everybody with respect and good fellowship.

—**Frank Goodyear**, Former Director of The Heard Museum

GROWING UP

As a young lad, I knew Bob Duffy. He was a great star, very competitive. Our fathers were part of a group that founded the Katonah, NY Little League, which was great for many kids. Bob was a pitcher. A classmate of my older brother, Richie, Bob made the most of his opportunities including being a great inspiration on the basketball court. As a banker I watched him succeed in the broadcasting business, as well as many philanthropic activities. Thanks to Bob for showing us, in this book, how these attributes cross the lines from sports to business to philanthropy, leading to success!

—**Bob Mueller**, Senior Executive Officer, The Bank of New York (retired)

I have known Bobby Duffy since my preteen age. I remember that he was the only student at John Jay High School to wear a coat and tie every day. In business, I know of his enormous broadcasting success at Eastman, Christal, & Duffy Broadcasting. In sum, he is "a quality gentleman," and *MAKE IT HAPPEN* is a quality read!

—**John Suhler**, Co-founder of Veronis & Suhler Capital Market Co.

PREFACE

The grandfather clock is chiming with its count of seven, as that is the early morning hour on this, the first day of January 2014 that I take pen in hand and begin writing down notable events of my life. It doesn't take long for the significant obstacles that occurred to surface, and just as a smooth pebble skips across the placid surface of a pond, it occurs to me that those "obstacles" have had a profound ripple effect on my life. Not only did they provide me with the learning experience I needed to achieve, but they serve as a reminder of the exceptional life I might not have had without them.

I considered writing this book many years ago, so that I might share my life's achievements with my daughters, Kim and Julie. I thought they might appreciate how some of my experiences impacted their own. I also had my grandchildren, Jack and Erin, in mind. It is my hope that my story can be of some benefit to the fulfillment of their dreams.

It may have been the memory of my late wife, Bella Werner Duffy, who prompted my pen. She felt strongly that my life experience could inspire others to achieve their dreams. Bella passed away from lung cancer before I ever took to telling my story. For the last sixty days of her life, she faced death with great courage and resolve. She was an incredible example, a model for how to bravely, and with a full heart accept the inevitable. It was her resolve that sharpened my own, urging me to move forward with this book.

Friends and past associates have also rallied behind me, encouraging this endeavor. Their interest in my story gave me the additional motivation I needed. While considering the challenge of writing a book, as well as the time and effort it would take, I focused on two solid reasons to make the commitment. First, I figured the process could serve as a catharsis, validating how I was able to make multiple good decisions throughout my life, despite the many risks involved, and how I was able to find extraordinary success in a short period of time. Secondly, I had the comfort of research to back me up via the press, and many personal letters addressed to me from those in the world of sports, business and philanthropy. Citing facts from credible sources assures the reader of authenticity and truth.

The title of this book, *Make it Happen*, has been a reoccurring theme in my life. It has been my motto for as long as I can remember. From the time I was a young boy living in a small town, driven by the dream of becoming a professional athlete, to a time when I was a businessman, a radio professional breathing life back into a dying business, or a retired entrepreneur focused on making a difference in my community, the goal was always to "Make it happen!"

I am excited to share my life experience with you, along with the valuable lessons I learned along the way. No matter what your dream is, or where you begin, the world is a competitive place. Achievement must be earned! You have to put in the work. It requires bold decisions, calculated risks, dealing with random circumstance, and adjusting to the reality of setbacks. It takes action, even on those days when you feel you have nothing to give. As I reflect on these points, I realize how each played a significant role in my own achievement. I hope that by reading my story, you will see that you are capable of anything that you set your heart and mind to, if you'll only remain focused on your goal, believe in yourself, and stay positive! Obstacles, though inevitable, can and will be overcome, so long as you remain persistent. If you do these things, you can achieve your dreams!

My parents, Joe and Marian Duffy, taught me that life is what you make it. It doesn't matter where you come from. It only matters where you are headed. Mom and Dad were products of the Great Depression, unable to afford a college education for themselves. The Duffy family lived modestly, though we were rich in the love that was given to us. My parents provided me and my brothers, Rich and Don, with an abundance of encouragement, and direction. They were committed to us Duffy boys, particularly to our future. There was never any doubt about that.

The greatest gift Mom and Dad ever gave my brothers and me was their time. Their support and involvement in our lives inspired a great deal of confidence, instilling in all three of us the daring to dream big, and the grit to create a better life. In my mind, it was their dedication, determination, and desire that fueled us all to succeed. And so, this book, at its heart, was written in their honor, as much as it was written for you, my reader, so that you might go after your dreams with one goal in mind, to "make it happen!"

GROWING UP

Growing up takes guts, grit, and good parenting.

Pictured left to right: Don, Rich, Bob, Marion & Joe Duffy

ONE

The Katonah Kid

If you are loved, you are rich enough.

Madison Square Garden was a one hour train ride away from the small town of Katonah, New York where I grew up. However, in the young, impressionable mind of a boy with a dream of playing professional basketball in the NBA, it may as well have been a rocket trip to the moon. As big as my dreams were, it wasn't likely that a kid like me would ever play professional ball in The Garden, let alone have the train fare to get there. The odds of being drafted into the NBA, even in its early days, were never in my favor. But that didn't stop me from living and breathing basketball. It didn't stop me from believing that it could happen. After all, some of the greatest success stories in history started from such humble beginnings.

I was born September 26, 1940 in Cold Spring, New York

a tiny township that sat at the deepest point of the Hudson River. I arrived just a little more than six years before the birth of the NBA. I was given the name Robert Joseph Duffy, but like all young men, was put on this planet to make a name for myself. At least that was the expectation in the Duffy household.

My mother, Marian Elizabeth Duffy, was 26 years old when she had me. I was her firstborn. She would often regale in the day we met, sharing with me how her hospital bed faced the most exquisite view of West Point — the United States federal military installation, turned military academy established by Thomas Jefferson in 1802. It was the tail end of The Great Depression, a much-needed turning-point toward recovery for the world market.

Cold Spring, much like the rest of the world, had fallen upon hard times. For more than a decade the newspaper headlines told how the world's economy had hit an all-time low and unemployment had hit an all-time high. Cities all around the world came to a crashing halt, particularly those whose manufacturers were involved in heavy industry. Rural areas, farmers mainly, suffered the most. Crop prices fell, and people's spirits right along with them. Those were tough times. However, the people who lived through them were tougher, including my parents. I was a product of my time in that, like the straining economy, it would be my struggle to achieve that would essentially define me. And it would be my love for the game of basketball, and my parents love for me, that would take me from the most modest of beginnings to a life that has been quite special.

In those days, Mom and Dad didn't lead a handsome life. It was a modest one at best, but by all accounts, it was good. They met while working at the Wingdale State Asylum. Mom worked as a nurse, and dad as an athlete. While she would care for the patients, he would entertain them with his incredible ball-handling and batting skills. Mom and Dad eventually fell in love and were married in Buffalo, New York on October 9, 1936. Mom left her job and stayed home to care for me. Dad picked up the financial slack by working two jobs and returning to school in his spare time, which was usually a random accumulation of evenings and weekends. He was determined to advance himself professionally. He and my mother's younger brother, Don Howerth, drove three hours round-trip to New York City every week to take evening courses on the topic of law enforcement. Dad wanted to be a police officer.

Somewhere in between working two jobs and going to school, he landed a position at the Great Meadow Correctional Facility in Comstock, New York as a prison guard. He was paid to secure hardened criminals, the likes of whom were a real menace to society. He kept watch over guys like Lucky Luciano, the father of modern organized crime in the United States. It was a hazardous job, one that would lead to his being stabbed in the gut by an angry inmate. Fortunately, Dad survived the attack. While it may have shaken his confidence, it didn't keep him from returning. As soon as he healed, he went right back to his duties as a prison guard. I'm not sure if that made him hard-headed or hard-wearing, either way I grew up wanting to be just as determined as he was.

In 1942 Dad was hired as a police officer in the New York township of Bedford, which consisted of three separate towns known as Katonah, Bedford Hills and Bedford Village. When I was just two years old we moved to his hometown of Katonah, a quaint, little hamlet with a tiny train station that connected our rural roots to Manhattan's Grand Central Station. The three of us settled into a small apartment nestled over the Kellogg and Lawrence Hardware Store downtown. The building, as well as the store are both still in existence today — all these years later.

In May of 1943 the three of us, soon to be four, as Mom was pregnant with my younger brother Rich, moved from downtown Katonah into a humble, little 1,482 square-foot house in the suburbs — 36 Huntville Road. Mom and Dad rented the clean, modest residence from my paternal grandfather, Joseph Patrick Duffy. It was one of three properties that Grandpa Duffy owned as a result of saving his earnings as a blacksmith. I spent the better part of my childhood in that house, up until the time I left for college. My younger brother Rich was born July 27, 1943, nearly three years after me. Like me, he grew up participating in youth sports. He was an outstanding catcher in baseball, a scoring guard in basketball, and a terrific quarterback in football. College scouts showed an interest in Rich's early sports career. Syracuse University picked him up, giving him a full basketball scholarship. Rich was strong, determined and very competitive. After college he was drafted by the Detroit Tigers baseball club as a catcher. I was always proud of him.

My little brother, Joseph, was born in 1946. He died that same year — a hiccup in time. I was young, no more than six years old when we lost him — bless my Mother's heart. I remember it being particularly hard on her. The memory of my little brother's death is still very clear. Mom had placed Joseph beneath the cool shade of a lilac tree in the front yard to sleep. When she returned to bring him inside after a short while, he had passed away. Mom and Dad were devastated, and yet they saw their way through their grief so to protect my brother Rich and me from too much emotional damage. It's hard to describe the sort of sadness that seeps into a home when a child dies. Many tears were shed. Watching my parents, two of the sturdiest people I knew, deal with their loss was especially difficult. As the firstborn son I felt an unspoken demand to be strong, but losing Joseph was more than I could wrap my young heart and mind around. I still think about him to this day, and wonder what kind of man he would have been. I like to think that he, too, would have shared our families affinity for sports and that all of us brothers would have become great friends. Joseph was third in line of the Duffy boys, and the first to be called up to heaven.

Don, the youngest of the brood, was born September 1, 1947, just a little more than a year after we lost Joseph. He spent the first two years of his life in the hospital. Born with a blockage to his stomach, Don had a lot of health issues. After being released from the hospital, Don contracted polio, a viral disease that led to partial paralysis. This was devastating to his childhood. Nevertheless, Don never let it obstruct his resolve. He was determined, particularly when it came to sports. Even though he never got to participate, he always loved rooting for those who did, no one more than the New York Yankees, the New York Knicks and his two big brothers. I don't know if it was because he was born with that fighting Irish spirit or because he wanted to keep up with Rich and I, but Don was one of the first people to prove to me that not much can detour a kid with a positive attitude.

TWO

The Love of the Game

Make a living doing what you would otherwise do for free.

Sports were my first love. I was particularly smitten with baseball and basketball. I had a long love affair with both, giving them my heart and soul and the better part of my youth and innocence. The NBA was born June 6, 1946. I was scarcely six years old, growing up in a small suburb in the shadow of New York City. I was ruined for all other careers the day I learned I could get paid to be a professional athlete. I wanted to be one of the greats. By the time I reached adolescence, both baseball and basketball were in my blood. The thought of playing professional ball is what got me out of bed in the morning. It got me through the day. And at night, I took that big orange ball to bed with me. I would stretch out onto my bed, one hand tucked behind my head, and I'd chuck that thing up into the air and catch it with the same

7

hand. I would do this over and over again until my arm ached. Then I would switch hands and repeat the process. I did the same thing with a baseball. I'd chuck that ball up in the air and catch it over and over again until I could catch it with my eyes closed. Since I wasn't born with exceptional height or skill, I was bound and determined to develop the parts of me that I *was* born with. After all, success in any one thing — whether it's baseball, basketball, or business — doesn't happen by accident. While random circumstance can certainly play a role, it takes a great deal of patience, practice and persistence to become a success.

You also need to be fearless in the face of adversity, not putting too much stock in what others think of you. Believe it or not, not everyone is going to root for your success, not even some of your closest friends or family. While I had a lot of support from my parents, I had my share of naysayers. I was often told that I was too small to go pro. Not only that, but I didn't show a whole lot of promise in the classroom. According to public opinion, things weren't looking good for me. The unsolicited and, sometimes, negative perceptions of others can easily crush a young boy's dream. Those voices get inside his head, and if he allows them to stay there, it can ruin any chance he has of making his dream happen. Thank goodness for my parents' belief in me. It was their positive reinforcement that drowned out all the other noise. It was their belief in me that gave me confidence.

Much of what I know and love about sports can be directly attributed to my Dad. He was an exceptional athlete. I looked up to him. When he wasn't working as a police officer, he was coaching varsity baseball and basketball at St. Mary's Catholic High School. I spent much of my free time watching him coach the varsity boys. I used to pretend that I was one of them.

When Dad wasn't patrolling the streets or coaching high school sports, he was organizing and managing many of the local baseball and basketball leagues for Katonah. Those leagues were a big part of our township, not to mention a better part of what connected us to surrounding townships. It was that special brand of competition that brought neighboring settlements together for some friendly competition. As a kid I didn't know a lot about what was going on in the world, but I knew enough to understand that whatever *was* going on could be set aside long enough to squeeze in a ballgame or two. Those local leagues brought our community a lot of joy. No one got a kick out them more than the players themselves, young men between the ages of 18 and 35.

Over time many of those young men outgrew their baseball and basketball careers, but continued to live for years off of the memories that came from competing. We all took pride in our teams, so much so that towns would collect money to pay their players to perform. These semi-pro ballplayers went to the highest bidder for the season and, in some cases, depending upon how important the contest was, for one game. And, when players struggled to make ends meet, a hat was passed around the crowd to collect the financial support needed to cover personal expenses.

These leagues were a significant part of who we were as a

community. It was an important part of my childhood. One year I was hired as a batboy. It was my first real job. I was paid a small stipend, as if I needed money for that opportunity! I would have done it for free. Money couldn't buy me enough bubble gum and baseball cards to compensate for the thrill I got from carrying around baseball bats for these guys. Nobody had a better seat in the house than I did. My experience as a batboy was a stepping stone on my path to becoming a professional athlete. It introduced me to the possibility of making a living doing something I would otherwise do for free. This was an enormous lesson. From that point on, I pursued the life of a professional athlete.

THREE

Hard-Wired for Success

Hard work becomes you.

Opportunity has two very important elements, the first being random circumstance and the second being hard work. Because my Dad was a police officer, his path crossed with all sorts of interesting people, many of whom he considered to be a part of his inner-circle of friends. As his firstborn son, I was fortunate in that I was able to glean some pretty amazing opportunities from this inner-circle. These connections were, indeed, an incredible gift for a kid like me. They were circumstances beyond my control that thrust me in the direction of my dream. There were days I got to visit some of the wealthiest estates in New York and, in turn, got to meet some pretty impressive people. Among the most impressive, at least by the standards of a schoolboy in the late 1940s, was Mel Allen, the Voice of the New York Yankees. Mr. Allen was one of the most famous play-by-play sportscasters of his time. He and Dad developed a special friendship over the years and it was because of *that* connection that Dad and I were often invited to Yankee Stadium to watch the New York Yankees play ball. It was one of the greatest things to ever happen to a kid like me. We sat behind home-plate, high up in the announcer's booth with Mr. Allen while he called the game. Those were the days of Mickey Mantle, centerfielder and first baseman for the Yankees. Mantle was my idol. I wanted to be just like him!

Every time I visited Yankee Stadium I would focus on that pinstriped uniform, picturing it as a part of my future. I knew playing professional ball would be a long shot. It would also be a lot of hard work. There's just no way to get around the struggle of achieving one's dream. Everyone, even the likes of Mickey Mantle, has to pay their dues. The good news was I was no stranger to struggle. I knew what it meant to work hard. I have Mom and Dad to thank for that. They fostered a robust work ethic in our home, beginning with a daily routine of household chores.

As a kid you don't really connect the dots as to how helping your parents around the house can actually help you succeed later on in life, but the truth is those menial chores help to develop a good, solid work ethic. In that respect, the Duffy boys were hard-wired for success. Expectations ran high in our household and there wasn't a whole lot of room for negotiation. Discipline was a meaningful branch of parenting, so it behooved us kids to do as we were told. It wouldn't be until years later, when I became a parent myself, that I would realize what a gift that lesson was. Times were different then. Children were expected to share in the house-hold responsibilities, and while we didn't always like it, we certainly knew better than to question our parents' authority — out loud anyway. Mom and Dad were a part of the GI generation, a cohort of folk who grew up children of World War I and The Great Depression. At the time, the world was experiencing some serious growing pains: economically, politically, racially and religiously. The GI generation was an energetic group, the original go-getters of their time. They were doers! And so we Duffy boys were raised in kind. Like my parents, we were expected to work hard for what we had.

Both Mom and Dad held down two jobs while raising three boys. And while they never made headlines, history books or established great wealth, they did provide a good life and a good example for us boys. Looking back my parents knew exactly what they were doing when they began delegating household chores, and encouraging us boys to pick up odd jobs in the community. Growing up I mowed lawns, shoveled snow and even cleaned windows for local residents in Katonah. It was a lot of work for little money. However, the money I made did buy me certain freedom, which begged the question, "What if I had even more money?"

When I was just 16 years old, Dad found me a summer job at the local golf and tennis club. As I mentioned, Dad had developed all kinds of relationships in the community, one of which was with the superintendent of the Bedford Village Golf and Tennis Club. It was that particular connection that got me the job.

I think he and Mom were more excited about it than I was, since the hours would cut into my summer vacation.

Like clockwork Mom would drag me out of bed at 5 o'clock every morning. She would feed me breakfast and then drive me to the club. It was a 10 mile commute on narrow, winding roads. Punching a time clock became my routine — the religion of the working class. While it wasn't exactly how I wanted to spend my summer break, I learned a lot about the demands of physical labor. Mostly, I learned that I did *not* want to spend my life working for somebody else. There had to be a better way. At 16 years old, I wanted more control over my future, and I was bound and determined to find a way!

FOUR

You Better Believe It

Mindset, even more than money, makes a man wealthy.

The good news was I didn't have to look far to see that it was possible to have control of my own future. Financial independence ran in my family, sort of. As it turned out, my Grandpa Duffy was a savvy entrepreneur who ran his business out of the trunk of his car. You wouldn't know it by looking at him, but in addition to his trade as a blacksmith, he soaked much of his hard-earned money into three separate housing properties, renting two of them for extra income. Grandpa Duffy had no formal education, but what he did have was a good head for business, and like many a good Irishman, a great deal of pride. He worked hard shoeing horses, saving a good percentage of what he earned.

Grandpa Duffy was strong. The man had big forearms as a result of his work. He spent long days lifting a large anvil, building fires, and handling horses. And he knew that when it came to investing his hard-earned money, real estate was a smart idea. He worked hard, but he also worked smart. And so while the man died with calloused hands from years of manual labor as a blacksmith, he left my grandmother an amount of two hundred thousand dollars, all of which had been deposited in several bank accounts throughout Westchester County. That was a lot of money in those days, especially for a laborer.

I like to think that I inherited some of Grandpa Duffy's business-sense. After working a handful of summers as his apprentice, I wouldn't doubt that some of his work ethic rubbed off on me, as did some of the soot. Grandpa Duffy and I spent a lot of time together working for wealthy landowners on rolling green estates in Westchester County, New York. He exposed me to real wealth at a young age. Many of those landowners came from old money. They were known for hosting elaborate parties which were publicized in the papers as being the social events of the season. You wouldn't find my name on any of their guest lists, but you would find me — the blacksmith's apprentice — tending to their horses, and occasionally rubbing elbows with the wealthy landowners themselves. My presence on those affluent estates was much more inconspicuous than the politician or the movie star. However, in my mind, it was no less special. Working on those estates gave me a vision as to what my life could look like, so long as I had the audacity to believe it. It was just the sort of exposure to make the ambition of a young boy like me unstoppable. And it was not hard to see what separated the wealthy man from the poor man — money and mindset. That is all it is and all it will ever be.

A man can make money his whole life and never know great wealth. However, if his head is in the right place, as well as his heart, the money will follow. I could see it in the steady gait of those high-powered industrialists. Their net worth, what made them wealthy people, was something born on the inside of them, long before it materialized in their bank accounts. I could see it in their confidence, in the way they spoke and in the way they carried themselves.

One of the most impressive of all the estates where I had the privilege of working as a kid was the Rockefeller estate in Pocantico Hills, New York. This was the home to John D. Rockefeller, renowned oil tycoon and American business magnate. It was magnificent! The house looked like a castle. It was enormous and magical, designed originally as a steep-roofed three-story stone mansion. It was situated on 249 acres that spooned up against the Hudson River, as if doing the famed waterway a favor. The entire estate was nearly as big as my birthplace in Cold Spring, New York, not to mention just a mere 28.7 miles south of there. It might as well have been a million miles away from the life I knew.

Men like John D. Rockefeller motivated me to think big. And while I wasn't exactly sure what a kid like me would have to do to achieve financial independence, I had enough sense in me to know that achieving such a dream would be hard work. I had nothing against the working class. After all, my parents and people like them built this country in such a noble way. However, I wanted more control of my future and I was more determined than ever to make it happen! However, I would first have to conquer grammar school.

FIVE

An Educated Man

Get a good edge-ucation.

Katonah was an idyllic place to grow up. It was peaceful and safe, a sublime piece of landscape set in the late 40s and 50s. My days in grammar school were particularly impressionable. Those years were the beginning, and nearly the end of my academic career. The truth was, when it came to school, I wasn't all that invested. I was an average student. I made the grade, but I had no desire to focus on my studies. It wasn't that I was failing. It was just that I was more concerned, if not consumed with sports. Katonah High School was a combination school at the time, housing kindergarten through the 12th grade under one roof. Katonah wasn't a big town. In fact, I estimate that the entire population was less than 3,000 people, including me.

Our class size was small. And while that made for a better

learning environment, it made it hard to be invisible. The teachers of Katonah High School were especially committed to a child's education. They weren't afraid to exercise discipline when necessary, which, incidentally, was a meaningful branch of learning in those days. I was raised "old school," a time when children respected their elders. When you were told to do something, you didn't take it into consideration. You just did it. We were brought up to be respectful and obedient of authority. There was not a whole heck of a lot of room for negotiation in that regard.

From kindergarten through to sixth grade, I was an underachiever — academically-speaking. Like most boys my age, I was more concerned with balls than books. Playing ball was a boy's business, and if what I was doing didn't involve running bases or shooting hoops, I wasn't interested. My time and energy was best applied on a baseball field or a basketball court, and so the first 11 years of my life were spent to that end. Sports were like a drug, and the fact that they were so accessible to me did nothing for my desire to achieve in the classroom. If anything, being the "coach's kid" only fueled my desire to focus on sports. I'm sure my parents and teachers would have loved to see me exude as much passion and energy into my schoolwork. However, in my mind, there was no comparing the two. Sports were my life. School was a distraction. And if I had to choose between the two, sports would win every day of the week, and twice on game day!

Unlike school, baseball and basketball came easy to me. By

the age of 12, my name was making local papers. Jimmy Powers, longtime sports editor of The Daily News out of New York City, and a journalist who supplemented the reach of his "Powerhouse" column with a parallel career as a boxing commentator on NBC television's Gillette Friday Night Fights, wrote, "Bobby Duffy, age 12, of Katonah, pitched two no-hitters in his first two Little League starts at Bedford, N.Y."

As I transitioned into the seventh grade, I hit that awkward stage of pubescence. My limbs got lanky. My voice changed. I started noticing girls. I was developing as both a young man and as a ballplayer. I was so consumed with all of those recent developments that I didn't even see her coming, the spark that would light up my academic world. Her name was Maureen Costello. She was an enthusiastic, young schoolteacher who had been hired by the town of Katonah to teach and inspire its middle school students. She personalized her teachings to fit the needs of each of us as individuals. I didn't realize it at the time, but she would inspire my desire to learn. Ms. Costello had such a zest for life and learning, a gift she handed down to me and many of her students. She lived in Mahopac, New York, which at the time was quite a distance away from Katonah. There were no major highways between our two towns. There were only trains and two lane winding back-roads, both of which necessitated a long commute.

Miss Costello was dedicated to the teaching profession, making my initial resistance to participate in her classroom almost pointless. It was her brand of enthusiasm, kindness and overall passion that helped me to develop good study habits and a real appetite for learning. My parents were thrilled since sports, up until to that point had ruined me for education. It didn't take me long to realize, however, how much easier life was in the classroom when I actually applied myself. Similar to sports, I finally saw the classroom as a field designed for competition, an arena that had me competing academically against myself and others. I liked that!

Not only did Miss Costello change my mind about learning, but she essentially changed my life. This wonderful teacher came from a big, Irish family. As it happened, she had a younger brother named Joseph who was my age. Joe was special, someone I had met while playing organized basketball in the sixth grade. Like Little League baseball, the Catholic Youth Organization provided basketball competitions for young boys to compete and to develop their ball-handling skills. I played for the St. Mary's Catholic Youth Organization in Katonah. Joe was the star player on the St. Joseph's Catholic Youth Organization in Mahopac. Miss Costello thought Joe was someone with whom I had a lot in common and should spend more time with. So, one weekend, she arranged for me to visit her family. Joe and I became fast friends. He was an excellent student, a boy of faith, and a talented athlete. This was a pivotal time for me. For the first time in my life, I could see the value of having both a good education *and* athletic ability. And it was at that point I began to ask myself,

"What do you *really* want to do with your life?"

The answer came down to basic economics. In life and in the economy, there is always the challenge of having limited resources with which to fulfill both your wants and your needs. As a result, you're left to make some pretty difficult decisions. I didn't want to be limited with my resources, not in any way. I certainly didn't want to be just another athlete, limited to my talent, and beholden to the threat of a career-ending injury. I wanted to be a man of options, an educated man who was just as successful off the field as he was on. This would require a college education, and so I found myself redesigning my future.

With this newfound thirst for higher education, I realized that I would need a plan — a good one. I also realized that I would have to lean on basketball more than ever in order to achieve that, since college scholarships in baseball were rare in those days. The reality of my situation was that I needed a full scholarship if I was to attend college. In order to make that happen, I needed to stand out in the classroom as much as on the court or on the field, so that I could attract the right college. There were simply no other options for a kid like me. This knowledge changed everything!

SIX

History Starts Today

Prove your critics wrong.

When I was promoted to the eighth grade I was bound and determined to improve my grade point average. The older I got the more I could see the value of a good education. Learning never did come easy for me, not like baseball and basketball. In fact learning was a self-inflicted struggle, and what made it even more unpleasant that year was my history teacher's lack of faith in me. Mr. Lazarro was a good teacher. He just lacked confidence in my ability. It wasn't like he was the first. There were others like him, mean kids mostly, who would tell me that I was too small or too short to become a professional athlete. However, I refused to internalize their opinions of me. I realized early on that it was much harder to actually achieve one's dreams than it was to cast gloom on someone else's. So rather than get angry or discouraged,

I got determined. I developed thick skin, and by the time anyone told me that I couldn't do something … I was already doing it.

It wasn't that Mr. Lazarro was a bad guy. The truth is I respected him. I would go so far as to say that I liked him. I thought he was an excellent teacher. And even though he could be opinionated at times, not to mention narrow-minded where my future was concerned, his lessons in history could be quite entertaining. Perhaps his lack of faith in me was an occupational hazard. After all, he was a history teacher. His job was to study and teach the past, not determine the future.

"Bob's just not college material," Mr. Lazarro said from across a large, wooden desk. His hands were folded in front of him, as if he were almost apologetic. I'll never forget that night. It was a parent-teacher conference. I would have much rather been holed up under the covers with a bad case of the stomach flu than sitting there with my parents listening to his less-than-stellar report of my academic future. My parents' faces were stoic. Mom pursed her lips, trying to conceal her frown. Dad shifted uncomfortably in his small wooden seat.

Mr. Lazarro looked at me with a detached smile, having no idea the brand of disappointment his remark brought to the two biggest supporters in my life. Just like that, he had written me off. At least that's what it felt like. The man, who had no tangible notion of what I was made of, or *who* I was made of, had thrown me back into the pond like a fish too small to keep.

It may have been my pride swelling, but I suddenly had

the urge to prove him wrong. His doubt fueled a fire inside of me. Had I let Mr. Lazarro's doubting words get inside my head, it surely would have kept me from achieving much success in my life. However, I was more determined than that. And I could tell by the squinty look in my parents' eyes that they were also determined that I prove him wrong. I would show him! I was no small fish, unfit for a college education. I may have been too focused on sports, but I was a boy motivated with big dreams that no one, least of all Mr. Lazarro, would see coming. Suddenly I was all about college!

What Mr. Lazarro hadn't considered was that I came from a long line of remarkable people, some of whom had survived World War I and The Great Depression. We weren't the wealthy sort, certainly not like those living on the affluent estates I had visited as a kid — not even close. My pedigree was a bit more unassuming. However, it was no less extraordinary!

Mr. Lazarro didn't know that I had Grandpa Duffy's blood running through my veins, a frugal blacksmith who died with two hundred thousand dollars of honest, hard-earned cash in his pocket. He didn't know that my Dad had been stabbed in the gut by an inmate and lived to tell about it. He didn't know that my Mom, the unassuming woman sitting across from him with a determined smile on her face and perfectly coifed hair, had buried a child, a wonderful boy whose teachers she would never have the opportunity to conference with.

Mr. Lazarro had no idea the vast reservoir of resolve stored within the heart of my brother Don, a kid who had spent the better part of his life fighting to survive. And he certainly didn't know me, not the *real* me, the kid who had dreams big enough to fit inside the likes of Madison Square Garden and Yankee Stadium. He didn't know that I, the determined kid from Katonah, would wind up being financially independent six months before my 43rd birthday. How could he have known?

Mr. Lazarro may have been well-read on the subject of history. He may have even had twice the education of both my parents put together, but he had a lot to learn about the future of Bob Duffy. The future is, and always has been built upon the dreams of determined kids like me, kids marked for failure — or worse, mediocrity. And here's the thing about history: It starts today! And no one's opinion of you, for better or for worse, can change that. Only you have the power to determine your destiny!

It's sad to think that people aren't more supportive of one another, that the opinion of one person can negatively affect the outcome of another's dream. It takes so little to encourage someone, to give them confidence in themselves. A little belief goes a long way!

I didn't know it then, but I would run into that same brand of negativity throughout my life. It's not something you ever grow out of. No matter where you are in life, or at what stage, count on the naysayers. Nevertheless, I always managed to move forward with a positive attitude and a renewed determination. With time, and with each obstacle, I fought harder for control of my future.

After that parent-teacher conference and the experience of feeling discounted, I was better able to recognize and overcome situations that could have very easily limited my desire to achieve.

SPORTS

Hold onto your dream with both hands.

Bob Duffy, John Jay High School 1958 —
First Team All-County.

SEVEN

The Boy in the Backcourt

You don't have to follow suit.

It took a lot of hard work and discipline, but I eventually graduated middle school in 1955. I was promoted to the 9th grade. At that point I decided to transfer from the Katonah Public School system to St. Mary's Catholic High School. My attraction to St. Mary's was two-fold. For starters, the school had a reputation for quality education. It also had an impressive history of basketball and baseball accomplishments — a remarkable feat for a school that averaged no more than 150 students per year. St. Mary's was known for competing against bigger schools in the area. I liked that! I have found that you can learn a lot about yourself and your measure for success when you put yourself in the face of it. I admired St. Mary's gumption, standing up to the proverbial giants. They didn't back down just because they were a smaller school.

Instead, they stood up and competed. I could relate to that brand of determination. I wanted to be a part of that program, a part of that mentality, partly because I was always up for a challenge and partly because my dad was the head coach of St. Mary's varsity baseball and basketball teams. It made sense for me.

Apart from being a police officer at night, Dad knew how to coach a winning team. There was no doubt about it, and I wasn't the only one who thought so. There were a handful of public schools in the area that had vied to hire Dad as their head coach. However, because he hadn't attended college, he was unable to coach at the public school level. Some schools were so hung up on hiring him that they tried to circumvent his lack of education — to no avail. Although he never came right out and said so, I think it always bothered Dad that he wasn't qualified to pursue those opportunities. I have no doubt that's why he pushed me and my brothers so hard to get a college education. He understood the value of it, not the least of which was to open doors.

Another big draw for me to attend St. Mary's was that my best friend, Joe Costello, was attending. As freshmen, Joe and I were both starters for the boys varsity baseball and basketball teams. That year we won nearly 80-percent of our games against bigger schools, institutions that had five to 10 times the enrollment we did. This was an incredible achievement and we knew it! To round things out, I was sustaining a better than 90-percent average in the classroom. Miss Costello would have been proud! Where she sparked my desire to learn, the strict nuns at St. Mary's fanned the flames. It was clear that I was evolving both academically and athletically. My dreams were beginning to take shape, and Dad was beginning to take notice. As the varsity basketball coach, he didn't let on too much, but I got the feeling he leaned on me a little harder than he did the other players. It stood to reason. I was his firstborn son, the first one out of the gate. I was also a talented left-hander who was just over the six-foot mark in a sport that necessitated extraordinary height. And I was still growing!

While I wouldn't swell into the likes of NBA superstar Bob Pettit, a 6'9, 200-pound power forward who would later become a fellow teammate, Dad saw something in me that spurred him to push me even harder. He believed I had what it took to go all the way, and so, he played me as a guard my freshman year alongside Steve Fiacco, a 5'9 senior.

"It isn't likely that you'll be tall enough to be anything but a guard when you're playing in college or for a professional team," Dad said. "So you ought to learn backcourt work from the start."

That became our game plan, not to mention the match that would set off a firestorm of criticism from other coaches later on in my high school career. As uncomfortable as this tactic made them, I trusted Dad. He knew what he was doing. He appreciated that I was one of the tallest men on the team. Most coaches couldn't see the point of having a guard who was more imposing in stature than their forwards. Since guards are generally the smallest man on the court at the high school level, our "game plan" didn't make sense. However, I didn't allow the other coaches' doubt get under my skin. Dad's confidence in me brought out my best, and I knew it would all work out. Dad believed in his heart that I was an effective guard and so I had no reason to believe that I wasn't. I worked hard to prove him right. Sometimes I think I still do.

℃℥

Near the end of my freshman year at St. Mary's, Dad arranged for me to attend Camp All-America at the New York Military Academy in Cornwall on the Hudson. Dad was friends with Honey Russell, head basketball coach of Seton Hall in New Jersey. The two worked together as professional baseball scouts. They sought local talent at the high school level for the New York Giants baseball club. Coach Russell, the first head coach for the Boston Celtics from 1946-1948, and inductee in the Naismith Memorial Basketball Hall of Fame, arranged for me to be showcased at Camp All-America.

I was just a 14 year old kid, but I was old enough to appreciate the gravity of this opportunity. I was set to spar against guys much more pronounced in size and experience. A number of them were college-athletes. I was ready! Coach Russell and a fellow by the name of Clair Bee, one of the most highly acclaimed college basketball coaches of his time, and the head coach for the NBA's Baltimore Bullets, watched me perform.

Coach Bee was a big name in the business of basketball. Firstly, as the famed coach for Long Island University from 1932 – 1951, he had two undefeated seasons and two NIT titles under his belt. The NIT was the most significant college championship title in those days. Secondly, he officially retired from college basketball in 1951. However, he continued to hold the record for "highest winning percentage by a coach whose basketball team is a current Division One member by winning more than 82% of his games." Thirdly, somewhere in between coaching the Baltimore Bullets from 1952-1954, Coach Bee had a hand in implementing a couple of game-changing rules in professional basketball. Aside from being responsible for creating the 1-3-1 zone defense, he helped to put into practice the three-second-rule violation, a tenet that limits the time a player can stand in the lane in front of the team's defensive basket. He also helped the NBA develop the 24-second shot clock. Basketball hasn't been the same since! Games could get pretty boring before those two rules took effect.

Meanwhile, back at Camp All-America, everything was going great until Coach Bee learned that I was 14 years old. The minute he got wind of my age, he yanked me off the court. Truth be told, I was too young to be playing at that level. The fact that I was participating with those older players could have meant certain trouble for him. Coach Bee had already experienced enough trouble in his career. The last thing he needed was another negative headline on his hands. I am, of course, referring to the scandal that ended his college coaching career in 1951 when eight of his players at Long Island University were accused of accepting bribes in order to fix games. This was a serious offense, violating a bill that had been passed by the New York State legislature in 1945, establishing that it was illegal to attempt to bribe a participant in a sporting event, amateur or professional. All things considered, Coach Bee was erring on the side of caution. While I was disappointed, he had every right to do what he did. Technically, I wasn't old enough. That's not to say that he didn't see something special in me.

A few days later, Coach Bee called my Dad and offered me a working scholarship at Camp All-America that summer. In return for my camp experience, I would work in the dining hall. It wasn't ideal, but there was no way I was going to turn it down. After all, I had been brought up to work hard, and so each and every day, beginning at 6 a.m. sharp, I set up for breakfast, followed by lunch, and dinner later in the day. I even waited tables as fellow campers and camp counselors ate their meals. Afterward, I washed dishes and mopped floors. It wasn't glamorous, but it was a means to a very important end. It was a very exciting time for me, a real tipping point in my life, as a boy and as a basketball player.

In between meals I participated in activities with the other campers. We played basketball from sun up to sun down. Coach Bee would often show up for days at a time, offering campers special clinics. I got to rub shoulders with some of the biggest names in college basketball, coaches and players, men whose names would astonish you if I said them aloud. I learned a lot that summer, not the least of which was that Mom and Dad were right. The long list of chores I was asked to do around the house and community, though far-removed from my boyhood dream of being a professional athlete, did, in fact, pay off! It was my ability to tackle my responsibilities in the dining hall, discreet details most kids miss, that provided me the opportunity of a lifetime. The instruction, competition, and introduction to top college coaches like Adolf Rupp of Kentucky, Frank McGuire of North Carolina, and Joe Lapchick of St. Johns gave me the opportunity to perform and, ultimately, reach a step higher in achieving my boyhood dream.

Best of all, I had a shot at making a good impression on one of the greatest basketball coaches of all time. Coach Bee saw something in me, and so he took a chance. I wasn't about to let him down. Not on the court and certainly not in the dining hall. I was more motivated than ever! As exciting as all of these new developments were, I still had a lot of work ahead of me. After all, I still needed to finish high school.

EIGHT

A Man of Options

If it's not working, try another approach.

In the fall of 1956, I returned to St. Mary's as a sophomore. I was more serious than ever about my education. Whether it was Latin, French, literature or math, with the help of some very dedicated nuns who demanded progress, I continued to improve in the classroom. I was as committed to my education as I was to sports. And because St. Mary's only had two team sports, basketball and baseball, I knew I was soon going to have to give my whole heart to one of them. This was not going to be an easy decision. The only thing I knew for certain at that point was that I wanted to be a professional athlete. This year was a definite turning point for me, as there were two rather significant incidents that took place that nudged me in the direction of basketball.

The first incident happened during the last game of our

varsity basketball season. The team, led by me and Joe Costello, was 17 and 0 on an 18 game schedule. Our final game was slated against Katonah High School. Katonah had the home-court advantage. This would prove to be a significant contest, if for no other reason than St. Mary's was determined to defend its undefeated record. Both schools were from the small town of Katonah, making it a very competitive and physical game.

Just before half-time I wrenched my ankle pretty bad. Dad, Coach Duffy, was angered by this development. He took little mercy on me, making it clear to everyone in the locker room during halftime that I was to play the second half, despite my injury. He laid into me pretty hard in front of the team. At that point, my ankle looked like a swollen eggplant, and it hurt when I applied any pressure to it. Nevertheless, I wasn't about to disappoint Dad or my teammates. Clenching my jaw, I hobbled back out onto the court and finished the game, pushing past the pain as best I could. In the end, it didn't make a bit of difference. At the final buzzer, we lost the game to Katonah High School. It was a tough loss. I'm not sure which hurt worse, ending an undefeated season with a loss to our fiercest rival or seeing the disappointed look on Dad's face.

Baseball season began the following spring — 1957. This marked the second incident that steered me toward basketball. I had just settled in as St. Mary's first baseman. My good friend, Joe Costello, was our pitcher. Dad, Coach Duffy, strongly believed the infield warm-up before the start of the game was crucial to a team's success. He felt a smooth and snappy performance, as the other team looked on, could duly impress and intimidate the competition.

One day as our team was warming up before a game, Dad hit a routine ground ball to first. With zip and accuracy I scooped the ball up into my mitt, tagged first base and hurled it to the catcher at home plate. In my haste, the ball skimmed the ground just before hitting the catcher's glove. Angry with my performance, Dad proceeded to hit one ground ball after another in my direction. The balls came hard and they came fast. Feeling my confidence begin to wane, I failed to connect with the ball, let alone the catcher at home plate.

"Stick your nose in there, Duffy!" he hollered, hitting several line drives in my direction. At that point, I had no choice but to block the balls with my body. Dad was deeply flustered, and I was worried. After a while, the rest of the team stood at ease, as they realized Coach Duffy had set his crosshairs on me.

It's been more than sixty years, and Joe Costello still remembers that day. I don't know if it was because I was his firstborn son and he felt he needed to lean on me a little harder than the other players, or if he was just testing my conviction. Either way, practices were becoming particularly painful. As Coach Duffy's son, I soldiered through as best I could. However, after that day of fielding balls with my body, it became painfully clear to both Mom and me that it was best I leave St. Mary's.

Playing for Dad was no longer a good idea. While I knew

he was trying to develop a particular set of skills in me, the underlying angst — both his and mine — was eating away at our relationship. It was time I venture out on my own. I certainly wasn't a young man without options. There were a few prep schools in Connecticut and New York showing an interest in me, offering full scholarships to play basketball at their schools. I put a lot of thought and consideration into my next move.

I was being touted as one of the greatest basketball players ever developed in northern Westchester, described as "second-to-none in my playmaking ability" in the interscholastic basketball competition. Therefore, it was a good time to seek out new opportunities, seeing as I was making a name for myself. That year I was awarded a scholarship in a competition that included a large number of terrific student-athletes in the surrounding area. The scholarship was awarded annually to a "man of excellent character and ability," a member of the junior class chosen by a committee that represented the donors. I jumped at the chance, accepting the scholarship that included two full years of tuition to Hackley Prep in Tarrytown, New York. Focusing on my education had proven valuable to my future. It opened doors that otherwise wouldn't have been there for me.

It was a huge relief knowing that I had somewhere to go in the fall, a school that could take me to the next level, academically and athletically. Even though Dad considered my transfer to Hackley to be a blow to St. Mary's baseball and basketball teams, he supported me and my decision. I always appreciated that.

CR

I spent the following summer training under Clair Bee at Camp All-America. I was offered another working scholarship and, once again, received top instruction from some of the best college coaches in the country. Men like Frank McGuire from the University of North Carolina, Adolph Rupp from Kentucky, Everett Case from North Carolina State, and Branch McCracken from Indiana worked with me on my technique. And then there was Alvin Fred "Doggie" Julian from Dartmouth, the same man who coached Bob Cousy at Holy Cross and the Boston Celtics from 1948-1950.

I was in basketball heaven!

I grew up a lot that summer. My ball-handling skills were improving tremendously, as was the company I was keeping on the court. Physically-speaking, I was blending in more naturally with guys like Pete Brennan, Joe Quig, Tommy Kearns, and York Larese of the University of North Carolina. Spending time on the court with these fine athletes was extraordinary, seeing as they went undefeated (32-0) that year and, ultimately, clinched the 1957 NCAA tournament against Kansas, and First-Team All-American Wilt Chamberlain) 54-53. The idea of playing professional basketball was in the cup of my hand, or so it felt at Camp All-America.

NINE

A Man in the Making

Push past the pain.

In the fall of 1957, the start of my junior year at Hackley Prep, I hit the ground running. I had never felt more confident, and even though this would mark my first time living away from home, I was determined to make it happen. "Making it happen" was becoming a recurring theme in my life. I was fortunate in that I didn't have to worry myself or my parents with expensive tuition. I was mentally free to compete with highly qualified students in the classroom. These were not usual circumstances for most boys my age. In that sense, I had everything I needed to succeed.

Since its inception, Hackley's adage has been aimed at the heart of developing character and responsibility, particularly as it pertains to serving others. This maxim of "service" had a big impact on me, as did the campus. Hackley Prep felt a lot like how I imagined university life would feel. It even resembled that of Yale and Princeton.

Hackley was an all-boys school led by one very strict headmaster, making it a sight more rigorous than St. Mary's. Dorm life wasn't the most attractive, but for a 16 year old kid seeking autonomy, it certainly served its purpose. In many ways Hackley prepared me for living on my own. For starters, I learned to be fiercely independent. While I missed the comforts of home, particularly Mom's cooking and the best-of-three cutthroat one-on-one competitions with my younger brother Rich, it was the year I became my own man. In order to grow up and appreciate where he came from, a boy must venture out into the world alone. Only then can he truly begin to fend for himself and learn to form and make his own decisions.

I was young, but I had a pretty good head on my shoulders. I was never afraid to fail. I was more afraid of missing out on the opportunity to succeed. It was that mindset that spurred me through life, and so taking calculated risks, particularly those that weighed in my favor, became a habit for me in school, as well as later on in my sports, business, and philanthropic careers. Success demands that you venture outside of your comfort zone. You have to be bold in your intentions, as well as your actions! And you cannot avoid taking risks. I am here to tell you that success, particularly in its early stages, is going to make you very uncomfortable. It's going to make you question everything, what you know about yourself and your commitment. My experience at Hackley made me seriously question my future. It was one of the first *real* tests of my conviction and integrity. And as uncomfortable as it was, it was that challenging time in my life that ultimately led to my progression as a student, a ballplayer, and, ultimately, a young man.

Hackley demanded the best of me. It pushed me to be a better student, as well as a better athlete. It was often painful, but to have avoided the pain would have kept me from being my best. I was motivated to achieve at a much higher level. After all, that's why I chose Hackley. I knew its fast, rigorous academic pace would build up my academic endurance for college. Hackley was a first-rate school. The majority of its students were accustomed to its academic demand. However, I honestly didn't know if I could keep up. The classroom was an extremely competitive playing field. Almost immediately, I fell behind in my studies. It didn't help that I had joined the soccer team as center half that fall. While I enjoyed the athletic experience, the physical activity did nothing to relieve the stress I was under academically. In fact, it only added to the pressure of keeping my head above water. This was a turning point for me. I knew that if I wanted to remain at Hackley, my grades would have to improve — fast.

I thought back to my days in grammar school. I thought about how Miss Costello had incited a fire in me for education. She taught me good study habits. Those study habits could pull me out of this slump, and so, when I wasn't playing sports, I was studying. It was the only way to pull up my grades and maintain an acceptable GPA. In time I found my feet, and was able to turn things around. By the end of my junior year, I had lettered in three varsity sports — soccer, basketball and baseball — all while sustaining a favorable GPA.

At Hackley's annual father and son sports dinner, the New York Press presented me with a certificate acknowledging my selection as a member of the All-Ivy League Prep School All-star Basketball Team. I was chosen from the forecast players in the loop which included Poly Prep, Trinity (of New York,) Horace Mann, Adelphi, and Stony Brook Prep Schools. This was an unusual honor for a first year man, an honor that would not have happened had I not pushed myself as hard as I did to achieve. I was happy at Hackley. However, as I began to consider my senior year, I found myself at yet another crossroad. After experiencing two years at a Catholic high school, and one year at a preparatory boarding school, I made the decision to return to the public school system. The truth was I missed home, as much as I missed the coed experience.

TEN

You Don't Want to be Nobody

Listen to your mother.

In the fall of 1958, Katonah High School had merged into a regional high school named for John Jay, a founding father of the United States and the first Chief Justice of the Supreme Court. I couldn't wait to rejoin the ranks of kids I had grown up with in grammar school. Not only that, but John Jay had an extraordinary campus. Its playing fields and athletic facilities were impressive, state-of-the-art. John Jay High School was a drastic change from the older, more traditional schools I was used to. I was invigorated by all of the upgrades, including returning to the coed experience, which, by the way, is also a very important factor in a young man's education. I was also ready to hang up the traditional dress code that required a coat and tie for a much more casual (i.e. relaxed) dress code. During my stints at St. Mary's and Hackley Prep, I was

45

held to a much more formal standard. Students were expected to wear dress coats, ties and slacks every day to school. It was tradition.

My mother thrived on tradition, and she expected as much from her boys. There wasn't a whole lot of room for discussion in that regard. The woman was no more than 5'6 but her mental stance was 8' tall if it was an inch. Mom was a strict disciplinarian, a woman who was determined to see that all three of her boys had a good life and a successful career. It was her intention that we all attend college, so that we might achieve that which she and Dad never had the opportunity of achieving, a college education. That being said, Mom had an incredible influence on my life. I respected her. She worked two jobs and lived in a house full of men, one of whom she married and three of whom she had given birth. The woman deserved a medal!

Upon my reentry into public high school, before I had time to hang up my dress coat and tie, Mom made it clear that under no uncertain terms would I be joining the ranks of the casually dressed. She insisted that I continue wearing a coat and tie to school — public or otherwise. Lowering my standard of academic excellence was not an option in her eyes. There would be no blue jeans and no bad language for Bobby Duffy.

"You're better than that," Mom said.

"But Mom, nobody wears a coat and tie to public school."

Mom pursed her lips.

"Son, you don't want to be nobody!"

There was no point in arguing with her. The few inches I had over her at the time didn't hold much weight in the high court of her authority. Mom gave us boys a good amount of guidance, and the truth was she was *always* right. Looking back, Mom, in all of her infinite wisdom, was the first of my most influential mentors, and while I did catch a terrible ribbing from my classmates for dressing so formally to school that year, I walked away with an incredible lesson. The lesson being, a coat and tie will distinguish you from the crowd. Whether you are in the classroom, playing for the NBA, in a business meeting or on a date, clothes do, indeed, make a statement. Don't get me wrong. It was awkward showing up to class looking more like a teacher than a teenager, but it gave me a certain level of confidence. That old coat and tie (and Mom's persistence) changed my life. Thanks to Mom, I had an awareness to detail that I didn't even know I needed to pursue my dream. Mom's been gone for a handful of years now, but I can still hear her voice egging me on to do the right thing. If in doubt, wear the coat and tie! As determined as she was, she held onto life, and her driver's license, well into her late 90s. Those expectations Mom had for me are still as present today as they were all those years ago. And because I believe she and I will meet again one day, I don't intend to disappoint her.

CB

Because it was my senior year, I decided to sign up for John Jay's varsity football team. Even though I knew Dad would never approve, I was looking to prove myself in yet another sport.

Deep down, I knew Dad would never go for it. After all, he had my college education in his crosshairs, and because football could result in a game-changing injury, shutting down my chances of getting a basketball scholarship to a prominent university, this was nothing more than a bad idea.

I signed up anyway.

With my football equipment stuffed in my locker, I headed home that afternoon. I rehearsed my argument in my head. I carefully anticipated Dad's response, meticulously preparing my rebuttal. As much as I dreaded the conversation, I knew he was nothing, if not a reasonable man.

The conversation went just as I expected. Dad listened patiently as I presented my argument. He nodded, as if seriously considering my case. After my summation, he took a beat, and then leaned in toward me.

"Son, if you were to tear your ACL or suffer a serious concussion you would be ruined for basketball."

There it was … the Achilles' heel to my argument.

He was right. I knew he was right. Such injuries are all too common in football, and while I knew Dad loved me and didn't want to see me get hurt, I knew what he was really saying. He didn't want me to ruin my chance at a college scholarship. A college education was the end game. If I were to sustain even the slightest injury in football, it could erase any chance I had at receiving said college education. Dad, being the consummate diplomat, left it to me to manage my way out of the commitment.

Although it was embarrassing, and a bit defeating, I met with head coach, Marty Todd, the next day. I turned in my equipment. Looking back, it was Mom and Dad's consistent support and direction that put me on the right path. A young man doesn't always want to hear the unsolicited advice of his parents, particularly his mother. However, it is always to his advantage to hear them out, and to follow their advice. Your mother is never going to steer you wrong.

With football out of the way, I continued to improve in the classroom and on the basketball court. I pushed myself harder than I ever had before. As a result, I was selected to be First Team All-County in Westchester County, New York. No high school basketball player in the northern vicinity had ever been recognized. All the major cities in Westchester were south, closer to New York City. There were denser populations in cities like New Rochelle, White Plains and Yonkers that were home to the top high school athletes within a huge county. I was the first in my region. That was a boost to my confidence, no doubt placing me in a better position to be elected years later in the Con Edison Sports Hall of Fame located in White Plains, New York. I was a happy, young man.

ELEVEN

Expect the Unexpected

Take nothing for granted.

When I was a senior in high school, basketball was my life! All of the hard work I poured into the game had developed into the kind of talent that would one day afford me a college education, and earn me a shot at my dream of becoming a professional athlete. Growing up, I was always appreciative of what I had. Although I was young, I never took any of it for granted, particularly when it came to my dream of playing in the NBA.

One day in the middle of a blizzard, while driving home from basketball practice, I lost control of my parents' car on a thin, black sheet of ice. It was in that moment that I realized how quickly those things that meant the most to me could be taken away. My hometown of Katonah, New York had been hit by a wicked snowstorm. While it was a blessing in its summer months, that part of the world was particularly susceptible to winter's curse.

The roads were a mess, visibility limited. Normally I rode the school bus home. However, that day my dad let me borrow the family car, on the condition that I drive straight to school and back home after practice. That gesture of trust was a big deal to me.

After practice I offered to drive a buddy of mine home, a fellow teammate named Les Shepherd. It was a half hour commute and while the roads were impaired, I felt pretty confident about getting behind the wheel. While Les and I conversed about the three most important things in our young lives, girlfriends, basketball and where we planned to attend college, I cautiously maneuvered the weathered road ahead. Les plotted his educational path, sharing with me his plans for the future. Les was an excellent student, so it wasn't a surprise to anyone, least of all me, that he would have his choice of colleges. At the time Les had set his educational sights high — Amherst, Williams and Wesleyan. I admired his ambition since all three colleges were highly regarded. It inspired me to evaluate my own aspirations. We were just about halfway home when we came to a hill, an innocuous incline that didn't appear to impose too big of a threat.

I was wrong.

I had but a split second to react when I realized we had hit a mean patch of black ice. The car began to fishtail out of control. I glanced over at Les. His eyes were as big as basketballs and his mouth was gaping wide open. In an amateurish attempt to keep from banging up my parents' car, I jerked the steering wheel against the spin and slammed on the brakes. Unfortunately, it was that knee-jerk reaction that caused the car to flip side-over-side.

Mind you, this was long before seatbelts came standard. Suddenly everything went black, and Les and I were being violently tossed about in that big heap of crunching metal. Although it must have happened at breakneck speed, it felt as though we were moving in slow-motion, in one long, lingering movement after another. My body must have gone into shock because I didn't feel as much pain as I probably should have and my life flashed before my eyes without much consequence. After what felt like an eternity, the car (with the two of us still inside) landed in a soft snow bank at the bottom of the hill. There was no sound, no sensation other than a bizarre, dreamlike feeling that washed over me. For a brief moment I couldn't distinguish whether or not we had survived the crash. It wasn't until I heard Les' voice that I realized we might actually walk away from that mangled up mess. And it was in that small window of time that I began to appreciate those things that meant the most to me, beginning with my Mom and Dad.

ᘒ

Being a policeman in the town of Bedford, it was my Dad who got the call that day. There had been an accident on Route 35. As he pulled up to the scene, Dad immediately noticed that the big heap of metal embedded in the snow bank was, in fact, his car. I could see the concern welling in his eyes as he approached. He wasn't angry. He was relieved to find Les and me on our feet.

While he could be tough on me when it came to sports and school, Dad demonstrated nothing but love where and when it mattered most. I was grateful for that, especially since I had just totaled his car. As a father, I can't even begin to imagine what he must have been feeling when he realized it was his son in that embankment. His concern for me was never more apparent, or appreciated, than it was that afternoon when he held me tight in his arms.

My parents had already lost one son to crib death. I could feel in Dad's embrace that he wasn't prepared to lose another. He put his big hand on my sore shoulder and gave it a good, hard squeeze. I winced in pain, as the shock was beginning to wear off and minor injuries were slowly introducing themselves in my right arm, shoulder and lower back. Dad let out an audible sigh of relief. I realized right then and there that I could have lost everything that was important to me that day, including my dream of playing college ball. That accident could have changed the trajectory of my life. If nothing else, my injuries from it could have certainly kept me from playing in the upcoming game against Horace Greely of Chappaqua, New York.

Not a chance!

With my right arm in a sling, I played in the game against Greely. I led the team to victory! Did I mention that I'm ambidextrous? With just the use of my left arm, I scored 17 points and made several assists. Nothing was going to get in my way. It's amazing what you can achieve when you push past the pain!

TWELVE

College Material

Consider your options carefully.

My senior year at John Jay High School was going well. I was making the grade. I was making a name for myself in varsity basketball. I was dating a great girl named Susie Woodfin, a varsity cheerleader who was bright, energetic and fun. Life was good! That being said, my senior experience was sorely overshadowed by the fact that I had a major decision to make. Because I had worked so hard, academically and athletically, I had an overwhelming number of colleges knocking at my door. The pressure to choose a school was at a zenith. My parents and I reduced the list of 73 universities to 12. The academic stand-outs were, of course, Cornell, Colgate, Dartmouth, Princeton, and Yale. Each of these universities had high academic standards and offered the best opportunity for post-graduate jobs beyond basketball, a

Plan B … should my sports career not pan out.) Also on the ticket was West Point, which, of course, included a political appointment. There were also many powerhouse basketball programs to consider, including the University of North Carolina, St. Johns, Syracuse, Seton Hall, Indiana, and North Carolina State. Each of these schools had my attention!

Because the scope of my options was so vast, I was having a difficult time choosing. On one hand, the University of North Carolina had a solid reputation for its intercollegiate men's basketball team. It was a championship team in the Atlantic Coast Conference. Much of its success had to do with their head coach Frank McGuire. He was known for being a great recruiter. I had the opportunity to work with Coach McGuire at Camp All-America. It was a great experience, and I knew it would be an extraordinary opportunity to play for him at the university level. The Tar Heels finished 32-0 in 1957, beating Wilt Chamberlain and Kansas in three overtimes for the first NCAA title won by an ACC school. It was a great game, one that put college basketball on the map! That game, alone, made the University of North Carolina a whole lot more attractive.

I was also drawn to St. Johns University, a school of similar caliber. St. John's head coach, Joe Lapchick, had an impressive resume. He played for the original Boston Celtics, later serving as head coach for the New York Knicks. In his 20 years with St. John's University, he captured four NIT championships at a time when the NIT was the nation's premier collegiate basketball tournament. He was also known for breaking the color barrier in the NBA when he signed the league's first African-American player in 1950, Nathaniel "Sweetwater" Clifton.

Besides its national presence in college basketball, and the fact that it was so close to home, St. John's was a real contender, if for no other reason than the school competed in Madison Square Garden, the home of basketball. Playing in the Garden was a huge draw for me, as was playing for Joe Lapchick.

I met Coach Lapchick once before at a small dinner celebration just outside of Katonah. Because St. Mary's varsity basketball team had been so successful that year, he was invited to sit at the head of the table right next to Dad — Coach Duffy. Coach Lapchick expressed an interest in me, inviting me to attend St. Johns. I was thrilled at the offer, especially since the university housed a very impressive law school. I figured if my grades were good enough, I could stretch my four-year scholarship into seven. However, after visiting my top five favorite schools, including those that offered the highest in academic standards, I was most attracted to Colgate and Dartmouth. Each had smaller campuses located in remote areas of the northeastern region, and both were a four hour drive from my home in Katonah. I liked that!

I was having a great time visiting these universities. It was sort of like shopping for a car. I was taking each one for a test drive. Dad seemed to like all the attention I was getting. I could see he was proud, and pleased that I had my choice of colleges. I could feel the enormity in this decision. Having Ivy League schools like

Yale, Princeton, Cornell, and Dartmouth knocking at my door was a real boost to my confidence. It was a big deal for a kid who was told he was not "college material." And while it may have been my high school basketball career that warranted the interest of some major basketball programs, it was my GPA and SAT scores that ultimately qualified me to attend these renowned academic institutions.

The Ivy League originally began as a collegiate athletic conference made up of sports teams from eight private institutions in the Northeastern United States. They included Brown, Harvard, Cornell, Princeton, Dartmouth, Yale, Columbia, and the University of Pennsylvania. The term Ivy League was derived in 1954, when the NCAA athletic conference for Division I was formed. At the time, the exclusiveness of these schools had more to do with their prestige in the realm of sports than academia. For me, this only affirmed that I was "college material" at the highest level, academically and athletically. And even though I knew I would have to work hard to keep up my grades at one of these institutions, I knew that it would be worth it.

03

One of the things that attracted me to Dartmouth was the school's head basketball coach, Alvin "Doggy" Julian. He was considered to be one of the best college coaches in the country. At one pivotal point in his career, he coached athletic superstar, Bob Cousy at Holy Cross. Cousy went on to have a sensational, professional basketball career in the NBA, going on to play for the

Boston Celtics. He was also named "Mr. Basketball" in the 1950s. Cousy was, and still is, known for saving professional basketball in its early days. He was my idol. So, the idea of playing for his former college coach was very attractive!

Dad and I visited Dartmouth twice before committing. It was during my second visit that I took a more serious look at Dartmouth's Tuck School of Business. Because, in those days, scholarships at Ivy League schools were based on financial need, and not on athletic talent, I wanted to be sure that I was making the right decision. Just as I was about to commit to attending Dartmouth, the director of admissions tossed an unnecessary fly into the ointment.

"Mr. Duffy, why is it you won't be contributing any monies to your son's education?"

It wasn't the question that bothered me so much as it was the man's tone. It struck me as arrogant. Dad shifted nervously in his seat. Suddenly the mood in the room went stale, the taste for Dartmouth along with it. I don't remember Dad's response. However, I will never forget the earnest expression on his face, and the way his fingers knotted together as he sat across from this man whose suit was more legitimate than his smile. Up until that point I had been ready to commit to both Doggy and Dartmouth. However, something about that gratuitous question changed everything for me. It was no secret that my parents couldn't afford to pay for my education out-of-pocket, so when Dartmouth's director of admissions needlessly put my dad on the spot like that,

I took it as a direct insult. I instantly had a change of heart. I had 72 other universities expressing an interest in me. I didn't need Dartmouth, and so I politely declined their offer.

Looking back, I believe it was an unfortunate lapse in judgment on the director's part. There was no reason to be so unkind. Doggy was both disappointed and disturbed to learn the reason why I declined Dartmouth's offer. I was just as disturbed and disappointed. The truth was even though I qualified for financial aid, Dad was too proud to consider it. He wanted me to obtain my education earnestly, in the form of an athletic or academic scholarship. And while turning down a great prospect like Dartmouth left me feeling a little hollow inside, it was a minor boost to my pride that such an offer existed at all.

With Dartmouth out of the running, I took a second look at Colgate University, a school that, in my mind, had a nice blend of academia and athletics. Like Dartmouth, Colgate was all men. It had a small student body, a beautiful campus, and based its scholarships on need and/or academic record vs. athletic talent. This was good news, since I maintained a better than average GPA throughout high school.

Bill Griffith, Director of Admissions at Colgate, and Howie Hartman, Colgate's head basketball coach invited me for a second visit of their school. Mom, Dad and I packed up the car and headed north. The moment we stepped foot on campus, Mr. Griffith made us feel right at home. Mr. Hartman was equally as welcoming and spoke very confidently about his basketball program.

Colgate was located in Hamilton, a small, rural town in Central New York. The campus was beautiful. I liked the fact that I would be competing as fiercely in the classroom as I would on the basketball court. Not only that, but Colgate wasn't restricted by the Ivy League. Its program played a more competitive basketball schedule, which could possibly help with my dream of playing in the NBA. It was that second trip to Colgate that turned the tide for me. I made the decision to enroll on the four hour car ride home. I knew Colgate was the right choice for me, and my parents couldn't have been more delighted!

To this day, I can't believe I chose Colgate over North Carolina. All things considered, North Carolina seemed like the right choice at the time and could have certainly given me a fine education, not to mention a great shot at the NBA. However, it was Colgate that was the academic standout, and while its basketball program didn't rival the Tar Heels, I decided to think big and accept the challenge of competing at a very high level in both the classroom and on the court.

THIRTEEN

All in Good Time

Enjoy the moment.

In 1958 Colgate had an enrollment of about 1,300 students, all of whom were eager young men. Colgate's emphasis was Liberal Arts. As a freshman, I was exposed to a variety of subjects and disciplines. For me, that included art, economics, geology, religion, and my two personal favorites, foreign language and philosophy. Great-thinkers like Plato and Socrates fascinated me. Their philosophies, matched with the diversity of my education would benefit my life tremendously, particularly in future matters of business and communication.

In addition to those great thinkers, I was also introduced to some special friends. If you ask me, it's the friendships you develop at university that become the better part of your education. Those human connections are invaluable, not to mention more tangible than what we learn in the classroom or read in a book. We won't always retain how Sparta established itself as a local power in Peloponnesus or how to formulate probability. However, when it comes to some of the greatest lessons learned in college, those happen in the midst of forging friendship with fellow undergrads. You can learn a lot about yourself and your fellow human while in the collegiate trenches. Most of those lessons are for life, as are the friendships that are formed.

I met one of my best friends, a guy by the name of John Jacobs, at the start of my freshman year. We bumped into one another while standing in line at "The Coop," the university bookstore to pick up our books for class. John and I met once before on the varsity basketball court back in high school. The encounter was brief, and somewhat blemished. We were juniors. He was at Horace Mann. I was at Hackley Prep. Our teams were competing. John had been assigned by his coach to injure me. Lucky for me, he refused. I hadn't seen John since that game 18 months earlier.

"I heard you were going to Dartmouth," John said.

"Yeah, I thought so, too," I chuckled.

From that moment forward, John and I were great friends. We shared a lot of common interests, including sports and the Russian language. I spent a lot of time with John and his family on weekends. It's been 56 years, and I still value his friendship today.

And then there are those fleeting friendships, the ones that are shorter than you'd like, but last a lifetime in your heart. I met a kid from Syracuse that same year. His name was Ernie Davis. You may have heard of him. He was an outstanding running back for the Orange football team. He was an All-American, and the first African-American athlete to win the Heisman trophy in 1961. Because we were both freshman, Ernie and I didn't get to play varsity sports, as was the rule at the time. We met while playing freshman basketball that season. Our teams competed, and I remember thinking to myself that there was something special about Ernie. It was the only season he played basketball for Syracuse. It was a time when the Orange struggled to find talent on the court. Ernie was a class act, not only as a student, but as an athlete, and as a friend. He was also a lot of fun to be around. He invited me and Dad to a big event hosted by Syracuse University at Toots Shores, a famous Manhattan club. The event was to celebrate his Heisman achievement. It was a great time, one I won't soon forget!

I was devastated when I heard the news that Ernie had passed away from a highly toxic form of leukemia in 1962, just six months after graduating from Syracuse. It's still hard to believe. He had a promising career in the NFL, having been drafted first overall by the Washington Redskins, and then immediately traded to the Cleveland Browns for a reported one hundred thousand dollars. He passed away before having ever played one snap in the NFL. It was a tragic loss. There was no one like Ernie. I will never forget him.

All things considered, my first year in college was going

well. The only drawback, in my mind, was that incoming freshman weren't allowed to play varsity sports. It was an NCAA rule. There was no skirting around it. The philosophy was books before basketball — period, end of story. Young and eager to begin my varsity basketball career at Colgate, this rule only infuriated me. Only now do I appreciate and understand the reasoning behind the rule, as it allowed young freshman to become acclimated to the rigors of college life. I was too stubborn to realize it at the time, but the NCAA rule forced me to practice the art of patience. I would come to learn that there is a time and a place for everything, not the least of which is opportunity. You can't rush success! I had no choice but to focus my energy on my schoolwork and honing my basketball skills on the freshmen team.

That season we were slated for twelve games, six of which were played against four neighboring schools: Cornell, Syracuse, West Point and, best of all, St. Johns in a four team Christmas tournament. I averaged no less than 25 points per game and, to top it off, our freshman team beat St. Johns at the Christmas Tournament Championship at West Point. This was a great accomplishment! I continued to work hard in an effort to make a name for myself at Colgate. I could see it was beginning to pay off, both in the classroom and on the court. I spent nearly all of my time studying, leaving little time for socializing.

While I had my nose buried in the books, my classmates elected me for Freshman Class President. That was a surprise. Around the same time my fellow fraternity pledges voted me the

Outstanding Pledge in the Delta Upsilon fraternity. While some might find this brand of recognition a good time to sit back and rest on their laurels, this made me even more determined to prove to them, and to myself that I was, in fact, "college material." I was already looking forward to the following year, my sophomore year. I couldn't wait to take part in a fraternity and excel even further.

Fraternities were a standard fixture on university campuses on the east coast in 1959. They housed a large percentage of students, not including freshman. Delta Upsilon was comprised of many student-athletes and that, no doubt, had much to do with my decision to join. A good friend of mine, a senior named Tom Flood, was already a member. Tom was a family friend, the son of Dad's best friend in high school back in Lincolndale, New York. It was Tom who inspired me to become a pledge.

For a freshman, I was doing well. Mom and Dad were both pleased. There were a couple of write-ups in the local paper that substantiated my achievements that year. The Patent Trader touted, "When he [Duffy] returns to Colgate in the fall, the backcourt star is expected to be one of the regulars on Coach Howard Hartman's varsity squad." It was the start of my interscholastic cage career. I had been named to the Patent Trader all-Star team and was All-County. Mom cut out that article, pasting it into a mounting scrapbook collection. Pasted next to it was another article that read: "It isn't very often that an outstanding collegiate athlete is also an outstanding student. But such is the case of Bob Duffy, son of Mr. and Mrs. Joseph Duffy of Katonah, who is just completing his freshman year at Colgate University. The John Jay High School graduate was named on the Dean's List with a 3.2 average on the four-point system. He was also given the Dean's recognition award for outstanding service to his class."

At the end of my freshman year, Bill Griffith, Director of Admissions, presented me and 13 other students with the George W. Cobb Award for outstanding character and leadership. That is one in every 100 enrolled at the university. I still have the letter Mr. Griffith wrote to me. His words continue to sustain my faith in hard work and personal commitment. He wrote: "Every year many students at Colgate make important contributions to life on the campus. We believe Colgate is a better place for everyone this year because of the contributions which you are making."

I was also presented with the Attis Chalmas Prize in Russian Studies by professor Dr. Albert Parry. Suddenly schools like Cornell, Syracuse, and West Point were beginning to take notice. They solicited my interest in transferring to their institutions. My hard work presented yet another major crossroad. I had to ask myself, "Do I really want to change schools?" I had just gotten my feet wet at Colgate, and while the sudden interest of these other schools was flattering, transferring would mean sacrificing another year of varsity basketball. It would also mean committing to five years of school versus four. That did not bode well with me. Regardless, I gave each of the schools a fair amount of consideration. In the end, however, I decided to stick with Colgate. And, as time would tell, that was a good decision.

FOURTEEN

The Bigger Man

Don't let others derail your dreams.

Summer came and went. Before I knew it, I was a sophomore at Colgate. I was looking forward to what the year would bring. A small part of me wondered if I made the right decision not to transfer to one of the other prominent universities. The better part of me, however, was confident in my decision. I went with my gut. I knew that Colgate was the right school for me.

With that said, I knew my sophomore year was going to be an adjustment, beginning with my living arrangement. I went from a single room in a freshman dormitory to a small bedroom that housed four grown men at the Delta Upsilon Fraternity — not the most favorable set of circumstances. Being in such tight living quarters with four adult men can be disruptive, not to mention choked with unpleasant realities of communal living. The upside to

Upsilon was that it was more than just student housing. It was a brotherhood. And the house, itself, was accommodating of large mixers. Those mixers were important. After all, Colgate was an all-male school and we were virile young men looking for a good excuse to fraternize with the fairer sex. Unfortunately, spending time with the ladies didn't happen as often as we would have liked, since it usually involved road trips to Syracuse, Cornell, Skidmore, New York City or Boston where my girlfriend Susie Woodfin was attending Katharine Gibbs College.

I enjoyed my visits with Susie. She made our time together special. With all of the partying going on at Colgate on the weekends, I would much rather have spent time with her. It didn't take long for my fraternity brothers to catch onto the fact that I was not much of a partier.

I didn't smoke.

I didn't drink.

I wasn't what you'd call a ladies' man.

One night my fraternity brothers pulled together one hundred dollars. They dared me to chug a tall glass of vodka mixed with orange juice, offering the money as incentive. I'm not going to lie. It was hard to turn down one hundred dollars. It was a lot of money in those days! And I certainly could have used it. I was living off nickels and dimes running the fraternity house soda machine. However, despite the fact the money could have come in handy, something occurred to me. Whatever it was I was tempted to prove was not in that glass. It wasn't in that room full of my fraternity brothers, and it certainly wasn't in the wad of cash on the table. It was on the basketball court. It was in the classroom, and so it was with a whole lot of resolve that I set the drink down, and pushed it and the money away from me. And do you want to know something? The decision wasn't as hard as I thought it would be.

The room let out a collective gasp. I received a whole lot of ribbing that night and for some time after, but I didn't care. I was determined not to let my pride get in the way of what I was trying to accomplish. I wasn't about to take my eyes off the road for any reason — pride or money. I was no prude. I was just determined to achieve my dream. I truly believed that drinking and smoking could affect my ability to become a professional athlete. Besides that, Colgate was no joke. I had to work hard just to maintain a decent GPA. Classes were small. Professors were dedicated. Courses were rigorous. Student-athlete or not, there was no place to hide your academic inadequacies. I was at a school where it didn't matter if I was a star athlete, scoring 50 points per game. The fact was if I wasn't able to maintain a good grade point average, I would have been asked to transfer out. It was the same standard for all students. While I thrived on that brand of discipline, it was hard to keep from stressing out. The rigor of college life was demanding, especially after making first team in varsity basketball. I was more determined than ever to make it happen. Looking back, perhaps I did err on the side of caution. After all, it was just one drink, one seemingly innocent dare. However, I had worked too hard. I was not about to take a chance on losing everything I had worked so hard for. Those seemingly harmless decisions have negatively impacted careers of better men than me. Even today, it happens all too often, young talent throwing away opportunity for such impetuous acts. My fraternity brothers didn't give me too bad of a time for not accepting the challenge. Some even respected me for it.

℞

Two games into the varsity season, in a match against Columbia, I suffered a serious injury. Somewhere in the clash of competition, I got kneed in the left quadriceps, and the contusion kept me on the bench for two weeks. It also kept me out of a two game road trip to Pennsylvania to compete against Penn State and Lafayette. That was frustrating! I think my pride suffered more than anything. I recovered after Christmas break, just as Colgate was slated to participate in a holiday tournament known as the Down East College Tournament in Bangor, Maine. On the bracket were Bates College, Bowdoin College, the University of Maine and, of course, Colgate. I was encouraged. It was my shot to prove myself. However, moments before tipoff, Coach Howard Hartman pulled me aside and told me that I would not be starting. Because our team had won both games in Pennsylvania, he didn't think it was fair to sit out one of the seniors.

"You'll go in as a substitute," he assured me.

That was of no assurance to me. In fact, the word "substitute" made me cringe. I didn't come all the way to Colgate to be a substitute. I was a blue chip recruit, and just as the rubber was about to hit the road, I was benched. It didn't matter the reason. I was disappointed, if not incensed. For the first 10 minutes of play I sat on the sidelines, nervous energy eating away at me. With each passing minute it became harder and harder to sit still. I was restless — fidgety.

My fists were tightened.

My knees were bouncing.

It took everything I had to sit still.

If that weren't enough, the Raiders were taking a beating on the court. Bowdoin was in complete control of the game. This only angered me more. I just needed to get my hands on that basketball. Just as my head was about to implode from frustration, Coach Hartman turned to me and shouted, "Duffy, get in there!"

I was off the bench and into the game before he even finished his sentence. Over the course of the next 30 minutes of play time, I scored 37 points, putting Bowdoin right back in their place. It was a beautiful thing! The Patent Trader reported: "In this game, the Bowdoin Polar Bears double and even triple teamed Duffy in an effort to keep him in check — but this was not to be done. Duffy finished with an amazing mark of 17 for 28 — an average of better than .600 for the game."

By the end of the competition, I felt vindicated. The 37 points I put on the scoreboard set a new tournament record. After all, I was there to play ball, not warm the bench. The Patent Trader officially set the record straight. "Bob Duffy, the sensational Colgate sophomore from Katonah, N.Y., established numerous records last week in the second annual Down East College Invitational Basketball Tournament held in the Municipal Auditorium. The 6'3, 19-year-old player set a new mark by scoring 37 points against Bowdoin and, in the three-game series, tallied 88 points — an average of better than 29 points per game. This boosted his season average to 26 points for six games."

I was branded the "big man" in that game against Bowdoin, and I sure felt like it. As I think back to that experience, all those years ago, I realize that the circumstances leading up to that game could have just as easily hurt my college basketball career. Suppose I hadn't been called off the bench. How different would my life be today? It's those random sets of circumstance that, by no fault of your own, can alter your life ... for better or for worse. And sometimes it can go either way.

FIFTEEN

School of Hard Knocks

In order to be the best, you have to be up against the best.

The closer I came to achieving my dream, the tougher the competition became. The summer before my junior year in college I found myself bleeding from the mouth, miles away from home in a basketball camp infirmary. I was left alone with a fat lip and injured pride. I wasn't sure which hurt worse, which makes this an important part of my story, the part that tested both my commitment and character.

In the spring of 1960, the second half of my sophomore year, I learned that Bob "Mr. Basketball" Cousy was holding a youth basketball camp known as Camp Graylag in New Hampshire on Lake Winnipesaukee. Cousy was my idol, a living legend in the world of basketball. I looked up to him. I studied him when he played point guard for the Boston Celtics. That spring I wrote to

73

Cousy. I inquired about a summer job as a camp counselor. I was thrilled when he responded, offering me a position assisting young campers with the basics of basketball. This was a big deal for me and a big step toward my future. I was getting closer to my dream of playing in the NBA. I would be learning from the best! I believed then, just as I believe now, that in order to become the best, you've got to go up against the best. It won't be easy, and don't expect a friendly welcome, especially if you demonstrate any kind of talent. If you are good at something, and you are gunning for a position in a fiercely competitive business, those in the business may see you as a threat, and you could find yourself sucking on an ice pack alone in the camp infirmary, wondering what happened.

I was an eager 20 year old kid looking for my shot at the big time. Being invited to Camp Graylag as a counselor was an accomplishment in and of itself. Not only was I going to be in the company of "Mr. Basketball," but I was also going to be in the presence of other basketball greats, fellow camp counselors whose reputation in basketball preceded them. One of the most memorable was 6'4 Celtic shooting guard Sam Jones. He was known for his quickness and off the backboard jump-shots. I didn't realize how fast he was until I was up against him. Guarding Sam Jones on the basketball court was kind of like trying to capture lightning in a Mason jar — impossible! Fortunately, it was a lot easier to get to know him off the court. Sam was an all-around great guy, a man of real character, someone I looked up to. What surprised me the most about him was that he was extremely humble, a rare and admirable quality in someone so famous.

I also got to know a guy by the name of Charlie Carr. He was an excellent basketball player — solid and energetic. Charlie graduated from Boston College. We had a lot of fun together and remained friends for a few years after camp ended. I regret that, had it not been for geography, we might still be friends today. Back then we didn't have the luxury of the Internet. There was no social media, cell phones, or Skype. People kept in touch with postage stamps and the occasional long distance phone call. Eventually Charlie and I lost touch. I still think about him, wonder how he and the others are doing. That time in my life, that summer spent at Camp Graylag was special.

Sam Jones would often instigate friendly competition amongst the counselors. We'd gather at the outdoor court in the evenings beneath the moth-ridden lights for a pick-up game. Cousy would often get involved. I think he enjoyed sparring with young blood. As for me, I thought I'd died and gone to heaven. I was playing with Mr. Basketball himself. Even if it was just a pick-up game, it was, at its heart, a boyhood dream come true! Growing up I had very specific goals, one of which was to emulate Bob Cousy in the next era of the NBA. What I hadn't realized at the time, but soon would is that our idols are only human. I was young. Moreover, I was green, unseasoned in professional sports. I was so eager to perform and make a good impression that I didn't even see it coming. Basketball, at its best, is a physical game. Throw in a couple of professionals who have knocked the ball around with big boys like Bill Russell, Jerry West, Oscar Robertson, and Wilt Chamberlain, to name a few, and it's a hard lesson waiting to happen. As eager as I was, I still had a lot to learn.

One warm summer night, campers and a number of their parents came out to watch some of our "friendly" competition. I volunteered to guard Cousy. Naturally, I wanted to do well. Like I said, if you ever hope to achieve, you have to compete against the best. This was my shot!

Cousy was a tremendous talent. He was built to be a superstar. Though he was only 6'1, not big by basketball standards, he had broad shoulders, large frying pan hands, and an extremely long reach. This made him dangerous. I had a couple of inches on Cousy, and what I lacked in experience, I made up for in determination. Keep in mind, Cousy was, and still is, regarded as one of the best guards in the world. The man had an incredible knack for controlling the ball. Not only did he have an uncanny ability to score, but his passing skills were out of this world. One minute you could see the ball, the next minute it was gone. With his signature long pass, he could send a ball sailing down the court and into the hands of his teammate, bringing a crowd to its feet and inspiring a roar so loud that the coliseum would tremble at its core. I could tell almost immediately that the only way for me to effectively guard Cousy was through swift and nimble motions. I figured that denying him the ball would be the only way of stopping him. However, you know what they say about the best laid plans — they don't always work out the way you imagine.

I stuck close to Cousy all night long. It was full-court press. Whenever his team had the ball, my hands and arms were up in his face. My initial, and somewhat naïve objective was to make a good impression. I wanted Cousy to recognize, if not appreciate my talent on the court. In hindsight, it probably wasn't the best idea I ever had. It was, after all, a pick-up game, not the NBA playoffs. I think all I did was make him sore. So, rather than look for the ball, Cousy jogged nonchalantly down the court. I was right there with him under the basket, leaving him very little room to move around. As he grew more flustered, Cousy clasped both of his hands together, knotting his fingers into a hard fist. And like a sledge hammer, he swung his arms upward, knocking me under my chin. Before I knew what hit me I was sprawled out on the cool, hard pavement, spitting blood as Cousy grabbed the ball and dribbled down the court. He never looked back.

That night I landed in the camp infirmary. My mouth was busted wide open, along with my innocence. My physical injury required a lot of attention, to say nothing of my pride. I was in a state of disbelief. As a kid who had always looked up to Cousy, I was crushed. To this day, a few decades later, I'm still a little disappointed in how it all turned out that night. For a long time I thought it might have had something to do with the fact that I had tried to show him up in front of his longtime fans, the campers and their parents. I thought maybe he had simply wanted to put on a show for the audience, rather than spar with a kid who was simply trying to impress him. It wasn't until many years later that Cousy revealed remorse for what happened that night in Bill Reynolds' book titled, *Cousy: His Life, Career, and the Birth of Big-Time Basketball.*

Though Cousy's recollection of the incident is quite different from mine, it gave me a little bit of insight into the man. Reynolds writes, "… but that wasn't the incident he felt most guilty about. That happened one summer at his camp when he was just a few years away from retiring from the Celtics. He was playing at a camp game when he and one of his counselors, a kid named Bob Duffy, who played for Colgate, went for a loose ball. In the struggle, Duffy inadvertently hit Cousy with an elbow, and as they both went to the ground for the ball, Cousy wrestled it away from Duffy, exhibiting more force than he had to, then hit Duffy with an elbow as he started back down the court — either intentional or not, he wasn't even sure — and continued with the play as Duffy lay on the ground bleeding. Moments afterward, he felt awful and later sat with Duffy that night, endlessly apologizing."

While our memories of that day differ, all that matters to me is that I learned from the experience. I learned that in the business of basketball, or any business for that matter, it's important not to take things personally. While achieving a dream is a very personal thing, those we are in the arena with, some of whom we are competing against, all come from different backgrounds and upbringings. Our motivations to achieve are all very different, as are the methods we use to achieve them. I realized that after reading another of Bob Cousy's books, an autobiography titled, *Basketball is My Life*, co-authored by Al Hirschberg, a renowned New York City sports reporter. The book reveals Cousy's family background. It identifies why he is so physically aggressive and willing to do anything to win. To this day, I admire Bob Cousy. He was a great basketball player and a wonderful person. I was fortunate to have had the opportunity to work with him. And I would do it again. To be a success at any one thing, you have to expect obstacles. Overcoming those obstacles won't be easy, and it certainly won't always be painless. However, if you can take them in stride, keep a good attitude, walk away with the lesson, and realize that even though a "busted lip" may feel personal, it really isn't.

SIXTEEN

You are the Storm

Showing up is half the battle.

In the fall of 1960, the start of my junior year at Colgate, I moved out of the Delta Upsilon house and into a dorm with two of my fraternity brothers. The dorm was located on the quad, within walking distance of class. It seemed like the ideal situation, considering my focus on academics had become the cornerstone of my existence. Living on campus, in the throes of academia, robbed me of any excuse not to dig deeper into my studies — not that I was looking for an excuse. I had never been more committed to my education. Dorm life provided me with much more personal space and the quiet that I needed to improve the quality of my studying experience. It didn't hurt that I was within a stone's throw of the library. My roommates and I each had our own bedroom, which meant we didn't have to compete with each other for space and privacy. Space and privacy are always a challenge in college.

I had just settled on Russian Studies as my major. I had boned up on the language as a curriculum requirement during my freshman and sophomore year. I enjoyed being under the tutelage of Dr. Albert Parry, the founder and chairman of the Department of Russian Studies at Colgate. Dr. Parry was born in Russia. He had witnessed the Russian Revolution as a high school student. This made him a great and knowledgeable lecturer on the subject. I found him to be engaging and committed to his students. Not only that, but we were literally in the midst of the Cold War, a time when the threat of nuclear war between the two world superpowers, the United States and the Soviet Union, was eminent. It seemed timely to study Russia's history, literature and economics.

Along with the excitement surrounding my choice of major, there had been much anticipation surrounding the upcoming varsity basketball season. Along with an impressive playing schedule, the American Broadcasting Company, otherwise known as ABC, had invited Syracuse, NYU, Holy Cross and Colgate to participate in a big college basketball event at an arena situated in Utica, New York — a double-header! This was an incredible opportunity since the broadcasting giant was introducing live sporting events on national television. The first big game, Syracuse vs. New York University, was scheduled to be televised. The second game, Colgate vs. Holy Cross, was not programmed to hit the airwaves. That made no difference to the Raiders. We were thrilled just to be invited. It was an exciting time in our lives and in the history of sports broadcasting. I remember that day well!

It was the dead of winter. New York was covered in ice and snow. It was one of the worst blizzards on record. Mayor Dulan called a state of emergency. As the event approached, the storm showed no signs of letting up. We all knew that if the dangerous road conditions didn't improve, or at the very least hold stable, we would be forced to forfeit the game and the event would be canceled. Syracuse and Holy Cross had already been forced to forfeit, as they could not safely make the drive to Utica. The weather was just too severe.

Meanwhile, New York University was already holed up in Utica, anticipating a worthy opponent, someone daring enough to make the drive. The only team left on the ticket was Colgate. The question was: Would the Raiders risk the precarious bus ride? I imagine there were some broadcasting executives holding out hope for one valiant act of defiance, one long shot to save the day. That's when Colgate, a long shot personified, stepped up and agreed to brave the storm. It was a terrible risk, the likes of which might have detoured far bigger and better men. However, with more confidence than common sense, the Colgate Raiders accepted the challenge. That day we braced against the elements, not to mention the odds, as we dashed from Colgate's Huntington gym to the team bus. The snow was coming down hard, though not so hard as to deviate the hour of our determination. The school bus, itself, seemed just as resolute and hard-headed. With thick, gray exhaust fumes spewing from its tailpipe and its determined engine shaking off the bitter cold, the Raiders climbed aboard one at a time until we filled the hull. The 40-minute trip turned into a two-hour slog through the winter sludge. Just as we thought we had conquered the worst of it, the team bus, a hero in its own right, reached an impasse just a few miles outside of our final destination. Traffic was choked up in both directions. The situation appeared hopeless. The team let out a collective sigh. Even the bus exhaled. We had come so close!

Suddenly, Ken Norum, our courageous team captain, stood to his feet. Without saying a word, he jumped out of his seat and pushed through the door and into the storm. Like a shot he crossed the street and cut through the blizzard. The team quickly rallied onto the driver's side of the bus, nearly tipping it over onto its side as we watched Ken soldier fearlessly in the direction of a farmhouse situated just off the road. He was nearly swallowed whole by the thick, icy vapor, the lake-effect snow blowing off of Lake Erie and Lake Ontario. The team bus was quiet as we waited for Ken's return. Minutes felt like hours. Our eyes were pasted to the cold, wet window panes. There were people dressed in heavy coats, scarves and mittens milling around in the road, unable to push forward. We were in need of a miracle.

With NYU and ABC waiting in the wings, it seemed like Ken might never return. We had come too far to get stuck out in the middle of nowhere. Just as I was about to give up on the idea that we'd make it to Utica on time, Ken sprung out of the fog. His cheeks were as red as Washington apples. He had a big grin on his face as he sprinted toward the bus. Behind him, from out of the fog was a farmer on a large tractor to dig us out of the mess. The team let out a loud cheer. We had found our miracle.

The day had been saved!

As the bus pulled up to the event, the Raiders were met with a loud roar of applause, followed by a huge sigh of relief from television executives. However, no one was happier to see us than New York University. We were greeted like rock stars as we disembarked from our faithful bus. ABC captured it on camera in real time. Suited up and ready to go, we wasted no time taking the court with just a few minutes to warm up.

NYU had an impressive program and the record to match. The Violets were ranked in the top 15 teams in the country, while Colgate had been coined the "28 point underdogs." The disparity of our record in contrast to NYU's made no difference to the Raiders. The only thing that mattered was that we were there, competing on national television against one of the best teams in the country. And to top it off, the longtime voice of the Boston Red Sox and American sportscaster, Curt Gowdy, was calling the game.

I scored 26 points that day, as did senior forward Dave Davenport, who played his best game ever. Bill Salisbury, another senior contributed 13 points to the scoreboard. John Doyle, my backcourt classmate, scored nine points, three of which were free throws in the last 30 seconds of the game. Those last three points sealed Colgate's victory over NYU — 80-75. Turns out, we were the storm! It was a game that college basketball fans across the country would talk about for years to come, no one more than my parents. We, the "28-point underdogs," had beaten a nationally-ranked team in a game that wasn't even officially scheduled. It wouldn't have happened if not for the snow storm. Sometimes circumstance sets the stage for those who are determined to succeed.

I managed to average 22 points a game that season, putting me among the top 25 scorers in American college basketball. The Rochester Democrat and Chronicle heralded, "Colgate's Red Raiders will come … with one of the top backcourt men in the East leading the way. Junior Bob Duffy, a 6'3 ball-handling whiz who is averaging 22 points per game, last year broke the school's sophomore scoring mark with 445 points."

I guess you could say I was determined to succeed. I wasn't about to let anything get in my way, least of all the weather. Success is all about what you've got going on between the ears, and once you've committed to your dream, there is no other way to go but to the top, no threat of snow storm or traffic jam can stop you.

SEVENTEEN

When Push Comes to Shove

Be intentional with everything you do.

At the start of my senior year, I was selected to be a part of the Maroon Key Honorary Society by Bill Griffith, Dean of Students. I was also chosen to represent Colgate in the 1961 — 1962 edition of the "Who's Who among Students in American Universities and Colleges." This honor was accorded by a joint student-faculty committee after having been nominated one of 25 students by the Colgate student body. The criteria comprised of student scholarships, participation and leadership in academic and extracurricular activities. It also consisted of good citizenship, service to the school, and promise for future usefulness. While the nomination was a surprise, it was satisfying to me that all my hard work was paying off. I had never been more focused or intent on achieving my dream. I was prepared to make any and all necessary changes to "make it happen," including my living arrangements.

While boarding with an 80-year-old woman isn't the ideal college experience for a senior student-athlete, I had decided to move from the college quad to a more private setting. I was looking for a quiet space so that I could focus on my studies. In order to accomplish this, I rented a clean, comfortable bedroom from a kind, elderly woman who lived alone. Her house was just a few hundred yards off of the Delta Upsilon lawn, close enough to keep me connected to all of the fraternity's activities, most of which were daily meals and social events, and far enough away that I might hear myself think. It was the best of both worlds. Dick Egan, one of my fraternity brothers, and a football player at Colgate, was also renting a room from the same woman.

I had a lot weighing on my mind that year, particularly as it related to my future. One of my favorite college professors, Donald L. Berry, a faculty member in the Department of Philosophy and Religion helped me wrap my head around the road ahead. He taught me how to be more thoughtful and intentional in both mind and body. One day in class he posed these three very important questions.

What is good?

What is real?

What is happiness?

Those three simple questions kept my focus sharp, so that I might look at my life in a deeper, more meaningful way. I was nearing college graduation, standing at the foot of my boyhood dream of playing in the NBA. I worked so hard to get there. I didn't want to complicate matters by straying from that which mattered most to me, and so I never lost sight of those three things.

☙

During the 1961-1962 varsity basketball season the Colgate Raiders lacked one instrumental requisite for success on the court — height. There are a lot of things a basketball coach can do in order to win games. However, the one thing he can't do is coach size. Our height deficit was particularly obvious in our center position. On average, college centers stand somewhere between 6'6 and 6'10. Our starting center wasn't even close. This shortfall could have proven lethal to our season since the sport all but demands exceptional size and stature. However, what we lacked in height, we made up for in tenacity. In an interview with Dell Sports Magazine, Bob Cousy even posed the question. "Where will the rebounds come from?" He was, of course, referring to Colgate's height deficit. Surely, he wasn't the only basketball aficionado to wonder. In that same interview, Cousy stated, "Duffy is rated the best back court prospect in the east."

I was very appreciative.

Cousy's unsolicited remark did a lot for my confidence, especially after having taken one in the chin from him just two summers earlier. That statement planted a seed, inspiring me to take control of my future. Colgate's lack of height could have proven to be a real problem for a 6'3 guard like me. Guarding a man who stands 6'10 with an equal wingspan is no easy feat.

This problem became evident when the Raiders were matched up against the University of Illinois and Loyola of Chicago in back-to-back games during a Christmas tournament in Chicago. The University of Illinois, otherwise known as the Fighting Illini, had our front line — a team of men standing somewhere between 6'2 and 6'5 — competing against a band of giants who stood anywhere between 6'6 and 6'10. We were literally in over our heads.

The University of Illinois' All-Big Ten guard, a man who stood 6'4 tall, did an outstanding job defending me. He was put on point for the box-and-one defense that was intended to neutralize me. The box-and-one-defense is a cross between man-to-man defense and a zone defense. It was designed to shut down a dominant scoring threat, forcing that "threat" to score against a man-to-man player, and a supporting zone. From the sidelines, I overheard the head coach shouting from the opposing bench, "Stop Duffy and Colgate cannot win the game!"

The strategy worked. We got clobbered 88-50. I only scored 18 points that game. And as for that All-Big Ten 6'4 guard, he was none other than Jerry Colangelo, the very same kid who would later build a sports empire that included the Phoenix Suns and the Arizona Diamondbacks. He would be the man to resurrect the American basketball program, and would be named in the Basketball Hall of Fame for his achievements. I suppose if I was going to be shut down by anyone it may as well have been to a guy like Colangelo. After all, a player is only as good as those he competes against. The next game wasn't any easier!

Loyola of Chicago had a front line that stood between 6'7 and 6'10. I was able to score 24 points that game, respectively. Unfortunately, it didn't keep us from getting shellacked. The Raiders had no idea what they were up against. Loyola didn't even bother with the box-and-one-defense. They spent much of their time double-teaming me and winning the game based on raw talent alone. Loyola went on to win the National NCAA Championship that year.

Meanwhile, the Raiders season wasn't looking good. Nor were my chances of playing in the NBA. I was beginning to realize how difficult it was going to be to achieve my boyhood dream, especially coming off of a losing season in college basketball. If I was going to "make it happen" in the NBA, I would need to stand out and fast! I was running out of time. I needed a plan, one that would require a quick adjustment in how the Raiders were handling the ball.

After much consideration, and very little input from my teammates, I devised a game plan, one that would give the Raiders an edge and me the opportunity to score more points. It was clear that I needed to take control of the situation. In order to do that, I had to ensure that I had control of the ball, as well as our offense. In order to accomplish this I would have to make sure another guard took the ball out of bounds. This approach would allow me to take the ball up the court. With a plan in place, things immediately got better! During our first big matchup against Cornell, I scored 29 of the Raiders' 46 points — 63-percent of the baskets. In the following game against Buffalo, I scored 27 of the 55 points — 49-percent of the baskets. My game plan was working, and so I continued to maintain control of the ball. At the final buzzer against Navy, I scored 30 of the Raiders 66 points. Against Bucknell, I scored 39 of the 66 points. My personal best was against Niagara when I scored a total of 40 points. Though a winning season was a long shot for the Raiders, I was seeing positive results in my own personal performance.

I hadn't given much thought to how my "game plan" would affect my teammates, though I began to sense their reluctance to pass the ball to me. Considering we were without significant height and overall talent, I felt as though I had no other choice but to take things into my own hands. It wouldn't be until years later that I would read a passage in a fellow Raider's memoir. Mel Watkins, *Dancing with Strangers*, told how he and some of our teammates "harbored some resentment toward me" for taking the initiative. Mel, who was among Colgate's all-time rebounders, wrote, "We sometimes sarcastically referred to [Bob Duffy] as Gatling, because of his predilection for shooting. I still remember a 30-foot, left-handed hook shot that he heaved during a close game while I stood unguarded under the basket. Several times during the 80 or so games we played together my irritation reached a point where I refused to pass the ball to him; an ill-advised tack since he was a guard and handled the ball most of the time ... In retrospect, since we were often overmatched against bigger, more talented teams, it's difficult to fault him for exploiting the situation to showcase his own talent. If I had been in his shoes, I might have done it myself. Moreover, it worked."

While the Raiders had endured many losses that season, we did have one big notch in our belt. We beat Syracuse. That's saying something, considering the Raiders haven't been able to beat them since. I contributed 28 points in that game against the Orange. I'm still proud of that accomplishment! I competed against Syracuse eight times in my college career, 320 minutes in total game time. They had a time-honored tradition at the end of each basketball season. The team would take a vote, nominating their most earnest competitors. That year, for the 1961-1962 season, Syracuse unanimously selected me, alongside Detroit's All-American, Dave Debusshere. That meant a lot to me.

It still does.

My final game as a Colgate Raider was against the University of Connecticut. We lost 94-78. I scored 36 points, despite being double-teamed. Colgate didn't have much of a season. I, however, averaged 26.1 points per game, making me the 9th leading scorer in college basketball in the country. I set a Colgate record of 1,591 points, and I did it in just three years as a varsity ballplayer. In those days, we played a 23 game schedule compared to today's 32, and, at the time, there were no three-point shots. I broke the three-year scoring record of 1,411 that belonged to Jack Nichols, a 6'7 center for Colgate and, for awhile, the Boston Celtics.

Sports Illustrated had a nice write-up, stating, "Colgate

University basketball guard from Katonah, N.Y., an A student majoring in Russian broke the school all-time one-game scoring record with 48 points against Rochester, and went onto beat the college center totals of Jack Nichols and Ernie Vandeweghe (who had a nice career with the New York Knicks)."

If that weren't enough, Jack Nichols sent me a telegram, congratulating me. He wrote, "Couldn't have happened to a better fellow. Good luck in the professional ranks. I will be watching you on television." That telegram meant the world to me.

Draft Day was just around the corner. I was nervous! I had the attention of men like Marty Blake, General Manager of the St. Louis Hawks. He was there the night I scored 40 points against Niagara. Eddie Donavan, head coach for the New York Knicks, was also in the stands. The pressure was on, and I was feeling it. Marty Blake invited me to participate in an all-star game in Binghamton, New York. The event was backed by a regional trucking company. It attracted a handful of all-Americans, including Terry Dischinger of Purdue. Marty and the Hawks' new head coach, ex-Knick player Harry Gallatin, evaluated the talent at the game. Competition was fierce. Once again, I had but a small window to stand out, and so that's exactly what I did. I scored 31 points in all and was named MVP. Come January, the offer letters came rolling in. The St. Louis Hawks, the New York Knickerbockers, the Detroit Pistons and the Chicago Packers were calling.

EIGHTEEN

The NBA Draft

Waiting for the call can be the loneliest time of your life.

I knew I would be drafted into the NBA, but by whom or at what level was the question. Even though I was confident I would get *the* call, it didn't make the wait any less difficult. I had several NBA scouts show up to games, looking to catch a glimpse of my performance throughout the season. A handful of the nine teams had sent me letters showing an interest. Those same teams were simultaneously soliciting my interest, looking to see if I was serious about joining the National Basketball Association. Believe it or not, joining the NBA wasn't as attractive an offer as it is today. The salaries weren't nearly as compelling. By today's standards, it seems ridiculous to think professional basketball teams would have to solicit an athlete's interest in being a part of the pre-eminent men's professional basketball league in North

America — if not the world. Most athletes today would give their eyeteeth for the opportunity to play professionally. However, in the early days of the league, the NBA rivaled big name corporations, companies that provided full-time jobs in the off-season on top of the opportunity to play professional ball. A job offer at a corporation was intensely more attractive to most players since it provided a long-term future in business in addition to the short-term excitement of being a professional ballplayer. It was a built-in Plan B in the instance a player's basketball career didn't skyrocket into the superstar hemisphere.

For example, there was the oil and gas giant Phillips Petroleum Company. Their organization sponsored a team called the Phillips 66ers, also known as the Oilers. The 66ers were an amateur team out of Bartlesville, Oklahoma. They participated in the AAU, the Amateur Athletic Union Basketball club. This was the nation's premier basketball league before the NBA. Some of the most successful teams in the United States during that time were sponsored by corporations like Phillips. They were very successful in attracting some real talent from the college ranks.

Playing professional basketball wasn't about fame and fortune in the early days. As a matter of fact, because salaries were based on ticket sales, there wasn't a lot of fortune to be had, even if you were famous. Most players had to hold down two jobs. In the 60s the NBA was comprised of nine teams that were spread out across the country. There wasn't a whole lot of attraction to play at that level. Money wasn't motivation enough.

Comparatively, professional superstar basketball players, the cream of the crop, earned what the average school teacher earns today — somewhere in the ballpark of thirty thousand dollars, respectively. So, in an effort to recruit, those nine teams that made up the NBA would annually distribute surveys to graduating student-athletes, soliciting their interest in joining the organization. This step saved recruiters the trouble of using a pick in the draft on an athlete who wasn't serious about a career in the NBA. Professional basketball was in its infancy. There was no promise of multimillion dollar contracts, and there certainly were no commercial endorsements — not like there are today. Be that as it may, my hopes were pinned on this phone call.

As I nervously paced up and down the narrow hallway of Delta Upsilon, staying as close to the house telephone as I could, I thought back to every decision I had ever made, every risk I had taken and all the hard work I had turned in to get to this point. This was *my* moment of truth. There was no one else to look to, no one else to blame if the telephone didn't ring. It was all on me. I had not been born with extraordinary privilege, height or brawn. What I did inherit was my family's resilience, an extraordinary mixture of courage, determination and grit. I was counting on those qualities now more than ever.

The first round selections were usually dominated by the big centers and forwards; the emphasis being on centers. With Wilt Chamberlain, one of the greatest and most dominant centers in NBA history, and Bill Russell, a five-time MVP, teams were on the lookout for productive centers that were big enough and strong enough — physically and psychologically — to match that same brand of competition. Therefore, picking centers and forwards in the first round was common practice. Guards were generally targeted in the second round. In today's market NBA guards are drafted early on, along with the big centers and forwards. This is done for two reasons: First, there were only nine teams in the NBA at the time, compared to the 30 teams in the league today, which more than triples the amount of talent selected in every round. Second, the three-point play was introduced decades later in both the NBA and in college. Both of these changes had a huge effect on the game and enhanced the value of the guard position.

Feeling the heat with each passing minute, I was comforted by something Howard Hartman, Colgate's head basketball coach, said to me a few short months earlier. We were sitting inside of Madison Square Garden, watching St. John's play in the NIT Tournament. From out of the blue, Coach Hartman turned to me and said, "Bob, you will be the number one guard drafted into the NBA."

I respected Coach Hartman. I trusted him, and so I held fast to that statement. In fact, those words meant so much to me that I replayed them over and over again in my mind as I waited for the call. Coach was, of course, comparing me to Kevin Loughery, a highly regarded guard at St. Johns. Those were big shoes. By the time the telephone rang, I was full of fire and adrenaline. I picked up the telephone receiver and I heard the voice of Marty Blake,

General Manager of the St. Louis Hawks. Coach Hartman was right. I was the first guard picked in the 1962 NBA draft. Detroit followed, selecting Kevin Loughery of St. Johns. Rounding off the second round picks were Chet Walker of Bradley (Syracuse), Bud Olson of Louisville (Cincinnati), Hubie White of Villanova (Philadelphia), Gene Wiley of Wichita (Los Angeles), and Jack Foley of Holy Cross (Boston). Loughery, White, Foley and I were all guards, expected to be the best in the business. Soon after I received *the* call, Coach Hartman told the Colgate Maroon, "I think Bob is made to order for the pro game. He has a good outside shot and is quick enough to get it away with the professionals. Very few boys have better shots."

Bob Duffy, Colgate Raiders, 1961

NINETEEN

The St. Louis Hawks

Not everything is as it seems.

Bright and early the next morning, Emil Barboni, a scout for the St. Louis Hawks, showed up at my doorstep sporting a smart suit and a friendly smile. He shook my hand, introduced himself, and handed me an airline ticket. It was a one-way flight to St. Louis to meet the Hawks' owner and general manager. Mr. Barboni was my official welcome into the NBA, as well as my ride to the airport. He and I chatted during the one hour drive to Clarence E. Hancock Airport in Syracuse, now known as the Syracuse Hancock International Airport. Barboni was a good guy who had nothing but encouraging things to say about my performance on the court. Still a little nervous, if not naïve, I found his kind disposition reassuring, giving me the impression that the NBA was a kind, friendly place — a fair place.

On the ride to catch my flight, Mr. Barboni and I discussed life and the love of basketball. Our conversation became so involved I missed my flight to St. Louis. As a result, I was forced to catch a later flight. I didn't think much of it at the time. However, all these years later, I wonder if my missing that plane wasn't an omen. I'm not a superstitious man, but knowing what I know now, it makes me think.

Marty Blake, General Manager, met me at the airport terminal in St. Louis. He handed me a jersey, number 24. Then, with zero fanfare, he dropped me at the Jefferson Hotel downtown. I stood in front of that hotel, soaking it all in. It was all a bit hard to believe — the NBA! I went to bed early that night, although I didn't fall asleep right away. I wanted to be on my best game, fresh and ready to meet the Hawks' owner Ben Kerner the next morning, as well as to be introduced to the press. This was the start of a whole new chapter in my life. I moved to St. Louis that summer. I was living out of a hotel. While it wasn't anything to write home about, it was an upgrade for this kid from Katonah. I had made it to the big league. Everything in my life was about to change.

ॐ

Apart from our official NBA contracts, the top four draft picks for the Hawks were hired to give basketball clinics during the summer of '62. We were expected to serve as ambassadors for the team. It was a clever marketing tactic, a way to encourage ticket sales for the upcoming season. We trekked across the city of St. Louis during those warm summer months in a large van with a picture of a Hawk painted on both sides, the words "Here come the Hawks!" splashed beneath it. Along with the team's new head coach, Harry Gallatin, the "marketing team" consisted of (in draft order) Zelmo Beaty, Bob Duffy, Charlie Hardnett, and Chico Vaughn. We were literally being paid to perform in front of crowds, large and small, teaching kids the basics of basketball at local high schools and playgrounds. It was a good way of keeping us boys busy during the off-season, providing us with some much needed income.

One day Coach Gallatin was out sick. Marty Blake asked that I take Gallatin's position, putting me in charge of our little traveling show. I was given the keys to the van, as well as the bull horn so to direct my fellow draftees as they demonstrated the basics of the game for an audience. As we drove up to a local high school, I could feel a certain amount of tension building. Nobody said a word, but it was becoming increasingly uncomfortable. As soon as the four of us stepped out of the van and onto the basketball court to start the show, with a few hundred parents and children in the stands, my teammates crossed their arms tightly across their chests, refusing to perform. It was clear they resented me for having been put in charge. I was embarrassed and extremely uncomfortable with the responsibility. I hadn't asked to be placed in that position, and so the clinic that day fell short.

Still a little green to the ways of the world, I was perplexed as to why they had chosen to act out against me. It wasn't until about a month later that a fellow teammate of mine, Bill Bridges of

Kansas, enlightened me as to why Beaty, Hardnett and Vaughn had challenged me in front of all those people. It hadn't occurred to me that we were in the midst of the Civil Rights Movement and that my three black teammates took my being put in charge as an affront. I hadn't meant to offend anyone, least of all my peers. I had been placed into an awkward position where I felt I had no control.

"There will be blood in the streets," Bill Bridges said. Bill was African-American, and he was referring to the discrimination that was taking place across the United States. Those were precarious times in our country's history. Coming from Katonah, I had no idea how bad racism had gotten, but I was learning fast. I, too, was feeling isolated. Along with the incident that had just occurred with my teammates, I had a sneaking suspicion that Gallatin didn't care for me. The man looked right through me. It hadn't occurred to me at the time, but his angst may have had something to do with the fact that the Hawks' owner, Ben Kerner, had invited me to have dinner with him and his girlfriend at the famed Chase Park Plaza Hotel on two separate occasions. If that hadn't rubbed Gallatin wrong, it may have had something to do with Marty Blake selecting me to represent the Hawks every Sunday over breakfast on KMOX Radio. The show was known as, "Hawks Highlights with Jack Buck and Bob Duffy." It was a breakfast radio show aired from the Chase Park Plaza Hotel, a first-class inn located on Kings Highway and Lindell Boulevard in the heart of St. Louis.

Jack Buck was a well-respected broadcaster in St. Louis. Years later he became a national celebrity. I'm not sure why the Hawks' administration chose me over Gallatin to co-host the radio show with Jack Buck. All I knew was that I was a rookie in the NBA. I wasn't about to question the man who signed my paycheck.

With all the attention I was getting, the press started referring to me as the "Ivy Leaguer." Considering the season hadn't even started, it was much more limelight than I deserved. While it had its perks, I felt that brand of attention put me at a disadvantage with Coach Gallatin and the other rookie draftees. It certainly didn't make it easy to build effective working relationships. The truth is I couldn't wait for basketball season to begin so I could actually earn the attention I was receiving. Basketball is, after all, a team sport, not a one-man show. I had confidence when training camp began that I'd prove myself as a player, and I did. When I did play, even at practice, no one was running over me. I held my own!

TWENTY

The Real World of Sports

Mental toughness is the greater part of success.

When you reach the big leagues, the competition becomes especially fierce. Training was more rigorous and, at times, bloody. I was competing for a guard position on the St. Louis Hawks ball club. I went from college ball, a relative cake walk, to sparring with superstars like Bob Pettit, Cliff Hagen, and Lenny Wilkens — all seasoned veterans with one sole objective: To protect their job. And as tough as the seasoned veterans were, it was my fellow rookies who were the real threat, as they had shown up to fight for the open positions. It was a battle of elbows, fast breaks, and intimidation tactics — both physical and mental. There were drills and double sessions and it wouldn't end until there were only 12 men standing. It was do or die and that was just practice. It didn't take me long to realize that if I didn't brace for this fight, if I didn't give it everything I had, and then some, I'd be eaten alive. It was dog-eat-dog, and I had decided at a very young age that I was not giving up my dream without a fight.

John McCarthy, a backcourt starter for the Hawks, made it his mission to get between me and the basket. He made no qualms about it. McCarthy was a graduate of Canisius College, a private university in Buffalo, New York. He never said as much, but I could see in his eyes that he was not about to give up his position on the team, not without a hell of a fight. He had been a guard with the Hawks for two seasons. It was up to me to change that. I had the burden of proving myself.

There were times when full court press felt more like a backroom bar fight. McCarthy gave me his worst and I, the kid from Katonah, gave it right back to him. Fortunately, for me, McCarthy was cut from the team after just a few days. It's a good thing, too, because this game is an endurance race. The truth was I was relieved. I knew it could have just as easily have been me.

There was still a long way to go, so I quickly pushed that thought from my mind. When you are competing against the best, there is no room for doubt and fear. When push comes to shove, the trick is to push harder and longer than the next guy and don't let fear get in the way. I realize that's easier said than done. Vying for position in the National Basketball Association was one of the toughest things I've ever had to do. It was exhausting, painful at times. If I was to keep up with a 100 game season that included an exhibition season and playoffs, I would need to build up endurance for this sport and its competition. In addition, I had learned how physically fit one needs to be in order to compete in the NBA. One day after the second session of practice, Emil Barboni, the scout who recommended me to the Hawks, stopped by. He pulled me aside and said, "You're doing a fine job, Bob. The Hawks are really impressed with you."

I needed that!

I was still young, naïve and very much in the fray. I was also worried about what had happened over the summer with the "traveling show" and how that might affect my chances of making the team. That was my only real concern. I knew I belonged in the NBA. I was built for that brand of competition.

The season before, the St. Louis ball club had collapsed. They had failed, for the first time, to make the playoffs. Owner, Ben Kerner, had plans of rebuilding the Hawks around Bob Pettit, Cliff Hagen, and Lenny Wilkens. He also had a brand-new head coach named Harry Gallatin. Gallatin, who played his college ball at Northeast Missouri State Teachers College and starred in the National League with the New York Knickerbockers and Detroit Pistons, had established a successful coaching career at Southern Illinois University. It was obvious the Hawks were gearing up for a successful season. Because of my ball-handling ability, I was aware via quotes in the press that my role was to be, what today is known as, a point guard. With Wilkens out with an injury until late October, Cliff Hagan and Bob Pettit, otherwise known as the "greatest one-two punch in the game's history" (at that time) were certain starters. I was known as the "handsome back-liner from Colgate University" and promoted as an "Ivy Leaguer" to make me more interesting to the press and prospective ticketholders. It's no secret. Professional sports are good at marketing their product. However, despite all the hype, I focused on making a difference and maintaining my self-confidence.

In between practices, the Hawks scheduled a huge promotional event designed to showcase the new team, boost ticket sales and generate anticipation within our fan-base. It was exciting to watch as thousands of fans piled into Kiel auditorium. My heart raced as the show kicked off and the entire auditorium went pitch black. The crowd went wild, cheering, stomping and applauding. There was a feeling of white heat emanating from my soul, an intensity so moving that I could hardly breathe. A spotlight spilled onto center court and one-by-one the Hawks were introduced. I couldn't see the crowd. I could only feel the vibration from their presence. The whole experience was a real turn-on for me.

As I stood nervously along the dark sidelines, waiting to be introduced to all of St. Louis, there was a small group of attractive young women standing nearby. They were some of St. Louis' top models. I watched as they quietly prepared to model fine clothing at the event. One woman, in particular, had my attention. She was beautiful and for a moment the entire auditorium disappeared. Her name was Sandra Nelson. At the time I was single, a free agent so to speak. Susie Woodfin and I had broken up a while back and so I felt inclined to introduce myself. Sandy smiled and I was ruined for all other women. Just then my name was announced over the loud speaker. This was it, my big introduction as one of the St. Louis Hawks. The announcer's teaser made me out to be some sort of a basketball god. It was an out-of-body experience as I dribbled the ball to center court, the blinding spotlight in my eyes. Even though most of it was just hype, exaggerated publicity at that point, I bought into it and so had the crowd. Much of the buildup and excitement would disappear when the lights were turned on. None of it was real. Underneath it all, I was still just the kid from Katonah and, at the end of the day I had to be good with that. Even though I was publicized as being the number one college guard in the country in the NBA draft, I still had to prove that would hold true in the professional arena.

ଔ

The sixteen-game exhibition season began on September 27, 1962. The Hawks competed against Chicago in Wood River, Illinois. In a month's time we played five of the eight NBA teams in a host of cities. It was a highly effective way for the NBA to boost regional interest. Six of those exhibition games were against the Boston Celtics — consecutively. Talk about your traveling circus! The Hawks were tired, having visited cities that included Bloomfield, Missouri; Parsons Kansas; Galesburg, Illinois; and both Nashville and Memphis Tennessee, to name a few. Playing that many games on the road, in the short stretch of 20 days was a real eye-opener. It revealed the kind of commitment and physicality that was required. In order to accomplish that, I needed to stay in shape. That meant keeping active, eating the right foods, and getting enough water. And sometimes even that wasn't enough. The one thing that made the biggest difference to my stamina was the encouragement of the fans. Their faithful support was what fueled me when nothing or no one else could. Life on the road was rough, but I gave it my best effort.

Up to that point, I hadn't seen much game time. I was growing concerned. Then, on October 4, 1962, in an exhibition game against the San Francisco Warriors, I saw 14 minutes of play in the second half. I was credited with seven assists, and Coach Gallatin was credited for this quote in the Patent Trader: "We scouted every top back court player in the nation and we feel that Duffy is the best prospect. He is a great shooter, has good size (6-foot-3), is extremely fast, and knows the Eastern style of play that is essential in our league."

I was relieved.

A couple of days later I received word from the Hawks' office that Zelmo Beatty and I had been selected to play in the College All-Star Milk Fund Game. We were slated to compete against the New York Knicks at Madison Square Garden in New York City on October 12, 1962. Zelmo was the Hawks' number one pick in the 1962 draft. I was number two. Zelmo and I flew to New York. We were both excited, not only because this was a great honor, but also because we were being teamed up with fellow draft picks John Havlicek and Dave Debusshere, just to name a couple. Together, in front of 18,000 people, the four of us were slated to compete against the New York Knicks. We were confident and ready to prove ourselves.

I had a tough time containing my excitement!

Each of the college all-stars had been hand-selected by a committee that included Kenny Norton of Manhattan College. Norton would be our coach for the upcoming all-star game. The man was highly respected in the basketball community. His college all-stars included LeRoy Ellis and Kevin Loughery of St. Johns, Bill McGill of Utah, Len Chappell of Wake Forest, Wayne Hightower of Kansas, Dave DeBusschere of the University of Detroit, Jack Foley of Holy Cross, John Havlicek of Ohio State, Zelmo Beaty of Prairie View A&M in Texas and me, Bob Duffy from Colgate University. It was quite a mixture of talent. I was grateful to be a part of it!

The team was put up at the Hotel Manhattan for a few nights. We spent our days practicing at Fordham University under the tutelage of Coach Norton. Our nights were spent resting up for the big game. Practice sessions were brisk and we were braced for a fight. According to the press and the high court of public opinion, the all-star team was not expected to beat the Knicks. And why would we? They were the New York Knicks!

The Knicks had far more experience and superstardom going for them. However, tell that to a team of eager young men looking to make a name for themselves in professional basketball.

As rookies, we may not have had the confidence of sports fans and sports-writers, but we did have confidence within ourselves. That's half the battle! Call it naivety, but that inexperience can be a blessing, especially when stepping into the lion's den. It actually never occurred to us that we could lose.

The competition kicked off with the Boston Celtics versus the Syracuse Nationals. Bob Cousy, Bill Russell, Tom Heinsohn, and Sam Jones were to set compete against Dolph Shayes, Johnny Kerr, Larry Costello, and Hal Greer — to name a few. It was a double-header. 18,500 tickets had been sold. It was the largest crowd I had ever played for!

By the time we were asked to warm-up for the highlight game, the Knicks versus the college all-stars, my adrenaline had reached its peak. I was busting at the seams, as was The Garden. The roar of the crowd was intense. I took a deep breath as I stood at the center of it all. For a moment everything went quiet. Those questions Professor Barry posed came flooding back to me:

What is good?

What is real?

What is happiness?

The answer to all of those questions, for me, was Madison Square Garden. I had made it! I thought about all the times Dad brought me to The Garden as a young boy to watch basketball. Because of him, and the time I spent with him in those stands, I grew up daydreaming about playing ball in that arena. As a matter of fact, I thought of little else.

I scanned the crowd, knowing that Mom and Dad and my brothers Rich and Don were somewhere up in the stands. I don't know who was more thrilled, them or me. I was moments away from competing against superstars like Richie Guerin, Willie Naulls, Johnny Green, and Gene Shue. It was hard to wash the smile from my face.

In the first half of the game, all 10 of the college all-stars had their fair share of play time. The Knicks led the way at the end of the first quarter: 33-32. By halftime we trailed 60-54. It was a tight competition. The crowd was on its feet. My teammates and I had never been hungrier for a win. After halftime the Knicks came out strong! "Jumping" Johnny Green made most of his 30 points before the end of the third quarter. Despite his incredible speed and high energy dunking ability, we all-stars never gave up. We were young and inexperienced, but we had a lot of heart!

Before we knew it, the Knicks had a 28 point lead. Things weren't looking good. That's when Coach Norton made some pivotal roster changes. He put me back in the game, alongside John Havlicek, Dave DeBusschere, LeRoy Ellis and Bill McGill. It was a magical combination because the five of us managed a comeback. Paced by Ellis, Havlicek and DeBusschere, we were able to close a twenty point gap. The Knicks had us at 103-98 with six minutes left in play. Just as things were heating up and it looked as though we might take the lead, Coach Norton called an unexpected time out. This line of attack seemed counterintuitive, considering we were prepared to drive home the victory.

I was shocked!

However, the real kick in the teeth was when Coach Norton

yanked all five of us boys out of the game and replaced us with players who had been resting warm and comfortably on the bench. This change-up came from out of nowhere, our thrust toward the finish thwarted. I didn't know what to do with all of the adrenaline coursing through my body. The only thing I could do was sit on the bench, both knees bouncing nervously, and bide my time until the game-ending buzzer sounded. I was beyond frustrated and so were the other players. We were on the brink of breaking the Knicks lead, upsetting their expected victory and Norton, for whatever reason, slammed on the brakes. And the worst part of all was that there would be no explanation. Dave DeBusschere and John Havlicek, two fierce competitors, questioned Norton's decision out loud while huddled during a time out.

"Someday you will understand," Coach Norton grumbled.

At the time I doubted I would ever understand such a half-cocked move. It didn't take the Knicks long to catch on. It was hard to watch them adjust their offense and defense from the bench and squash us in a final score of 132-112. As a young team we were angry, but more than that we were discouraged.

After the game, three of my teammates and I took a long walk through the streets of New York. We had to. We needed to recalibrate. It was becoming clear that professional basketball was a whole new ballgame. Coach Norton knew what he was doing, since the game itself was only meant to showcase the Knicks' franchise, and to boost season ticket sales, their main source of revenue. We figured that was the reason we were taken out of the game so abruptly. It might not have been in the Knicks' best interest to lose against a team of rookies. Again, it all came down to "hype!" That was a tough pill to swallow for a group of college all-stars who had something to prove.

I was young and I was hungry — too hungry for my own good, especially when I realized that I didn't have control of how the game played out on the basketball court — much less my life.

Zelmo Beaty and I boarded a plane and left New York the next morning. I tried my best to remain positive. I figured, if nothing else, my performance at that game would earn me more playing time in St. Louis. It might even earn me the respect of my coach and teammates. Only time and tenacity would tell.

St. Louis Hawks, 1962

TWENTY-ONE

Warming the Bench

Achievement starts between your ears.

It was time to suit up for the big exhibition game in St. Louis. Beatty and I were still reeling from the all-star game in New York, having had very little rest in between competitions. It was an exciting time! Up until that point, the Hawks had been on the road. It felt good to be back on our home court, our fans cheering us on in the stands. This game marked my first in Kiel Auditorium. The energy was electric!

Being the consummate professional, as well as my mother's son, I showed up a couple of hours early, sporting a freshly pressed suit and tie. Old habits, and Mom's expectations, die hard! The truth was, even though I had suffered some minor disappointments, I'd never been more content. I felt like a million bucks as I strutted into the locker room.

As I made my way to my locker, I noticed a number of new players suiting up. I got the feeling they were avoiding direct eye contact with me. That's never a good sign. Something was wrong. Just as I was about to put two-and-two together, Coach Gallatin met me in the middle of the room. "Duffy, you are not suiting up for the game," he barked.

Before I could process what had just happened, Gallatin was gone. There was no explanation, no eye contact — nothing. And there never would be. The other players went about their business of lacing up shoes, taping up wrists and ankles, and mentally bracing for the big game. I, on the other hand, was suddenly the odd man out. My confidence had been shot down, right there in front of everyone.

From the corner of my eye I could see a new pair of guards — John Barnhill and Nick Mantis. They were shiny, new arrivals from the American Basketball League. I didn't know it at the time, but the ABL was going out of business. The organization was just a few years old and had proven to be a bone of contention for the NBA, particularly when it came to recruiting talent. I assumed Barnhill, a 6'1 guard from Tennessee State and Mantis, a 6'3 shooting guard from Northwestern, had just fled the ABL and would be suiting up in my place. If the college all-star game against the Knicks wasn't a kick in the teeth, this would be. Nothing could have prepared me for this side of professional sports. Not knowing what else to do, I turned around and walked out of the locker room, clutching as much of my dignity as I could.

If Barnhill and Wilkens were first and second guard and Chico Vaughn (who played for Gallatin in Southern Illinois) replaced me as third guard, I would be pushed back to the position of fourth guard. In case you didn't know, fourth guards in the NBA achieve very little playing time — if any. This random circumstance could have easily cost me my job or, worse, my boyhood dream!

I was in shock.

I wanted to be long gone and hard to find.

Looking back, I am not proud of my reaction to the situation. I could have handled it better. After all, the NBA is a business, not a babysitter. Nevertheless, playing professional ball was very personal to me. So when I realized how impersonal the business really was, I let it get the better of me. It was a hard lesson to learn.

Feeling let down, just two hours before game time, I stood on the hardwood floor in the middle of the basketball court. The empty auditorium had a different feel. It lacked the initial exhilaration I felt when I had first been introduced to all of St. Louis. At the farthest reach of the arena was a stage. It was used for concerts and a variety of other entertainment venues. A heavy wall of velvet curtain stretched across the face of the platform, closing it off from the basketball court. Wanting nothing more than to disappear, I pushed through the mouth of those velvet curtains and skulked into the darkness. Feeling disoriented, I sat down in an empty chair. It is difficult now to describe what I was feeling then, but I will say, if the Hawks' management was trying to break my spirit, it was working. I couldn't understand why they would select me as the number one guard pick in round two of the NBA Draft if they hadn't intended on playing me.

I was sick to my stomach.

As I sat in the empty belly of that dark room, I began to doubt myself and everything I had worked so hard for. I thought about my parents. I thought about how proud they were of me. I wondered how proud they would be of me, knowing that I would be riding the bench, knowing that I was sitting alone in the dark, choking back tears because of it. I dreaded Dad's disappointment more than anything else. In the blink of an eye, I had gone from a backcourt hero at Colgate University, one of the best ball-handlers in the country, to a discouraged franchise rookie, shrunk in the shadows of Kiel Auditorium.

I was alone.

I was shocked.

Worst of all, I was worried.

All of the emotion, the disappointment, and the upset began to well up at once. I couldn't hold it together any longer. All that I could do was rest my head in my hands and cry. Behind the curtain, I could hear the auditorium coming to life. The familiar sound of basketballs bouncing and players' shoes screeching across the hardwood floor brought me back to reality. I had to pull myself together. I took a deep breath, cleared my throat, wiped away the tears, and found my feet. The ground was a little loose, uncertain, but I was able to make my way back into the auditorium and up the steep steps to the announcer's booth. I was feeling a little lost, and it showed as I was met with the renowned voice of the St. Louis Hawks, one of the best basketball play-by-play sportscasters around — Buddy Blatner. He and Jerry Gross were preparing to broadcast the game on KMOX. Both men seemed surprised to see me standing there dazed and red-eyed, although neither went out of their way to acknowledge me. Just then the telephone rang. Buddy answered. With that friendly smile of his, he held the telephone receiver in my direction.

"It's for you."

It was Marty Blake.

"Duffy, get down here and get on this bench," he shouted.

He was angry.

I wasn't surprised, disillusioned yes, but not surprised.

I handed the telephone receiver back to Buddy and headed downstairs without a word. As far as I was concerned, the exhibition season couldn't end soon enough. The few minutes of total play time that I received, at that point, did nothing for my confidence but spur anxiety and disappointment. Gallatin wasn't helping matters. Not one person from the Hawks' organization took the time to give me feedback, much less reassure my future with the team.

I was on my own.

That was clear.

One week later, just before the start of the regular season,

Nick Mantis, from the ABL, was traded to the Chicago Zephyrs. With Mantis out of the way, the Hawks settled on Wilkens, Barnhill, Vaughn, and Duffy as their guard lineup, in that order. I had officially made the team, by the skin of my teeth.

The St. Louis Post Dispatch ran the story on November 19, 1962. The headline read: "More Play for Duffy, Hawks Trade Mantis." Reporter, John J. Archibauld quoted Gallatin: "Bob just needs to get over the original excitement of playing in the NBA. I think it is obvious he has a great speed advantage over Mantis, and that he is a better ball-handler. Poise is his lack right now. After he watches guards like Oscar Robertson and Jerry West enough, he'll learn when to go and when to take it easy."

That was the most feedback I had ever received from Gallatin, and so, even though I had no control over the situation, I accepted it. What mattered was that I had survived! Over the next few weeks I received some good press, reporters recognizing me as one of Colgate's leading gunners and scorers and one of the Hawks' first non-starters to accumulate 16 scoring assists in just 46 minutes of play. Having absorbed all the good feedback, and seeing that I was slowly building a healthy reputation in the eyes of the press, I began to look forward to the game again. My enthusiasm and confidence began to resurface, despite the fact Gallatin was still holding out. Occasionally, as if in a last ditch effort, he would throw me in during the last couple of minutes of the fourth quarter. I was embarrassed, but mostly I was frustrated because I had no control. Nevertheless, I kept my chin up.

It wouldn't be until years later that I realized Gallatin's indifference toward me was actually a good lesson in life and leadership. Not only did this disappointing turn of events teach me humility, patience and persistence, but it also taught me the value of depending on myself. My destiny was not determined by what was written on someone's clipboard or in the newspaper. I had more control over my destiny than that. In life, there will always be obstacles. That is a guarantee. The good news is that achievement begins between your ears. It's what *you* tell yourself that counts! That's not to say that it doesn't feel good when others recognize your talent. In my mind, even though I was warming the bench, I refused to see myself as a bench warmer.

Halfway through my rookie season, Robert L. Burnes, the sports editor for the St. Louis Post-Dispatch, wrote "Bob Duffy could be the whole answer. The people's choice, Duffy on Saturday night moved the ball better than any other back-liner, made his forwards run and hit them well with passes. In the remaining time before the playoffs, he should get enough work to earn him regular turns in tough competition. There never will be another Cousy or Dougie Martin, but in a lot of ways a Bob Duffy could come close to it, especially in the knack of pulling fans out of their seats as Dougie (Martin) and the Cousy always could."

This was encouraging, as I was struggling to keep my confidence in check. I was young. I lacked experience, and I allowed my confidence to be affected by someone else's plan for my life. In that respect, Gallatin taught me a very important lesson, and that was that I would never allow someone to make or break my confidence again. This newfound conviction changed everything.

In the second half of my rookie season I finally got my chance to start for the Hawks. As we prepared for another home game inside Kiel Auditorium, Gallatin ended our locker room pregame strategy session against the Chicago Zephyrs by announcing the game starters.

"Duffy! You are guarding Green!"

I was going in for John Barnhill, assigned to guard Si Hugo Green from Duquesne University. I was both stunned and motivated! We won the game against Chicago. As it turned out Barnhill needed the rest. His break turned out to be my big break! I walked away from that win against Chicago feeling euphoric. I thought about that game for a long time afterward, replaying some of the big plays over and over again in my mind. The one that stood out above them all was when I led a second half fast-break for two points. With sheer determination I dribbled the ball down the court, eyeballing the basket. Even though I was surrounded by thousands of people, and at least nine other men on the court, my focus had narrowed so dramatically that I saw nothing but the hoop. It was just me, the ball, and the basket. Relying on my peripheral vision, I dropped a no-look bounce pass behind my back to 6'7 Barney Cable. The crowd jumped to its feet as Cable palmed the ball and rose into the air as if there were rocket boosters spitting fire from the bottom of his shoes.

He stuffed the ball for two points!

The crowd went wild! It was one of *the* most memorable experiences of my life. I was confident that it would be an important development in my career. I looked forward to the next four games on the road, as I was sure that I would see more playing time.

I was wrong.

Nothing changed.

It was business as usual. Gallatin made sure that I warmed the bench, even though my recent performance on the court had been validated by the points on the scoreboard, by the press, and by the applause of St. Louis fans. I can't say I was surprised.

Ↄ

Our last game on the road was scheduled in New York City. We were slated to play the Knicks in Madison Square Garden. The Hawks put us up at the Madison Hotel which was just a short walk from the Garden. A few hours before tipoff, I took a stroll through the city. I needed the fresh air.

A couple of hours later, I returned to the hotel. Gallatin was standing in the lobby, near the elevator. He was alone. I saw this as my chance to open up a dialogue with the man. I had spent the better part of two hours mulling over my options while walking the streets of New York. I realized what I needed now, more than anything, was Gallatin's support. I was a 22 year old kid desperately searching for my place on the team. I couldn't move forward, not without knowing how he felt about me and my future with the Hawks. And so I walked up to him. He stood facing the elevator, his hands dug deep into his pockets. He had a serious expression on his face. I was nervous, though I dared not show it.

"Hey, Coach!" I said, clearing my throat. "I was wondering if there's anything I can do to increase my game time."

Gallatin looked at me without any sort of commitment. I looked to him earnestly, waiting for his counsel, a word or even a hint of encouragement. In exchange for the nerve it took me to approach him, I would get nothing. Gallatin turned away from me and stepped into the open mouth of the elevator as though I weren't even there. Our eyes locked as the doors shut between us.

I was in trouble.

That was clear.

In a contest against the Syracuse Nats, I was, according to the box score, on the floor for 15 minutes of play. I scored a total of eight points. Not bad statistically-speaking. The Hawks beat the Nats, 128-100. The next day, reporter John J. Archibald of the St. Louis Post-Dispatch, the same journalist who had nothing but good things to say about me just a week prior, wrote, "… Hawks' management feels he [Duffy] might someday become another Bob Cousy. In his occasional appearances in games, however, he has shown much razzle but too little dazzle… Duffy a smiling Irish boy who already has a corps of rooters, was in for 15 minutes in all. He did a little of everything: 8 field goal attempts, 3 field goals, 2 free throw attempts, 2 free throw points, 2 rebounds, 2 assists, 3 fouls and eight points. And where, Gallatin wonders, is the column that totals such Duffyisms as that which happened in the fourth quarter when Bob found himself under the basket with ball in hand. The coach could only clutch his forehead in despair as he recalled the sight of the oh-so-green Irishman suddenly turning away from the basket and flipping the ball over his shoulder toward the rim. And missing!"

That was a low point in my rookie career. The best I could hope for, in that situation, was to be traded before I did or said something I would regret.

The Hawks' season ended in the second round of the 1962-1963 Western Division Championship playoffs. We lost to the Los Angeles Lakers in the seventh game. Bob Pettit and Elgin Baylor traded big offensive games and rebounds. Cliff Hagen was averaging 26 points per game while wearing a cast on his left hand. He had suffered an injury in game six. Due to some foul trouble in the backcourt, I was thrown in during the fourth quarter, mainly to control the ball and assist our two superstars, Petitt and Hagen. We lost by six points — three baskets!

It was a disappointing blow!

On the flight back to St. Louis, we were each given a check, a playoff bonus of fifteen hundred dollars. That was a lot of money in those days. Still, it was of little consolation to such a big loss. We were but one victory away from competing for the 1963 NBA Championship against the Boston Celtics who, in fact, won that year!

St. Louis Hawks warm-up before game against
Chicago Zephyrs in 1963. Pictured: Zelmo Beatty,
Bob Nordman, Cliff Hagan, and Bob Duffy (#24).

TWENTY-TWO

The Army Draft

Take responsibility for your part in the problem.

I enlisted in the Army in the summer of 1963. As a young man growing up in that era, I saw it as my patriotic duty. It was also a legal requirement, otherwise known as conscription (i.e. the draft.) Unlike the NBA draft, Uncle Sam mandated that young men enlist in the Army at the age of 18. The only exception to that rule was for those young men attending university. A student was deferred by law until graduation or the end of his last academic year in college. The Hawks' administration recommended that I volunteer my service early. Because of my bachelor's degree, I could have enlisted as an officer. However, Hawks' management advised me against it, since they lost Lenny Wilkens for a full year after he enlisted in the Army as an officer. They did not want that to happen to me. Truthfully, after my disappointing rookie season, I was surprised Hawks' management was even showing an interest in keeping me around. However, I took their advice. I enlisted as a Private First Class, reporting to duty at Fort Leonard Wood in the beautiful south central Missouri Ozarks. The odds were I would be released from the Army after six months and back on the Hawks' roster by fall.

I learned a lot from my experience in the Army. I was also able to spend my free weekends with Sandy. She was just a two hour drive from Fort Leonard Wood. Spending time with her did wonders for my morale. After six months of basic training, I returned to practice with the Hawks. The time spent away from professional basketball, and its inherent hurdles provided me some much-needed perspective. I was better able to assess my rookie season, as well as recalibrate my attitude. Sometimes all a man needs to do is take a hard step outside of a situation in order to wrap his head around it. That summer I realized that I, myself, was a big part of the problem. I had always been hard on myself, even as a kid. When my performance wasn't up to snuff, whether in the classroom or on the basketball court, I would beat myself up. I had a hard time accepting setbacks of any kind. This inflexible behavior made it difficult for me to focus on those things that needed to change in order to improve. And, more often than not, the thing that needs to change is how one effectively reacts to life's hurdles. I was never going to change Gallatin's opinion of me or the unpredictable business of professional basketball. If I was going to change anything, it would have to be how I dealt with those types of obstacles. I spent the better part of my rookie season feeling sorry for myself. I was disappointed and blaming others. There's no glory in that. It was time for me to deal with reality.

The discipline I received in the Army helped me overcome that sense of self-pity. The military does great justice to a young man's character. A man's service to his country reveals something important about him, his willingness to fight for something bigger than himself, and to die for the man next to him. That soldier mentality makes men hard to defeat, and it changed me as both a man and a ballplayer. If I was going to be effective on a professional level, I needed to emphasize my ball-handling skills, as well as call attention to my ability to be a team player. I had to accept my role, work to get better no matter the circumstances, and deal with obstacles with a positive approach. With two scoring superstars like Pettit and Hagen, being a team player was the perfect game plan. The problem was, however, that my own scoring talent, the thing that made me a standout, was not being capitalized. I needed more opportunity to shoot the ball. The question was: Would Gallatin give me the chance? Without his buy in, or the hope of being traded, there was no guarantee I had a future in the NBA. It was up to me to turn things around, beginning with my attitude!

TWENTY-THREE

Traded to the Knicks

Adjust, adapt, and move on!

In the fall of 1963, I went back to the business of competing for a job with the St. Louis Hawks. I was prepared for the effort — mentally and physically. Hawks' management had drafted two more guards: Lee Mitchell of the University of Mississippi and Gerry Ward of Boston College. Both were talented players, and both presented a reasonable threat to my position as a guard in the Hawks' franchise. The stakes had been raised!

There were 13 men vying for a position on the team — six of whom were guards, and we were all very aware of our precarious situation. The number would whittle down to 11 before the opening of exhibition season. Tensions were high, and practice sessions were painfully physical. Lee Mitchell was the first to be cut. This left Gerry Ward and I wondering who would be next. As physical as practice was, the mental game was far more grueling. I fought hard to stay focused, but I couldn't keep myself from mentally measuring up my competition. Ward was a good guy and an equally good player. Where I had speed, Ward had height — a good inch over me. And, as in life, sometimes all it takes is that one inch advantage to make or break hearts. And so, Hawks' management went with Ward and traded me.

☙

On October 1, 1963, a little more than a month before President John F. Kennedy was assassinated, I became a New York Knickerbocker. It was a relief, the fresh start I was looking for. I was expected to report to the Knicks' locker room that Tuesday and play against the Hawks at Madison Square Garden on Wednesday. Unless you're a fan, there's not much room for loyalty in professional sports. The rosters are in constant flux.

During my rookie season with St. Louis I played 42 out of 82 regular season games, averaging 3.7 points. And while I had high hopes for my sophomore effort with the New York Knicks, I had to wonder if it was going to happen since this acquisition put the Knicks over their active roster maximum, exceeding the NBA player limit. The press labeled me the "extra man." Despite the uncertainty, I never stopped believing in my boyhood dream. It was hard, especially since no one from the Hawks' management team ever contacted me to inform me about the trade. I learned about it while driving to practice that morning. I was listening to KMOX radio when I heard that the Knicks had traded their star guard, Richie Guerin, for me. I wasn't surprised. However, I was shocked. Guerin was a bona fide all-star. I, on the other hand, was a bench warmer. The trade didn't make sense. Nothing up to that point did, so I made a giant U-turn and went home to pack my things.

I was headed back to New York. The Knicks coach, Eddie Donovan, contacted me later that afternoon to firm things up. After speaking with him, I jumped in my car and headed back home to Katonah. I drove 24 hours straight. I couldn't get there fast enough. I read in the papers that I had been bought for a waiver price. That hurt! However, there were no hard feelings. I was learning fast the importance of moving forward. All professional sports, the NBA included, are a business, and so I quickly became a realist. After quickly settling in at Mom and Dad's house, I reported to practice at Madison Square Garden the following day. I was given a jersey with the number nine, a locker, and a schedule. An official photo was taken of me, and the start of my career as a New York Knickerbocker had officially begun. As exciting as this new opportunity was, all of the stress from it had caught up with me. My resistance was low and within a couple of practice sessions I had come down with a miserable case of the flu. It took me three days to fully recover, and even though I had "moved on" from the Hawks, I was struggling to keep my confidence. Being sick didn't help.

I was trying to find my feet, as well as my place as a guard with the New York Knick franchise. While I was adjusting well to my environment, and bonding with my new teammates, I was still beating myself up over what had happened with the Hawks. It was hard for me to keep my eyes on the road ahead when I was still trying to make sense of the road behind me. I was looking for an explanation that I would never get, not from Gallatin or Kerner. It was a struggle to move forward, but move forward I did.

My first game as a Knickerbocker was against the Boston Celtics in a double-header at Madison Square Garden. I scored 10 points. I was one of five Knick players to score in the double digits. At one point I drove to the basket and, out of necessity, lifted a left hand hook shot away from the outstretched arm of Celtic's 6'9 center Bill Russell. The ball bounced in off of the backboard. The fans loved it! Russell, however, did not. For the remainder of the game, as we kept pace up and down the court, he let me have it. It was a physical and mental skirmish.

Russell, who scored 18-points in that game, was a powerhouse player. And for whatever reason, he took a strong disliking toward me. I had met him on the court once before during my rookie season with the Hawks. That interaction was just as brutal. It was as if he had waged war. At the time I chalked it up to the nature of the sport, the clever use of mind games to gain the advantage on the court. Being that it was the 60s, however, and there was a lot going on with the civil rights movement, it might have been something a little bigger than basketball.

The Knicks took a terrible beating against the Celtics that night. Tom Heinsohn and John Havlicek were the Celtics' leading scorers with 27 points each. And while the loss took a mental toll on the team as a whole, I was feeling grateful for a fresh start. Even though my appearance on the Knicks' roster was more of a formality than a formula, it felt good to start over. And although Coach Donovan, and assistant coach Red Holzman, were cordial toward me, they didn't go out of their way to provide me direction or reassurance that I had a future with the team. It wouldn't be long before I knew why.

TWENTY-FOUR

Tricks of the Trade

In a fickle business like basketball, rent shelter — don't buy.

It was Christmas Day 1963. The New York Knicks were scheduled to compete against the Detroit Pistons in a double-header at Madison Square Garden that evening. I was looking forward to the game, as were my folks. Between practice sessions, photo shoots, and preparing for my future with the New York Knickerbockers, I hadn't much time to look for an apartment in the city. I was staying in Katonah with my parents. My girlfriend, Sandy, flew in just a couple of days earlier for a visit. It was the first time she would meet Mom and Dad.

Early that morning, before the Christmas turkey had been prepped and placed into the oven, the telephone rang. It was Eddie Donovan, head coach for the Knicks. The moment I heard his voice, I knew something was wrong. He cut right to the chase.

"Duffy, you and Donnie Butcher have been traded to Detroit. Pack your bags and report to the Piston locker room tonight. You're leaving with the team for Detroit after the game."

The phone went dead.

In the short time I had been in the NBA, I got the sense that there was neither the time nor the luxury for formality, let alone good manners. With my heart in my throat, I did exactly as Coach Donovan ordered. I packed my bags and I reported to the Piston locker room just before game time.

No questions asked.

I did my best to keep my chin up. I was handed a jersey with the number 25 sewn on the chest, and with a brave face, I searched for my place in the locker room. While the team went about taping up their wrists and ankles and lacing up their shoes, I got the sense my being there was of very little consequence to them. However, in truth, when it comes to professional sports, when a new player ambles into the locker room, and that player is vying for a position on the team, it is of significant consequence, though you dare not show it.

It was my second season in the NBA and I still hadn't found my place. Life, at that point, went sideways and it showed in my performance. That game against the Knicks, my first as a Detroit Piston, was some of the worst basketball I ever played. Despite my poor performance, the Pistons won 107-103.

I scored a whopping one point.

After the game, I caught up with Sandy and my parents just

outside of The Garden. We huddled together, bracing against the cold. A charter bus hummed alongside the curb, waiting to transport the team to the Piston's private plane. I didn't want to leave New York. Under my breath, I exhaled a four letter expletive. Mom, ever the presence of practicality and protocol, gently placed her hand on my shoulder and whispered firmly, "Bob, you're better than that."

I was struggling, and she knew it. Mom always had my back, not to mention a way of keeping me grounded. The truth was I wasn't simply struggling. I was rethinking my whole career. More than anything, I wanted control of my future. That just wasn't happening in the NBA.

As the bus pulled away, I watched Sandy and my folks shrink into the distance. The further away I moved from them, the sorrier I felt for myself. This was not becoming behavior for a professional athlete. I knew that. I could still hear Mom's voice, "Bob, you're better than that."

I was upset. If it hadn't been for Mom and Dad, and their constant love and support, I'm not sure how I would have managed to get through that night. It was hard to stay focused. I had to keep reminding myself that I belonged there, and that I actually had talent. The problem was it hadn't been fully realized. I just needed somebody to give me a chance.

The next day I picked up the paper and read all the details about the trade. Turns out, it was a three-way, month-long transaction between the New York Knicks, the Detroit Pistons, and

and the Cincinnati Royals. It involved five players. I was one of them. Suddenly it all made sense. My time with New York was only temporary. I was in a holding pattern in between trades. The Knicks were in a rebuilding phase. They had acquired Billy McGill, Len Chappel, Tom Hoover and Art Heyman — a draftee who had been named the college basketball player of the year at Duke University. Somewhere along the line I got tangled up in the deal, likely so that the Knicks could obtain big man Bob Boozer. In a league that consisted of only nine teams, I had already played for three of them and I hadn't even broken a sweat, except to pack up and move my things from one team to the next.

In between competitions, I drove home to Katonah. Not only did I need a breather, but I needed to pick up Sandy and some of my things so that I could settle down in Detroit. After a couple of days of rest and relaxation, Sandy and I packed up all that we could fit into my brand new Oldsmobile convertible, and headed back to Motor City. It was a long drive and I was glad to have the company. After a couple of hours behind the wheel, I struggled to keep my eyes open. I was tired and I needed my rest for a game the following night. Sandy kindly volunteered to take the wheel.

I pulled over onto the shoulder of the road, where she and I swapped seats. It was freezing outside with flashes of snow streaking across the roadway. Shaking off the cold, I crossed my arms and shrunk into the passenger seat and closed my eyes. I don't know how long I had been asleep before I woke to a loud, piercing scream. My car was spinning out of control, sliding across a thin, black sheet of ice. Instinctively, and without hesitation, I palmed Sandy's head in my hand, jerking us both in the direction of the floorboard, and not a moment too soon. The car flipped onto its soft top. I don't know how we survived.

Sandy was pretty shaken up. She had been navigating a fierce snowstorm while I slept. It was fortunate for us both that a Good Samaritan stopped to help us, otherwise if the accident hadn't killed us, the bitter cold weather surely would have. Law enforcement eventually showed up, and not long after that an ambulance came to carry us to a hospital in Harrisburg, Pennsylvania. My adrenaline was through the roof — emotions amplified. Riding in an ambulance, having just escaped death and reeling in a spontaneous act of pure abandon, I turned to Sandy. "This is ridiculous!" I exclaimed. We should just get married!"

She said yes, making me a fortunate man — twice in one night.

⋆

Life with the Pistons was looking good. Phenomenal players and personalities like Bailey Howell, Dave DeBusschere, Ray Scott, and Don Ohl made for a much friendlier, less strenuous work environment. I could finally focus on my game, and not the hidden agendas that sometimes prey beneath the surface of professional sports. Coach Charley Wolf was upbeat and more sensitive to his players. He seemed to genuinely appreciate my contributions to the team and looked for ways to utilize my talent.

Team owner, Fred Zollner, put a lot of his faith in his

coaching staff and in his players. He didn't waste his time, not to mention ours, micromanaging the team. Unlike Hawks' owner Ben Kerner, Zollner let us do what we did best, and I took that as my cue. Within a month, I was able to adjust my game. Life was beginning to feel normal again. Little by little, as the second half of my second season in the NBA evolved, I was feeling like my old self.

I was strong.

I was confident.

It felt good.

With each game, I earned more playing time. My scoring record was improving. In a game against the San Francisco Warriors, I scored 13 points. Wilt Chamberlain, a 7'1 center for the Warriors, was the leading scorer on the court that night with 38 points. My ball-handling skills were picking up. I was more effective in the backcourt, and it couldn't have happened at a better time.

Late in the season, the Pistons were scheduled to compete against the St. Louis Hawks at Cobo Arena in downtown Detroit. I couldn't wait. It meant squaring up to Coach Gallatin. Deep down, I still had something to prove to him. Come game time, I watched as Gallatin paced nervously up and down the sideline. He ran four plays in a row, each of them designed to isolate me in the left corner against his guards. I was his defensive target. That was obvious. I wanted him to give me his worst, so that I could prove him wrong, once and for all.

"Post up Duffy!" Gallatin shouted, his arms waving wildly.

He sent Lenny Wilkens in after me first, and then Charles "Chico" Vaughn. He seemed determined to prove to the press and, most especially to the St. Louis fans that he had been right about me all along.

I didn't let that happen.

St. Louis needed this victory if they were going to the playoffs. A victory was of such eminence for the Hawks that owner, Ben Kerner, made the trip. I could see Kerner pacing nervously behind the Hawks' basket. Like Gallatin, his arms were flailing as he screamed at Sid Borgia, one of the top referees in the game at the time. Borgia was known for coining the phrase, "Yes! And it counts!" after a player was fouled and was still able to score a basket in the process.

With each call Borgia made against the Hawks, Kerner got hotter under the collar. The worst upset was when Hawks' superstar, Bob Pettit, the tall, thin forward, was thrown out of the game for arguing a foul that had been called against him. It was unusual to see Pettit so upset, as most of the time he was above such behavior. However, this was a crucial game and emotions were loaded. Detroit maintained a strong lead. Don Ohl led the Pistons with 28 points. I put seven points on the board with as many minutes on the court. I couldn't have been happier with the final results.

The Pistons got the W — 106-96.

Things were finally starting to fall into place. Sandy and I tied the knot in April of 1964 at St. Mary's Catholic Church in my hometown of Katonah, New York. She and I settled down in an apartment in a small suburb in Detroit. Our neighbor was a fellow teammate named Jackie Moreland. He was a forward/guard out of Louisiana Tech and first round draft pick in the 1960 NBA Draft.

Sandy and I became good friends with Jackie and his wife Jeannette. Jackie, standing at an impressive 6'7, was an incredible shooter and a fun guy to be around. His southern Louisiana drawl added to his natural charm and likeability. Sadly, he died of pancreatic cancer in December of 1971, not long after his career ended in 1965. He was only 33 years old. That was a hard loss. To this day I have nothing but love for Jackie. I look back fondly on our time together — on and off the court. Losing a special friend in the prime of his life was tough. It taught me to accept reality and remain focused on the road ahead.

Bob Duffy, Detroit Pistons, 1964

TWENTY-FIVE

Don't Quit Your Day Job

Sometimes the biggest risk of all is to play it safe.

In the summer of '64, during the NBA off-season, I accepted a job with Fidelity Insurance, headquartered in Fort Worth, Texas. Where basketball was the dream, Fidelity Insurance was the job that supported the dreamer and his wife. In the 60s a professional basketball career didn't come with a six to seven figure salary. It wasn't padded with commercial endorsements. And it certainly didn't come with any guarantees. A career in professional sports is likely to end before it ever begins. Even if you're lucky enough to make a go of it, a career in the NBA usually doesn't last more than 10 years. A "normal" basketball career in the 60s averaged two years — tops!

With the NBA Draft, and the endless trading that occurred throughout the season, there was a high turnover of players. That is as true today as it was then. The percentage of turnover was much higher in those days, however, because there were only nine teams and a universe of about 108 players. The odds of an extended NBA career weren't great, and even if you did make a career of it, it didn't guarantee that you'd be able to make ends meet at the end of the month. Even if you were a superstar in the 60s, your salary was in the ballpark of thirty thousand dollars, bonus not included.

At one point, Ben Kerner signed three star players onto his roster, Pettit, Hagan, and Clyde Lovellette, for a combined one hundred thousand dollars. Most players in the league had no room to negotiate their salary, so they settled for about half of what the superstars signed for. The great Bob Petit, when interviewed, stated that his rookie salary was eleven thousand dollars. Lenny Wilkens stated that he made six thousand dollars as a rookie. Wilkens, along with Cliff Hagan encountered problems with their coaches, Red Holtzman and Paul Seymour, but thrived and wound up becoming Hall of Famers. Today's rookie can earn a few million dollars a year, and the super stars up to thirty million dollars, thanks to television revenue and the support of corporate giants. Fidelity Insurance, while not my primary pursuit, was an incredible experience. It gave me a glimpse into the world of business. My sales territory was the University of Michigan in Ann Arbor, home of the Wolverines. It was my job to crack the university student population, selling students enough insurance to guard and protect their future — and mine. I spent eight hour days holed up in an office the size of a small walk-in closet, taking on the tedious task of telephone solicitation. It wasn't a sexy job by any stretch of the imagination, but it was a valuable learning experience, one that gave me a lot of insight into the kind of competition that existed off the court. I was shocked to find that the competition in business was just as brutal as it was in professional basketball. Selling insurance was especially cutthroat, and while the nature of the business wasn't necessarily where my heart was, my parents instilled a strong work ethic in me. Therefore, I always gave 100-percent in whatever it was I was doing. Sales, like professional basketball was a good lesson in the art of rejection. If nothing else, I was developing thick skin, which would come in handy.

Near the end of summer, Fidelity approached me with an attractive offer to stay on permanently. Accepting the offer would mean walking away from the NBA, working in sales full-time out of Detroit. The salary Fidelity offered was more than what I was making with the Pistons. Having had several disappointments in the NBA, I seriously considered chucking basketball for a career in sales. The problem was I didn't have a lot of time to think it over. The Pistons' training camp was about to begin in St. Claire, Michigan in mid-September. I had to make a decision fast. My career in the NBA was still uncertain, while Fidelity was a sure thing. Logically, the decision was easy. Emotionally, however, I wasn't ready to give up on my boyhood dream. I knew I would regret it if I did. There would be other offers like Fidelity down the road, but there would never be another shot at the NBA.

TWENTY-SIX

All Good Things

Take it like a man.

September of 1964 marked my third year competing for a job in the NBA, this time with the Pistons. The experience turned out to be far more encouraging than it had been in previous years — or so I thought. Eleven men made the team, four of whom were guards — myself, Donnie Butcher, Rod Thorn, and Eddie Miles. I had been here before. I wasn't naïve enough to believe that there wouldn't be more changes made to the Pistons' roster throughout the season. Nothing in this business, with the exception of the stadiums in which we play is set in stone. And even those buildings get torn down and rebuilt from time-to-time. In between the trades and cuts, there is a lot of restructuring that takes place. Of course these things happen a lot less often when you are on a winning team. Basketball, after all, is a business.

The only thing worse than being traded in professional sports, is being cut. Unless you are a superstar, a name that brings the franchise a whole lot of money, the basic rule of thumb is to rent shelter, rather than buy because you might not be around long enough to actually close on a house. Unless you were a Bob Cousy or a Wilt Chamberlain, one never got too comfortable on any one roster. That is as true today as it was then. The only difference is there are 30 teams now, and only nine teams then, so more players are affected.

The whole business boils down to statistics, numbers, and, of course, the randomness of circumstance. Depending upon individual performances and a team's win-loss ratio, adjustments are essentially made to balance out the deficits. With the first choice in the NBA draft that year, the Pistons picked 6'5 "Jumping Joe" Caldwell from Arizona State University. It was a smart choice. At the time he was playing for the United States basketball team at the 1964 Summer Olympics in Tokyo, Japan. They brought home the gold. "Jumping Joe" came to Detroit later that fall after the season had already started. The Pistons also accumulated Terry Dischinger, a 6'7 forward and guard from Purdue and Rod Thorn, a 6'4 guard from West Virginia. Both were traded to Detroit before training camp.

To my surprise, I earned the starting guard position, alongside Don Ohl of Illinois. Our first game was scheduled in Philadelphia against the Syracuse Nationals. Today they are known as the Philadelphia 76ers. Coach Wolf quickly sized up the Nats, and because of their size advantage, I spent most of my time riding the bench. In the nine minutes I played, I scored six points and made a few assists. Future guard all-star and projected Hall of Famer, Hal Greer, scored 32 points with a hot hand.

We lost 125-113.

A few weeks later, and as many games, the team was working out at a local YMCA. The gymnasium was filled with the loud echo of basketballs bouncing against the hardwood floor, tennis shoes screeching with the occasional fast-break and Coach Wolf's whistle. Just as I was about to take a turn at the foul line, Coach Wolf called my name, motioning for me to join him in the bleachers. I passed the ball to the guy behind me and hustled over to the sideline, taking a seat next to the coach. I mopped the sweat from my face with my shirt, and then it happened.

"I'm sorry, Duffy. I've got to let you go."

His words hit me like a sucker punch to the gut. Everything went sideways. When a professional ball club fails to have a winning season, the organization is in a constant state of flux. There is the desperate need to improve, and when I say "desperate," I mean fraught with tension for everyone involved. If you look closely, you can see it, the volatility. Coaches and players are coming and going all the time. There's an invisible revolving door. It's impossible for most players and coaches to get too comfortable, even in the early days of the NBA. Not much has changed in that respect. Cutting players is a necessary evil. The word "cut" implies pain, discomfort. And while there was plenty of discomfort for me that day, I took the news surprisingly well. If I learned anything in that league ... I learned to never take anything personal. I also learned not to take anything for granted. Life, particularly as it translates to sports, is short and unpredictable.

With a brave face, I looked Coach Wolf in the eye and shook his hand. In the breadth of that handshake, my career in the NBA was over. I appreciated his candor. It made a positive impression on me. That hadn't always been my experience in the NBA. Coach Wolf leaned in and said, "You will be way ahead of these guys when their basketball careers come to an end."

I thought he was just being kind, letting me down easy. But the truth is he was right. All these years later, I can see how my future was being cleverly set up by this setback. It doesn't make it any less disappointing, as this was the end of a very important road for me. Trust me when I say that it was with a heavy heart that I headed for the locker room — alone. My teammates avoided eye contact. I was grateful for their detachment from the situation.

Who wants that kind of attention?

With the exception of those basketball greats who were guaranteed a spot on the team, many of those players knew they could be the next to go. As for me, my career in the NBA was over. I had been "infected" and so my former teammates couldn't risk getting too close. They didn't want to catch what I had — joblessness. This was a heavy defeat. The worst part was there was nothing I could do to change it. The only thing left to do was to take a hot shower, put on a fresh pair of clothes and let go of my boyhood dream. I had 94 regular season games under my belt. Spread out over the course of two-and-a-half years and three teams, that did not equal a successful sports career in my mind. I was disappointed, and yet, strangely relieved. It was time to write off my losses and focus on a career in the world of business.

Detroit Pistons, 1964

TWENTY-SEVEN

The Comeback Kid

The beauty of life is the constant ability to begin again.

Sandy saw it in my wet, blue eyes. It was the end of life as I knew it. Within two days we were packed up and headed back east to my parents' house in Katonah. In many ways, I was relieved. There would be no more uncertainty, no questions of whether I had done all I could. A decision had been made — for better or for worse. The good news was that I was 24 years old. I still had my whole professional life ahead of me. It was time for a new dream, a new plan and I was ready to get on with it. I had no idea what I was going to do. All I knew for sure was that I had to keep moving forward; lest I get stuck in my own disappointment.

As we pulled into my parents' driveway, Dad stepped out onto the stoop. He had an expectant look on his face. It was not the reaction I was expecting. I knew he was as disappointed as I was, if not more. However, you would never have known it, not with that hopeful smile on his face.

"Mr. Barnes called for you." Dad said, shaking my hand. "He needs to talk to you right away."

"Colgate's athletic director?" I asked.

Dad nodded.

I was shocked. I had no idea why Mr. Barnes would be calling me. The carcass of my basketball career wasn't even cold. After hugging Mom, I went straight to the telephone to return the call. The curiosity was killing me. My heart raced, as the front desk clerk at the Madison Hotel patched me through to Mr. Barnes' room.

He answered on the first ring.

"Bob!" Mr. Barnes exclaimed cheerfully. "It's good to hear from you, son. Do you think you can make a trip into the city this afternoon?"

"Sure!" I replied, as if I had any idea what I was agreeing to. The truth was I was exhausted from the long ride home from Detroit, not to mention defeated. I wasn't expecting much from this phone call. However, because I was curious, and because Dad couldn't wipe the grin from his face, I jumped in the shower, shaved, put on a fresh suit and headed for New York City. After all, when opportunity knocks, you answer!

Everett "Eppy" Barnes, a graduate of Colgate University, class of 1922, greeted me with a firm handshake and a knowing smile. He invited me into his hotel room, cutting right to the chase.

"Bob Dewey, the head basketball coach and assistant athletic director, is no longer at Colgate."

I nodded, unsure of where this conversation was going.

"I'm interviewing for Colgate's new head coach. I need to make a decision here, pretty quick."

"Yes, sir," I replied.

I assumed he wanted to solicit my feedback on prospective coaches. Had I known this meeting was a job interview, I might have been nervous, not to mention better prepared.

"Bob, I want to do something different this season," he said, leaning in. "I want to hire you as Colgate's head varsity basketball coach."

"What?"

Surely, I had heard him wrong. I didn't have any coaching experience. How could I be considered for the head varsity coach of a Division I University basketball program, the same program I participated in just a few years earlier?

"I'm prepared to make you an offer — today," he smiled.

I didn't know what to say, so I did the first thing that came to mind. I extended my hand, sealing the deal in a gentleman's agreement. At the tender age of 24, I had just agreed to sign on as Colgate's newest varsity basketball coach, the youngest NCAA Division I coach on record at the time, and I have been told, since.

"Last season we had a record of five and 18. Recruiting is going to be your number one priority," he said. "The season starts in two weeks. You start tomorrow."

A million things were running through my head.

"Your first two games are away," Mr. Barnes said enthusiastically. "It's Yale on Friday and Fordham on Saturday."

I was back in the game. Basketball wasn't done with me yet. The next morning Sandy and I loaded up the car and headed back to Colgate. Our life was changing fast, my career right along with it. The business world would have to wait.

TWENTY-EIGHT

Behind the Clipboard

Lack of experience is no reason not to try.

Sandy and I arrived in Hamilton, New York, home of Colgate University. We were full of anticipation. Hamilton was a quaint little town with a population of about 2,500, a far cry from the urban tangle of St. Louis and Detroit. Located in Central New York, Colgate was a one hour drive south of Syracuse and four hours northwest of Katonah. With its rolling green hills and rural character etched in its historic architecture, it was an idyllic place for Sandy and me to begin our new life together.

Sandy was pregnant with our first child. I was the new head coach at Colgate. We had a lot to look forward to. We checked into the Colgate Inn later that morning, our residence for the next few weeks. It was charming and cozy, and it kept its daily promise of clean linens on the bed and fresh slivers of soap in the shower.

After Sandy and I unloaded the car and got settled into our room, I put on a fresh shirt and headed straight for the Huntington gymnasium. I wanted to get there early, before practice was scheduled to begin. I couldn't wait to get started.

With the help of the equipment manager I was able to reacquaint myself with the gymnasium. I inspected my office and, of course, obtained the tool of the trade, a shiny new whistle. I strode into my new coaching career as though I knew exactly what I was doing. The truth was I had no idea what to expect. I had no experience to rely on, other than what I knew as a player. I figured looking confident was half the battle. The other half was keeping my wits about me, paying attention and learning as much as I could as fast as I could while turning in an honest day's work. I figured I could learn just about anything, even how to coach a winning team, if I worked hard enough.

The first (and hardest) step to any challenge is to not over think the situation. To over think any given situation can be fatal. I knew I had to jump in with both feet first, appearing confident, even though I lacked experience.

I was just 24 years old. I was two-and-a-half years out of college and coming off a disappointing career in the NBA. What made me think I could coach a major basketball program at a Division I University?

After being cut from the Pistons, I hit rock bottom. There was nowhere to go but up. The one thing I had going for me was confidence. I was confident that I could do the job. On the surface of things, I looked more like a big brother to these boys than their college basketball coach. Underneath it all, though I was determined, my adrenaline was high. There was a lot riding on this opportunity. In the world of sports, as any aficionado knows, the lifespan of a coaching career can be short, depending upon a team's ration of wins and losses. There's a lot riding on each and every game. It takes broad shoulders to be a college basketball coach because if he is unable to turn a program around, he will find himself out of a job.

ℭℨ

As Colgate's men's varsity basketball team huddled around me for the first time, I let it all soak in. I introduced myself to the squad of young men, many of whom hadn't even started shaving yet. I recognized some of the faces, as they were freshman when I graduated in 1962. Some of the players were aware of the records I had set my senior year at Colgate. They respected me for that. And although it was only for two-and-a-half seasons, the team was also up to speed with my NBA career. For that reason, I had their attention. Because I had competed with superstars like Oscar Robertson, Jerry West, Bob Cousy, Wilt Chamberlain and Bill Russell, this weighed heavily in my favor with these young men.

I recognized the hunger in their eyes. It was the very same hunger I had in college. Despite the disappointing end of my professional basketball career, these young men were impressed by the fact that I had made it to the big league at all. This was a valuable realization for me. What I had come to accept as a major failure on my part was, indeed, an achievement in the eyes of every young Raider looking up to me for direction. It didn't matter to them how long I played in the NBA. It only mattered that I played. And although I had never run a varsity practice session, let alone lead a team of eager, young men to victory, my instincts as a player kicked in almost immediately. I had three goals in mind:

1. Learn how to coach.
2. Teach these young men what I knew about the game.
3. Bring home Ws.

I started them off with basic drills. I needed to get a feel for their ability, as well as their motivation. Running, passing, dribbling, and shooting drills are a great way to identify talent and teamwork. As it stood, the Raiders were no favorite on the Division I schedule, only having won five of the 23 games played. However, I saw something in them that could change all that, perhaps not in heroic measures, but in brave strides. Recruiting over the next few years was paramount.

One of the major hitches in college recruiting in the 60s was that freshmen, as I mentioned before, were not allowed to play varsity ball. Both the NCAA and college universities considered it prudent for incoming freshman to adapt to their academics, as well as brace for university life before they delved into the rigor of varsity ball. Therefore, freshmen athletes played a small schedule of games, a fraction of the varsity schedule. The schedule itself was also limited to competition located close to home, cutting down the necessary travel time. This meant I would have to wait at least three seasons before I could effectively utilize the players I recruited. With that in mind, I built a four-year plan. On paper, I was confident I could build a winning team. In the meantime, I would have to manage the talent I had in front of me. To begin, the Raiders lacked in height and, no doubt, depth. What they did have going for them was intelligence and determination. That was a good start. With less than two weeks to prepare, it was going to be a rough road ahead.

On Friday morning, December 4th, 1964, the team and I boarded a bus headed for Yale University. We were scheduled to compete that evening. The players spent much of the four-and-a-half hour drive studying. I, perched at the front of the bus, spent that time developing a game plan. Yale had a good team. Their head coach, Joe Vancisin, was well-respected and had become an impressive fixture at Yale.

In the 60s, not many universities had the budget to hire assistant basketball coaches. Therefore, I was on my own. I had no coaching experience and no time to scout the opponent. It would be baptismal by fire! The most I could hope for was to have gleaned some wisdom from some of the coaching staff of my past. Throughout my basketball career — from youth ball to the NBA — I had both good coaches and inexperienced coaches. I learned valuable lessons from each. And, having been a player for so many years, I had a pretty good handle on what my team needed from me and what I needed from them.

That first game against Yale was encouraging. We had but

a few days to design and practice an effective offense and defense, one that could compete in that caliber of competition. At the time, there was no second clock in college basketball, so I elected to be methodical with our offense, just long enough for me to size up the players. Without much height going for the Raiders, I chose a Zone Defense until I could evaluate who could handle a man-to-man approach. So rather than each man guarding a corresponding player on the opposing team, each defensive man was given an area known as the "zone" to cover. It turned out that Yale was doing the exact same thing, creating a very close contest from beginning to end.

We lost the game by three points.

While I was proud of my players, I took the loss particularly hard. As a coach, losing was a lot harder than I expected. Technically, the Raiders weren't my team yet — not really. I was playing with a hand that had already been dealt. However, that's not to say I didn't feel responsible.

The very next day, the team loaded onto another bus and traveled an hour-and-a-half south to New York City — Fordham University in the Bronx. At the time, Fordham had a history of recruiting star players, and building exceptional teams. As far back as high school, I recall one of their biggest stars. His name was Ed Conlin. I admired his abilities as a forward. Fordham's coach, Johnny Bach, was also highly regarded and had been coaching their basketball program for a number of years. Later in his career Bach became a top assistant coach for the Chicago Bulls, alongside head coach Phil Jackson during Michael Jordan's reign. The 60s were the grassroots of basketball — both college and professional. There were a lot of big names that came from that era, many of whom made the sport what it is today.

The game against Fordham turned out to be a crushing defeat for the Raiders. Besides the Ram's stable long-term basketball program that included players who had been purposefully hand-picked years before, the team was a far bigger, stronger, and well-oiled opponent than we were prepared for. Not only that, but they had much more bonding time than we did, whereas the Raiders were still getting to know and trust one another.

We lost the game by 18 points.

I remember sitting frozen at the front of the bus on our way home at 2:30 a.m., the painful reality sinking in like a bullet through warm butter. Within just a few days as Colgate's head coach, I was 0 and 2. That was a wake-up call. I hadn't even been in my new role for a full week. I was concerned. Having been through a difficult struggle to achieve in the NBA, I was beginning to realize that I was onto yet another kind of struggle to achieve, only this struggle was tougher because I had even less control over my own circumstances than before. First, I was working against the clock to turn this team around. Time was not on my side. Secondly, I was up against bigger schools that offered athletic scholarships, to which I had none. It was becoming clear to me that things could get worse before they got better.

Meanwhile, Sandy and I were looking for a permanent place to call home. Life at the inn was becoming old. Jack Warner, the head track coach at Colgate, tipped me off to a nice, little rental at 16 College Street. It was owned by a professor and his wife who were looking to rent out the backside of their home. Sandy and I took a look at it, and although we didn't necessarily fall in love with the place, we felt it would fit our needs for a year or two. Within a few days we were moved in and ready to focus on our future.

TWENTY-NINE

The Raw Recruit

Inexperience has the luxury of predicting its own future.

Four months later, the 1964-1965 season was over. My first year as a head coach was complete. Our record was seven and 16, which was an improvement, considering I was working with the same players from the previous season. Overall, I was satisfied with the team's progress, as well as my own. In just four-and-a-half months I had learned what it took to be a good coach. In addition, I realized that I actually loved the job. I was more committed than ever to turn the program around. Even though our victory count equaled less than 50-percent of the games played, we had a number of what I like to call moral victories — wins that were marked, not by what was reflected on the scoreboard, but by the realization that we did better than we expected. Those "moral victories" were revealed in our motivation as a team. I knew that it was unrealistic to believe that we could be an overnight success. However, the challenge of overcoming that struggle excited me. It inspired me to hit the road in an effort to recruit talent and to secure what I, and the Colgate administration, expected within four years — a winning season. Somewhere in all of the excitement, I became a father. Our daughter, Kimberly Anne Duffy, was born January 8, 1965 at a hospital located on the Colgate campus. Becoming a father was one of the greatest moments of my life. Fatherhood inspired me to be a better man.

It still inspires me!

That spring I visited high schools up and down the northeastern coast. I met with a diverse collection of coaches, parents, and prospective student-athletes. I had set mighty goals for myself and for Colgate's basketball program. In the process of seeking smart, athletically-talented young men, I was occasionally invited to speak at luncheons and other high school events. These were terrific opportunities for me to grow professionally.

⁓

As a college basketball coach, the key to achieving success on the court begins and ends with effective recruitment! Once a coach has successfully collected the talent he desires, it is his job to design a game-winning strategy around that talent. Without the fundamental talent, a coach's options are limited to average results. No coach at the college level, I don't care who you are, will survive average results.

He will lose his job first.

In the summer of 1965, in between the business of reading books written by successful college coaches and recruiting players, I re-enrolled as a graduate student at Colgate. I decided to go for an MBA in education. As a non-traditional student, and as the breadwinner, I was preparing for a future beyond coaching. I was targeting a future as an athletic director. I had it all mapped it out in my mind. I figured I had 10 more years, give or take, to coach the Red Raiders to winning records. From there I could move on to a higher calling, as well as a higher pay grade.

Like professional basketball players, college coaches didn't make substantial incomes in the 60s. Therefore, I had to construct a back-up plan. I was always ambitious in that respect, always looking for a way to achieve more. I knew going back to school wouldn't be easy, especially since I, myself, was a raw recruit as a coach and as a father. It was a learn-as-you-go situation on both accounts. However, I was confident that if I put in the work and took the necessary risks, that everything would work out. After all, hard work and calculated risks are what I do best!

Along with the rigor of my post-graduate education, I began planning for the 1965-1966 varsity basketball season. My second season as the Raider's head coach was set to begin in November of 1965, marking one year of service at Colgate. I would have nearly the same roster as the season before, minus a few graduating seniors. Replacing those seniors would be a handful of sophomores moving up in the ranks.

In order to effectively compete against schools like Penn

State and Syracuse University, Colgate needed exceptional players on its roster. By Colgate's standards, these players were required to be equally as competitive in the classroom as they were on the court. This was one of my biggest challenges. You're not going to win ballgames unless you get the players who can compete on the same schedule, and yet we were not competing on a schedule with teams that had the same academic standards as ours. Athletically-speaking, it was not a level playing field. Colgate was independent, and historically had a tougher schedule than most. We were also a much smaller school, which increased our odds of losing games. Bottom line: Colgate was at a disadvantage, and it was my job to change that. It wasn't going to be easy. The Dean of Admissions, Robert B. Shirley, admitted that our record was a direct result of the lack of athletes with high-scoring GPAs. He was right, and since Colgate didn't offer athletic scholarships, like some of its competition, it would make my job that much harder. The only scholarships available to students were academic and, of course, those based on financial need. Therefore, when it came to recruiting athletic talent, I was not competing on a level field. I was going to have to present a compelling argument to overcome this disadvantage. I knew this, and I knew it wasn't going to happen overnight. When I brought the issue to the table, Director of Student Aid, Robert Jaycox, contended the fact. He said, "You can't tell me there aren't men who are good basketball players and also academically qualified."

It's normal to have contrasting positions on the subject of

recruitment. However, this was a red flag for me, a sign that we might have a problem. The harder I worked to recruit quality talent, the more red tape I got tangled up in. Administration wasn't budging. On one hand, they expected me to build a winning team, so to raise the stakes of Colgate basketball. On the other hand, they did not understand the hurdle I was facing. Putting Cornell, Princeton, and Yale aside, the majority of our schedule was with larger universities that had different standards. I had the confidence of Colgate's president and other administrators, which I valued as an alumnus. Unfortunately, they didn't have the experience to appreciate the combative world of recruiting, especially when you don't have the ammunition you need.

My second season as coach ended with eight wins and 15 losses with the same players I'd inherited. While it wasn't great, at least we were trending in the right direction, and I was able to provide a better life for my family. That fall we moved into a brand-new townhome situated on the west side of campus along Spring Street. It overlooked Seven Oaks, Colgate's golf course and club. Colgate's hockey coach, Ron Ryan, and his wife, Brenda, lived next door. We became great friends, and thanks to him I developed a love of golf.

THIRTY

Orange Crush

Win or lose, there is victory in having battled.

February 16, 1965 was a big day in Colgate history. Heck! It was a big day in my coaching career! It was in the middle of my first full season. The Red Raiders were competing against the Syracuse Orange in Colgate's small Huntington Gymnasium. The Raiders had been crushed by the Orange, 91-52, just one month earlier in Manley Field House, a multi-purpose arena that was home to the Orange's basketball team before they moved to the Carrier Dome in 1980.

The Syracuse program had methodically rebuilt the men's varsity basketball program from the bottom up, beginning with a brand-new approach to coaching and the recruitment of new and exciting talent. Some of the varsity talent had been farmed in from the freshman team, including Dave Bing. Bing, one of the greatest players in Syracuse history, and down the road an NBA all-star with the Detroit Pistons, and inductee into the Naismith Memorial Basketball Hall of Fame was among the Orange that night. He was a classy, young man who was inexhaustible in his scoring, passing, and rebounding. After his basketball career, Dave, as an entrepreneur, founded a company called Bing Steel, and ultimately was elected Mayor of the city of Detroit.

What an achiever!

Also on the roster for the Orange was Jim Boeheim, future head basketball coach for Syracuse University. Boeheim was a game-changer, who would one day coach the Orange to nine Big East regular season championships, five Big East Conference championships, and 28 NCAA Tournament appearances, including three appearances in the national title game. That night against Colgate, Boeheim was a walk-on. He was an excellent shooter who, would be an inductee into the Naismith Memorial Basketball Hall of Fame as a coach in September of 2005. Jim was a diversified achiever, who, along with his coaching career, was successful in the financial world and philanthropy. He and his wife Julie have been leaders in raising money to fight cancer.

Also on the Syracuse roster that night was Chuck Richards, a 6'8 ½ center. Richards broke the height rule as a cadet at West Point. He averaged 22 points per game as a plebe at Army, and he kept the same scoring average after transferring to Syracuse. After being selected as a basketball academic all-American, Richards had a long career with the FBI.

And then there was Rich Duffy, my kid brother, a senior at Syracuse, who I had grown up with. Rich was a tough competitor who could not only score, but drive the other team crazy with his ability on defense. He was also successful later in life in the world of consulting and marketing. Even though we were on opposing benches that night, each seeking victory over the other, I was proud of Rich and happy for his success. I know he felt the same.

Syracuse was rated in the top 10 college basketball teams in the country in 1965. Each of its players had been purposefully recruited over the course of three years by Coach Fred Lewis and his assistant coach Roy Danforth. Syracuse had the budget for two coaches, whereas Colgate could only fund one — me. This was a definite advantage for the Orange; forget the fact that I was the greenest coach in college basketball history. It didn't matter. As "green" as I was, I observed a few significant holes in the Orange line of attack. For one, they appeared overconfident. Syracuse had given my Raiders a pretty good beating in their last contest, so I figured they might naturally ease up their guard a bit, seeing Colgate as an easy mark. Despite the odds, I knew that Colgate hadn't signed up for another beating, particularly not while we had the home court advantage. Granted, Colgate was the obvious underdog. Its enrollment of 1,300 students was no match to Syracuse's 11,500. The Orange' strength was definitely in its numbers! That said, I wasn't about to count my Red Raiders out, nor were our fans!

As head coach, I scarcely had 12 games under my belt. The

losses my Raiders were taking were fierce and they were frequent, and they were beginning to take a toll on me and my players, mentally and physically. No doubt we would need to up our game, in order to improve our odds, if for no other reason than to save face until we could recruit both the size and the talent we needed to turn things around.

As both teams warmed up for the game, I took a short walk over to the opposing bench to shake hands with Syracuse's head coach Fred Lewis, as an act of good faith and sportsmanship. I was surprised with Mr. Lewis' response. Instead of mirroring my gesture, he sneered at me. Refusing to shake my hand, he made an unsportsmanlike comment and walked away. I didn't know it at the time, but Lewis was a close friend of Harry Gallatin. I'm not sure if that had anything to do with his reaction, but whatever the reason, it didn't feel good. As I walked back to my bench, I felt a warm rush of confidence wash over me. I could barely wipe the grin from my face. Something told me that the Orange weren't prepared for this game. Right then and there I knew that my Raiders had a shot.

At the opening tap, my 6'3 center, Alan Brown, got the jump on Syracuse's 6'6 Rick Dean. However, as luck would have it, Syracuse got the tap. My Raiders matched Syracuse play-for-play, controlling the ball on both offense and defense, following the game plan to the letter. In the first half, my brother Rich scored 17 points as we focused our zone defense on Dave Bing and Jim Boeheim.

Huntington Gymnasium was literally bursting at the seams. The energy of the crowd was explosive, but it didn't faze my Raiders. In fact the Raiders' performance remained steady and strong, and as the minutes turned into quarters, it was obvious something special was happening. The score toggled back and forth for a while, neither team getting too far ahead of the other. It seemed as though the contest was never-ending. Both teams were exhausted. At just 10 seconds left in the game, Syracuse had the lead by one point. Dave Bing was at the free throw line for one shot. The crowd came to a hush as Bing bounced the ball … once then twice. You could feel the collective anticipation of the crowd as he lifted the ball up over his head and released it into the air.

Bing sunk the shot!

However, the point never registered on the scoreboard.

Huntington Gymnasium, a small venue for such a historic game, was filled to capacity, nearly 1,300 fans. People were literally standing in the aisles. With 10 seconds left on the clock, the Raiders pushed the ball to midcourt, briefly losing possession. George Dalzell, our star player, regained control of the ball. He put up a last second shot and scored, appearing to give the Raiders a 74-73 victory over the Orange. The buzzer screamed. The game was over, and the crowd went wild.

Believing the Raiders had just achieved the all-time biggest upset of college basketball, Colgate fans flooded the floor. The human swarm carried me and the team out of the gym and down the stairs to the locker room on their shoulders. It was college basketball at its best!

Meanwhile, up in the gymnasium, Syracuse's head coach, Fred Lewis, was spitting mad as he paced up and down the floor. He knew that the score didn't reflect what had really happened. Deep down, beneath all of the euphoria and celebration, I knew it, too. I thought the game was tied, but because I had gotten caught up in all the excitement, I let it go. Johnny Gee, the game's referee, knew the score was wrong. He knew that Bing's free throw shot hadn't registered on the scoreboard. With a smile on his face, he fought through the crowd, pulled the Raiders out of our celebration, and reassembled both teams back onto the court. It took about 20 minutes, but we put on our game faces and squared up against Syracuse in triple overtime.

It was utter chaos!

Going into those last seconds, I figured our star player, George Dalzell, who had 25 points on the board, would be targeted defensively. Therefore, I made the decision to have Dalzell act as the decoy and swing the ball around to Tim Vigrass, who had a hot hand and who also had 25 points on the board. During our last time out of the game, I warned the boys against fouls. We had designed this critical play to clinch the game and the only way to mess it up was to foul Syracuse. To get their attention, I raised my voice to the rafters, "Stay away from the hoop when the shot is up in the air! Run up in the stands if you have to, but do not put yourself in a position to foul!"

At the whistle, it looked as though the strategy might

actually work. Vigrass was wide open. Dalzell swung the ball in his direction and Tim took the shot. The ball sailed through the air as the entire auditorium held its breath. Bouncing softly off the rim, Dave Bing leaped up and got the rebound. One of our boys reached in and fouled Bing, giving him a chance to win the game for the Orange. Bing put 45 points on the board that night, two of which were from the foul line, clinching the win. With only a few seconds left in play, Dave Bing gave Syracuse a 93-90 victory in triple overtime. The Raiders accepted the loss, but not the defeat!

That game was a lesson for me as a coach with only three months experience. I learned that I would never have total control over my team. A coach can lead and advise. He can even inspire, but ultimately his players decide the outcome on the court. In the heat of battle, and despite the best laid plans, mistakes can occur. That's life. That's basketball. I was proud of my men! I still am.

I stayed up all that night. No matter how hard I tried, I couldn't sleep. I replayed that game over and over again in my mind. To this day I still can't help but replay that last shot Dalzell took to tie the game, a shot that would have been considered a three-pointer by today's rules. Had it been a three-pointer then, we would have won the game, but that's neither here nor there. Victory wasn't in the cards for the Raiders that night. I have come to realize that there wasn't a single thing my men could have done to change the outcome. They did absolutely everything they could in that epic game against Syracuse, and at the end of the day, it was enough for me. We may not have won the game, but we truly achieved something special!

The next day I received two letters. The first letter was from Vincent Barnett, Jr., President of Colgate University. The second letter was from Robert Waldbillig, Captain of the USAF. Both letters still bring tears to my eyes. Barnett wrote: "I hope the boys are not downhearted as a result of last night's game. They earned more real respect by the courageous battle they put up than they could have gotten through several ordinary victories. I want to congratulate you and the team on a magnificent ballgame. Nobody who was there will ever forget it."

I appreciated his kind words. I also appreciate Waldbillig's words of encouragement. He wrote: "It is once or twice in a lifetime that one is privileged to witness acts of greatness. By being in Huntington Gymnasium on the evening of 16 February 1965, I was fortunate enough to see a great basketball team — Colgate Red Raiders. Of lesser importance, but something I will never forget, I saw the most exciting athletic event of my life. I've talked to many sports enthusiasts and coaches since the contest and they all endorse this fact. The essence of the whole story Tuesday night, however, is your courage. Your ability to bounce back, continuously, to force and control the situation despite overwhelming odds is what really counts. That is greatness. Congratulations!"

It was a legendary game! From my perspective, from the shoulders of Colgate fans, it was one of the greatest basketball games I ever got to be a part of as a coach and as a player.

THIRTY-ONE

Full Court Press

You've got to play every game like it's your last.

As my second season as head coach came to an end in March of 1966, I was able to sit back and reassess my new coaching career. On paper it didn't look too bad. Overall, I had secured 15 wins and 30 losses with basically the same players, guys who had won but 22-percent of their games before I arrived on the scene. After two seasons with me at the helm, we had improved our wins to 33-percent. Technically, I was not wholly responsible for the team's poor record. However, the reality of it, it was my head was on the chopping block. The coach's head always is. The Raiders had increased their percentage of wins with the same level of talent I had inherited, but it was not enough to secure my job. Most people fail to recognize the initial obstacles a new coach has to overcome before turning a team around.

I had to think fast!

I had to reach into my arsenal and pull out the big guns, especially if I was to boost Colgate's winning percentage. I had to recruit a star player ... and soon. Inching our way up the competitive ranks was not going to do it. I needed to make a hard move. Even without the benefit of athletic scholarships, the job was definitely doable over the course of a four years. It would mean months of concentrated recruiting. Fortunately, I had the help of high school coaches, like Dee Rowe of Worcester Academy in Massachusetts and Morgan Wootten of DeMatha Catholic high school in Hyattsville, Maryland, two great high school coaches who were kind to me and wanted to help.

Meanwhile, that spring we learned that Sandy was pregnant with our second child. With another baby on the way, it was obvious we needed a bigger house. Sandy and I committed to building a house in a new area one mile away from the university golf club. We moved in November 1966, almost two years to the day that I returned to Colgate as head coach. Excited about the birth of our baby, and the upcoming basketball season, I began to plan for the future of both.

December was proving to be a big month!

I was shouldering a lot as a husband, a father, a graduate-student and a coach. Yet despite all of that, I was feeling confident in my ability to do well. I was especially confident in my Raiders. To look at the schedule, one might consider Colgate the underdog. I didn't see it that way. I had more confidence in my Raiders (and in myself) than that. Although I had only been head coach for 18 months, I saw my third season as *the* season to turn things around. I had never been more optimistic! I felt we could put our "wins" into the double digits. We were definitely in a good position to surpass our losses by year four.

℃

We were looking at a 23 game schedule, starting with Yale, ending with Syracuse, and a whole lot of college basketball muscle in between. I had four solid weeks to get my Raiders ready. I was sure that we could effectively compete with these bigger schools, despite the fact that some of their student bodies were 10 times that of Colgate's. Dad's coaching career was proof of that at St. Mary's. The fact is bigger schools mean bigger budgets, and bigger budgets mean winning seasons!

Despite the odds not being in our favor, I was encouraged. The freshman recruiting class, the future of Colgate's varsity team, was showing promise. That, matched with the addition of Johnny Gee (6'6,) George Erickson (6'5,) and Dennis Cronin (6'4,) men who were physically more imposing than most Colgate players from previous years, had proven that size is, indeed, a factor in college basketball. With Gee, Erickson and Cronin, I felt we had a real shot at keeping our opponents' defense honest, adding a much faster pace of play.

Included in my arsenal was Colgate's 6'2 star guard George Dalzell. The 190-pounder came to play. Also in my lineup was Gary Blongiewicz, a guard who could hold his own, most notably as a sophomore against Syracuse in the "epic game." Blongiewicz, our team captain, had gained a great deal of experience in that game. And then there was the Raiders' 5'8 sparkplug Mike Barrett. As a guard, he was mature, not to mention unmatched in swiftness and agility. Barrett was a rabbit on the court … small, but quick and effective. Roster-wise, things were looking up for the Red Raiders in the 1966-1967 season.

☙

When it came to college basketball coaches, I was inspired by Rutgers' Bill Foster, a wonderful coach whom I had competed against during my stint as head coach at Colgate. I met Bill on December 11, 1965, just a few weeks into my coaching career. The Raiders were slated to play Rutgers University. Bill was head coach of the Scarlet Knights and fast-becoming known for his exceptional leadership. From coaching high school in Pennsylvania to coaching college basketball, he put Rutgers University on the map. His extraordinary recruiting success and uncanny ability to lead and inspire a team is what made him great.

Foster built his team that season around two outstanding guards — Bob Lloyd, a kid who often led the nation in scoring, and Jim Valvano, otherwise known as Jimmy V., who would later coach North Carolina State to an NCAA Championship. As the Scarlet Knights and the Raiders warmed up for the big game, each on their own half-court, Bill approached me, his hand extended.

"Good luck," he said with a big smile on his face.

His easy demeanor impressed me. It was quite a different

experience than the one I had with Fred Lewis that historic night the Raiders nearly clinched the game against Syracuse. There was nothing pretentious or pompous about Bill Foster. The man single-handedly rebuilt the Rutgers basketball program from the ground up, proving that with hard work and outstanding leadership, ordinary men could be elevated to championship levels. He was best known for his contribution to Duke University. He took over Duke's struggling program and proud history in 1973, leading the Blue Devils to an NCAA championship game in 1978. That same season he was named Coach of the Year by the National Association of Basketball Coaches, and was inducted into Rutgers Basketball Hall of Fame. He accomplished the same with Utah's program and later became the first NCAA coach to lead four different teams to 20-win seasons as a result of his accomplishments at South Carolina and Northwestern, as well.

From the moment I met him, I knew he was special, and although our teams were competing against one another, he was someone I looked up to. Bill Foster was a gentleman, a great coach, and a terrific leader. Colgate lost to Rutgers University that night, 92-82. While it was disappointing, I walked away having gained a lifelong friend, one of my most special friends. I took what I learned from Bill and put it to good use both personally and professionally. I am better for knowing him. Bill Foster helped me raise my game. He gave me hope that I could turn Colgate into a winning team. Sadly, Bill died in January of 2016. I miss him terribly. I will cherish our time together — always!

THIRTY-TWO

Lead with Your Gut

Quitting is not the same as giving up.

Recruiting was going well. I had reason to believe that my efforts were about to pay off, not only in the upcoming season, but well beyond. I had recruited a couple of freshmen who I knew had it in them to do good things, as well as a guard from Maryland and a forward from New York — each academically qualified to play for Colgate. I was especially excited about the latter two players. The pair was just *the* caliber of competition Colgate was looking for, on the court and in the classroom. I knew they would make a difference! However, it was a 6'5 forward named Bill Schwarzkopf who would be my secret weapon, the promise for a Raider turnaround. Schwarzkopf was a high school senior from Westlake High School in Westchester County, New York. Not only was this kid the poster boy for Colgate University, but he was voted in the top two of five All-County Repeaters, the cream of the crop according to coaches and the Westchester Rockland Newspapers' sports editors. He averaged 21.8 points per game his senior year, all while achieving excellent grades and SAT scores.

I spent a lot of time getting to know Bill and his family. I was invited to their home on New Year's Eve in 1966. I was certain that I had the inside track on Schwarzkopf. However, a few days after the New Year's celebration, before the champagne had gone flat, I received a phone call from his mother. Cornell was offering Bill a half-scholarship, whereas Colgate was not. The issue had to do with Schwarzkopf's biological father. He died years earlier and left a trust in Bill's name. Colgate interpreted that "trust" as financial means, even though it would not be made available to him or his family until he reached the age of 22.

Athletic scholarships at Colgate weren't an option. Unlike most Division I athletic conferences, the Ivy League, and similar universities, prohibited the granting of athletic scholarships. Any scholarship that was awarded to a student was based solely on financial need. This put an enormous crimp in my recruiting plans. Schwarzkopf had expressed to me on more than one occasion his interest in attending Colgate. More than anything, I wanted to make that happen for him. I even met with Vince Barnett, President of Colgate, to discuss Schwarzkopf's options. President Barnett was always supportive of me, so when I strolled into his office, I felt confident I could convince him to see my side of things.

I was wrong.

No scholarship or financial aid would be offered, and so it looked as though we would lose Schwarzkopf to Cornell on a technicality. Though both offers were operating under the same assumption, this was an unusual situation, potentially creating two opposing conclusions. This was known as the Princeton Plan.

I was in trouble.

I lost a lot of sleep.

I couldn't stop thinking about what a terrible loss it would be for Colgate. Bill's mother and stepfather needed the financial help. They assured me that if Colgate could match Cornell's offer, their son would attend Colgate. I had done my best to make President Barnett understand and appreciate the significance of this recruit. I knew that if I couldn't get administration to back me, it would not bode well for the team's future — or mine.

Colgate was strict with its recruitment and financial aid requirements. Meanwhile, the ideal recruit — academically and athletically — was standing in front of me with pen in hand, ready to sign, and I was not able to make it happen. The situation was reminiscent to my rookie season in the NBA. I had very little control of my future.

My hands were tied.

I loved coaching.

I loved Colgate. However, there were red flags, and it became evident early on that I had hit another crossroad.

Everett D. Barnes retired, and Hal Laher, Colgate's head

football coach, became the new athletic director. This changed things. I was forced to consider how he would react, knowing it could take even longer for the Raiders to achieve a winning season. I didn't have a choice, and so I resigned as Colgate's head basketball coach. President Barnett assured me that Colgate was impressed and happy with the job I was doing.

"I hate losing," I replied.

Resigning as head coach was a tough decision, but it had to be made. I had accepted the job with the understanding that I'd be given the tools and the capacity to manage the Raiders' roster. Colgate meant well, but I was about to lose the perfect recruit. I could not, in good conscience, coach a team which might be playing powerhouse schools like Syracuse, Penn State, NYU, University of Illinois, and the University of North Carolina and not have the means to build a team capable of matching them. I was not comfortable putting my team up against blue chip players who were receiving athletic scholarships, whereas Colgate was not. It was not a level playing field. Schools like Syracuse and Penn State were giving five or more full grant-in-aids a year, specifically for basketball. Today Colgate offers athletic scholarships for student-athletes. However, they are still based on high academic standards and financial need.

Being the consummate professional, and my mother's son, I offered to stay on as head coach and finish out the season to ensure a seamless transition for the team's future success. I was happy to do it. President Barnett was grateful for the offer. I was relieved that my decision to leave did not detract or detour the Raider's desire to win. Despite my resignation and my star player, Dalzell, being dismissed from Colgate for academic reasons, we managed to end the regular season with a record of 10 wins and 13 losses, compared to eight wins and 15 losses the year before.

In my mind, I had done what I had set out to do. I created a positive change in an otherwise losing program. Leaving Colgate was not a rash decision. After all, just three months earlier I had built a home and celebrated the birth of our second daughter, Julie Anne Duffy, who was born on Christmas day. I had a lot riding on this job. Regardless, I knew I had to move on. Like all my decisions, I put a lot of thought into the risks involved. Therefore, it was a calculated risk. Worst case scenario, I would rebound, find another job in a couple of months. There were no regrets.

My working relationship with Colgate, though short-lived, was mutually beneficial. Our time together was special. The hard part was explaining my decision to Dad. He put up a pretty good argument that I stay on. Because I respected him, as both a father and as a man, I gave his counsel some serious consideration. After all, Dad was a smart man. I knew he had my best interest at heart. Moreover, I knew he was right. Opportunities like Colgate were rare. However, I didn't want to hedge my bets anymore. I wanted to make things happen, and I needed the freedom to do it. Don't get me wrong. It was hard leaving Colgate, but my experience, as both a student and a coach, had prepared me for the best and the worst of my next important challenge in life — business!

Coach Bob Duffy with Colgate Red Raiders 1965.

Coach Bob Duffy with Colgate Raiders 1966.

BUSINESS

Business proved to be a lot more profitable than dribbling a basketball for a living in the 60s.

Bob Duffy
(© Pach Bros., New York)

THIRTY-THREE

Getting Down to Business

Take what you learn and apply it to your next venture.

As I begin the transition from my sports career to my business career, I would like to share with you, my reader, my thoughts and feelings at the time the transition was taking place. I would also like to compare those thoughts and feelings to what I thought just a few years later. The difference between the two is quite significant, not to mention how an individual can not only overcome a major setback in life, but use it to their advantage in achieving success at a higher level.

I can't say that my heart was broken the day I was cut from the Pistons — the NBA. While it was upsetting, I was more relieved than anything. Sure, my confidence was shaken. My boyhood dream of playing professional basketball was over. However, I was ready to move forward. It was disorienting at first, and in many ways I felt cheated, but the best plan of attack for overcoming disappointment is always to keep your eyes on the road ahead.

From the time I was drafted until the time I was let go, I did not have control of my future. In the business of professional basketball, a player is a commodity. Like a side of beef or a brand of beer, a player is a product that is bought, sold, and traded for profit. My first reaction to this experience was negative.

I was young.

I was angry.

I blamed others.

I came out of college thinking I was going to be the next Jerry West. But, as it turned out, size was a problem for me. I was 6'2 ½', and that was the era of the big guard. There were guys like Jerry West, Oscar Robertson, John Havlicek, Sam Jones, Gene Shue and Richie Guerin. All were 6'4 or better. I could always put the ball in the hoop, but I was being outmuscled.

It wasn't until years later, after much reflection, that I realized I was partially to blame for how my basketball career turned out. The truth was I failed to effectively handle the obstacles placed before me. I let myself down. No doubt I allowed the frustration I was experiencing at the time to get the better of me. Guys like Gallatin didn't hold me back. Disappointment and disillusion kept me from achieving all that I could have.

I had the wrong attitude.

I let the situation get the best of me. In effect, I lost

confidence. That was a monumental mistake! I was so focused on the negative reality of professional basketball that I failed to recognize that my future was always in my hands. Consequently, I became a shadow of what I could have been as a ballplayer in the latter portion of my rookie season. That was dumb, not to mention irresponsible and that "wrong attitude" never happened again the rest of my life, at least not where it mattered. Even today, as I think back to the discontent I felt as a rookie, and as I write this book, I realize how vital a positive attitude is to success ... to life!

A positive attitude should never be diminished by adversity. Without adversity, without the struggle, we have nothing to fight for and so we become complacent. It's the struggle to achieve that defines us and our attitude can be the difference between the miscarriage of a dream and the birth of one.

The resentment I felt toward Harry Gallatin expired a long time ago. Regardless of how I felt he treated me, his presence in my life was a blessing. His resistance fueled my determination. Gallatin taught me that there will always be obstacles to overcome. He, alone, wasn't to blame for my short career in the NBA. I had something to do with that. After all, I had competed and made the NBA roster, twice in St. Louis and once in Detroit, in two more training camps. I had the talent. I just didn't have the patience or the experience to deal with the situation.

The truth is, in hindsight, Coach Wolf did me a favor when he cut me from the Pistons. That decision thrust me into a brand new career, and so I took what I learned in professional basketball and I applied it to business. I found the same rules applied.

The world of business is just as competitive as professional sports. The only difference was, at that time, there was more money to be made in business than in basketball. As for obstacles, business had them, too. They presented themselves differently, but I could see them coming a mile away. My experience in the NBA prepared me in that respect, so that I was better able to distinguish and deal with them, and to come out on top. The truth is I was excited. This was a genuine opportunity to make real money, but it would mean starting at the bottom.

THIRTY-FOUR

Breaking into Broadcasting

Get busy with Plan B.

If someone would have told me that I would go from playing professional basketball in Madison Square Garden to delivering donuts for a living, I wouldn't have believed it. It didn't stand to reason. I had a college degree. I held Colgate's all-time scoring record in basketball. I had been nose-to-nose with superstars like Jerry West, Oscar Robertson, and Bob Cousy. Heck, I still had the afterglow from an unforgettable night when Raiders fans carried me off the court on their shoulders in a presumed win against Syracuse — one of the greatest college basketball games in history! So believe me when I say, delivering donuts, while a respectable trade, didn't seem to be the next logical step in my career. Nonetheless, upon my entry into the world of business, that's exactly what I did. I delivered donuts. To be honest with you, it was hard to tell if my business career was starting off at the bottom rung of the professional ladder or if it had simply hit rock bottom. Either way, I was mortified! It's a good thing I have a sense of humor and a strong work ethic, otherwise I'm not sure I would have gotten past this part of my story.

You can't take yourself or life too seriously. You have to be able to laugh at the folly life presents, and you have to be willing to put in the work to get the job done. It doesn't matter what business you're in, in order to reach the top you must first pay your dues. Sometimes that means starting at the bottom. This may be life's way of weeding out the competition, gleaning only those who are serious about success.

One of the first companies that stood out for me after leaving Colgate was The Eastman Company, a broadcasting business. Its headquarters, an office that faced Fifth Avenue, was situated on the second floor of Rockefeller Center, overlooking the ice rink. Bob Eastman, the company's owner, was a very charismatic fellow. He was well-respected in the radio business. He had heard of me through a close friend of his who followed my sports career. His name was Charlie Helms. He was the superintendent of schools in my hometown of Katonah. When I resigned from Colgate, Mr. Helms immediately reached out to Mr. Eastman. He believed I would be an asset to The Eastman Company. I had no reason to doubt I would be, so I accepted Mr. Eastman's invitation to interview with a few of his key executives at the Forum of the Twelve Caesars restaurant near the skating rink at Rockefeller Center.

In February of 1967, I found myself sitting in the company of some real business heavies, including The Eastman Company President Frank Boyle, Executive Vice President Joe Cuff, and Vice President of the Detroit office Bill Burton. I was particularly impressed with Mr. Burton. He was renowned for his sales smarts and his success in training people for the business of selling air-time to clients. I was intrigued by this circle of men, as well as excited by the organization itself.

The Eastman Company provided an invaluable service to its clients, radio stations throughout the United States. Each station had a local sales force competing for air-time revenue — the bread and butter of radio. However, due to cost restraints these stations were unable to afford the necessary sales staff throughout the United States to gather revenue at the national level. Therefore, companies like Eastman were hired to represent those radio stations. Known as rep firms, The Eastman Company and the like competed coast-to-coast to deliver revenue to radio stations. It was a cutthroat business and the reality was that The Eastman Company, and companies like it, were considered a "middle man," sort of like an advertising agency. For example, companies large and small, hire ad agencies to develop advertising campaigns and commercials to promote their products. These agencies then purchase air-time on broadcast radio and television to market their product. Because both rep firms and ad agencies attract a long list of clients, they can afford to provide a top notch staff. For any one individual broadcasting company, that cost, by itself, would be an unbearable burden. Hence, the term "middle man," a professional liaison contracted to make marketing happen at a more reasonable cost.

Though I had a number of other interesting prospects lined up with impressive companies in all types of other businesses, I was drawn to Mr. Eastman's offer. I trusted my gut and, therefore, accepted a job as a salesman trainee at The Eastman Company that day. However, there was a rub. It would mean moving back to Detroit, the same city that ended my basketball career. That stung a little bit. However, from that day forward I focused on the positive, seeing this new venture as a giant leap forward. As it turned out, that decision was one of the most pivotal in my professional life, as Bill Burton would become my boss, and he would have a tremendous influence on Bob Duffy the businessman.

CB

That spring I checked into the Sheraton Cadillac Hotel in downtown Detroit. I was familiar with the place. It was where I roomed when Donnie Butcher and I were traded to Detroit. It was a 10 minute walk to Cobo Arena, home of the Pistons. Sleeping so near to that arena resurrected much of the disappointment that came with being cut loose from the team. However, I was no longer that guy. I wasn't the disillusioned rookie. I was a new man with a new career, a salesman trainee at The Eastman Company, expected to perform in a business suit and tie. There was no number on my back, no one to hand the ball off to and, for the time being, there was no reason to believe I wasn't in complete control of my own future. It was a clean slate and I was determined to make a go of it!

As I strolled through the familiar streets of downtown Detroit, I thought about my parents. I thought about Mom and how she insisted I wear a coat and tie to school. I thought about Dad and how he urged me to get a good education. Both Mom and Dad had a hand in the man I had become, each nudging me to separate myself from the competition. Their encouragement meant everything, and it changed everything, too.

As I crossed the street to the Book Building, a rare jewel to the city skyline, I had a whole new bounce to my step. I gazed up at the unusual building where Eastman Radio and Bill Burton were housed. The building, itself, wasn't obvious in its beauty, nor was the start of my career in business. The truth was both were a little off-putting at first sight. However, that didn't matter. What mattered was that I was able to look past all that. I was able to envision a life much grander for myself and for my family. I was finally gaining control of my life!

THIRTY-FIVE

Dunking Donuts

No job is too small to achieve big things.

The first couple of months as a salesman trainee were spent apart from my family. I was living alone in a hotel room. Sandy and the girls were staying in Mt. Kisco, New York. It was a stressful time. Just before I left for Detroit to begin my new career, Sandy underwent emergency surgery. She was suffering from an infection and was admitted to the Westchester County Hospital in Mt. Kisco to have a kidney removed. Fortunately, her folks, Eileen and David Nelson, lived in the area. They looked after Sandy and the girls, allowing me to focus on my sales training in Detroit.

I found a brand new apartment complex in Royal Oak, a suburb of Detroit. It was a good neighborhood, a nice place to begin our new life. Just as soon as Sandy recovered from her surgery, she and the girls joined me in Royal Oak, Michigan. Kim was two-and-a-half years old and Julie was just seven-months. It felt good to be together again!

It was June 1967. I was adjusting to my new career in sales. Bill Burton became more than just my boss. In many ways, he was like a coach, one of the best I ever had. After a disappointing finish to my NBA career, and my college coaching career, I needed a guy like Bill Burton in my life. His guidance, support and belief in me helped me to find my footing at a time when my self-confidence had taken a hit. Bill introduced me to the world of sales, and it changed everything! I didn't know it at the time, but his expertise and generosity would help facilitate extraordinary levels of achievement in my life. It didn't take me long to realize that Coach Wolf was right to let me go from the Pistons. There was something more I was meant to do, and it would begin under the tutelage of Bill Burton, a gentleman known to the business world as Mr. Fabulous.

Bill was full of energy. He had high expectations of himself and of others. His motto: "Be fabulous!" Bill believed in outworking the competition, and so I was expected to be in the office at full force at 6:30 every morning. I didn't stop until 6:00 at night when most men were home, sitting at the dinner table with their families.

Those were long days!

Bill and I represented over 100 clients. Every night I boned up on one of the business of those clients, familiarizing myself with their radio station, so that I could write an effective sales pitch. Each pitch was due on Bill's desk no later than 6:30 a.m. the following morning.

I did my best to mirror Bill, represent his customer focus, his unique and affable demeanor, and his killer instinct for sales. Just as I had studied Bob Cousy's ball-handling skills in my youth, I studied Bill. I observed him while he wooed buyers at ad agencies and wowed executives at automotive companies. He had an incredible knack for winning the confidence of businesses, the bigger the budgets the better! Bill was good at exceeding client expectation, making sure they got their fair share, or more, of those advertising dollars.

Bill thought big!

Bill was brilliant!

Bill was Mr. Fabulous!

He would call on the executives at ad agencies and other big name companies, hyping up radio as *the* medium of choice. He knew how to get results and, with the same token, he knew how to send the message to our clients that our firm was the best in class. Bill wasn't about blowing smoke. He was a man of action, always looking outside of the box for ways to increase a client's revenue at the national level. Most salespeople rest easy at the buyer level because it's comfortable there.

Not Bill.

He didn't believe in staying "comfortable." He believed in being the best, and sometimes that meant stepping outside of his comfort zone. That, matched with his incredible work ethic and determination, was his strong suit, and it made me a better business man. Salesmanship is one of those skills that transfer into other areas of life. In order to sell any one thing, whether it's a car, a house, or an idea, one must first know how to sell one's self. At this, Bill was an authority!

He would say, "Bob, don't ever take no for an answer from someone who can't give you a yes!"

In other words, go straight to the top. That's where you'll find the decision-makers. Bill operated under this principle each and every day of his life. Long after his career ended, he lived as though he always had somewhere to be and something to do.

He was relentless!

Bill and I spent our days and some of our nights following leads, making cold calls and knocking on doors. I learned that no effort, big or small, is ever wasted in sales. That was a valuable lesson, considering I was delivering donuts at the time.

ൠ

Delivering donuts required a profound adjustment in my mindset. Because I trusted Bill, I kept a positive attitude. Each and every morning Bill would have me begin the day by visiting a local donut shop. There, I would purchase donuts by the dozen, boxes and boxes of them. In colored marker I would write a message on the top of each box, a simple missive that highlighted a key point about each of the radio stations we represented. For example, for our clients in New York City the message might read, "WMCA, home of the good guys!" That was WMCA's on-the-air motto. I would then deliver said donuts to our clients, local ad agencies. This job became the bane of my professional existence. I couldn't get over the fact that I had gone from dunking basketballs to delivering donuts, and yet I kept at it with a smile.

The experience was humbling, to say the least.

I would have much rather been signing autographs on basketballs than writing missives on tops of donut boxes. However, as discouraging as it was, not to mention embarrassing, I could see the positive effect my donut deliveries were having on the people at the advertising agencies.

They were always happy to see me!

Salesmanship is, after all, about making people happy. As simple as it sounds, these donuts separated me from my competition. Just as Pavlov's experiment had his dog's tongue wagging at the sound of a bell, our business was wagging with the warm, sweet smell of donuts — a minor expense for such a loyalty. Bill was always looking for ways to separate Eastman Radio from its competition.

After delivering the last box of donuts each morning, I would meet up with Bill at the first sales call of the day. One day, Bill asked me to go with him to a local bar to record the song, "Sweet Georgia Brown" off of the juke box. The bar was situated across the street from the University of Detroit, the alma mater of my ex-Piston teammate Dave Debusshere. I had no idea what Bill had up his sleeve. I was just along for the ride. After recording the song, Bill leaned in, put his hand firmly on my shoulder and instructed me to take a walk over to the Detroit Piston's main office. You can imagine my surprise! My heart was knocking hard against the inside of my chest when I realized he wanted me to go into that office and borrow a Piston's jersey, along with a basketball that bore the Piston's logo. I couldn't believe it! This was the last thing I wanted to do, since it was the Pistons who had uninvited me to the NBA, extinguishing my boyhood dream. I was embarrassed. I didn't know if I had it in me to do it. It would mean swallowing my pride, humbling myself for the sake of a sale. I started to fidget and tug at my tie.

"I'll meet you back at the office," Bill smiled.

He left me there, sitting alone at the bar, doubting myself and my decision to accept this job. In order for me to be a good salesman, I knew it would require nerve. However, I didn't know that it would require me making a complete fool of myself. I took a couple of deep breaths. What did I have to lose, other than the last shred of reputation I had left in that city?

Determined to succeed, I stood up and walked out of that bar with as much nerve as I could muster. Sick to my stomach, I marched straight over to the Piston's main office. I was nervous, but even more than that, I was humiliated. I hadn't walked through the doors of that office for three years. So to do so in this capacity, asking for a hand-out was one of the toughest things I ever had to do — up until that point anyway.

The first face I saw was Kathleen Roberts. She ran the Piston's office. Kathleen had become a good friend to both Sandy and me, long after my days with the team. Not only was she happy to see me that day, but she was delighted to help out.

I was relieved!

Kathleen gave me a numbered jersey and six basketballs — so much more than I had asked for. I was grateful, not just for the swag, but for her grace in handling my awkward request. There was no judgement on her part, just kindness. I still didn't know what Bill's intentions were for that stuff. What I did know, however, was that I had overcome a great deal of discomfort in acquiring it.

Bill Burton was a firm believer that every good salesman had to have a unique identity in order to separate himself from the competition. I could see he was bound and determined to carve out a niche for me. Bill was a smart businessman. He understood people. He knew what made them tick. When it came to my niche, my strong suit in sales, it came right down to my days in the NBA. He knew how much people loved and appreciated sports, particularly at a professional level. He knew that my professional basketball career, albeit short-lived, would give me an edge with the Detroit advertising market. It would be my ticket into a successful career in sales. Bill was all about making a fun and unusual impression on his clients. I, on the other hand, wasn't quite convinced. I figured being a salesman was going to be a demanding career. I just didn't realize how demanding it would be of my pride.

THIRTY-SIX

Be Fabulous

Take the basics of what you learn and make it your own.

I was feeling pretty good about myself when I returned to Bill's office with the Piston swag in hand. That was a big step for me. However, my face went flush when he instructed me to put on the Piston's jersey over my dress shirt and tie.

"Now I want you to take one of those basketballs, go out onto West Grand Boulevard and demonstrate your fabulous ball-handling skills to all of Detroit."

West Grand Boulevard?

I waited to see if he was kidding.

He wasn't.

This was a whole new level of humiliation.

"Excuse me?" I asked.

"Show them what you've got, Duffy!"

I had gone from being humiliated to being horrified in the time it took me to put on that Piston's jersey, something I thought I had done for the last time less than a handful of years ago. Things weren't looking good for me and my sales career, to say nothing of my pride. First there was the demotion to donut delivery boy and now I was being reduced to that of an ex-NBA player/street performer in downtown Detroit — in a Piston's jersey no less!

What was next?

Collecting loose change in an empty guitar case?

I was afraid to ask.

As I dribbled the ball onto the busy street corner, the echo of each bounce ricocheting off the pavement, cars and pedestrians passed by me without much consequence. Occasionally a car horn would sound and men in smart business suits would walk past me with looks of confusion. Mostly people just went about their business.

It was awful.

Regardless of my embarrassment, I did just as Bill asked. I dribbled the ball down West Grand Boulevard, facing the General Motors building. I looked up at the surrounding skyscrapers. I felt small and insignificant in the company of all that concrete, and yet I stuck out like a sore thumb — red-faced and embarrassed. Suddenly, from out of one of the high-rise windows, came a loud recording of the song, "Sweet Georgia Brown" — the Harlem Globetrotter's theme song we had recorded earlier at the bar. This was Bill Burton's idea of good publicity. I, on the other hand, wasn't so sure.

As the melody resounded in that big, open space, a strange feeling began to resonate within me. Suddenly I felt inspired. I surprised myself when I began to get fancy with my footwork, bouncing the ball in and out of my legs and behind my back. I lost myself in the moment. People started poking their heads out of high-rise windows, smiling and pointing at me. In a sense it felt good. Basketball had always been a big part of who I was. It was one of the great loves of my life. It felt good to handle a ball again, even if it was at the expense of my humility.

Suddenly, more car horns screamed as they drove past. Pedestrians stopped in their tracks, gathering around me with big grins on their faces. I couldn't tell if their expressions revealed pleasure or just plain pity for the former Piston who was clearly out of his gourd! The truth is I was too busy putting on a show to care. No matter what the reason, the crowd was clearly entertained. It was certainly no coincidence that I was positioned at the foot of the General Motors building, home to General Motors and a variety of local advertising agencies. As I mentioned, Bill Burton knew exactly what he was doing when he put me on that particular street corner.

Even though I was horrified, feeling more like a circus clown than a businessman, I was beginning to see the bigger picture. As a rookie in the world of marketing, Bill was establishing a brand identity that would take me to a higher level. Don't get me wrong; it was awkward as hell, one of the most uncomfortable things I've ever had to do. The 15 minutes I spent performing out on that street corner felt more like 15 hours. However, as horrifying as the entire experience was, I was beginning to see that there was a method to Bill's madness. Where my mother emphasized that I should not want to be "nobody," Bill was pointing out that I first ought to be "somebody!"

That day in Detroit, I heard that message loud and clear. Moments after performing my ball-handling skills on West Grand Boulevard, still sporting a Piston's jersey over my business suit, I stepped off the elevator into the Campbell Ewald advertising agency. I nearly jumped out of my skin when I was met with a roar of applause from its employees. Bill's game plan, at the expense of my humiliation, was a huge success!

"Be fabulous!" Bill insisted. It was then that I knew he was onto something. People talked about that performance for weeks. Even those who weren't there to see it for themselves talked about it, and for that reason I was able to generate a lot of business, not to mention a good laugh with my clients. From that day forward I learned quickly to incorporate my personality into my work, creating an environment of enthusiasm and fun, a place where people felt comfortable and cared for. That lesson was priceless!

CԱ

A graduate of Michigan State University, Bill Burton took the basics of what he had learned as a young salesman from the giant Minnesota Mining Company and adapted them to suit his own personality. He believed, as I do, that standing apart from your competition is crucial in sales. Take the basics of what you learn, whether in the classroom or out in the field, and make them your own. That goes for any industry!

You've got to love what you do, and be moved by whatever it is you are selling. If you are moved, your clients will be moved. Bill loved what he did. He was so moved by his purpose that even at the age of 83, decades later, he was still very much involved as a representative of the Detroit Radio Advertising Group, otherwise known as DRAG. He would call on CEOs and other leaders of Detroit-area companies, reminding them that, "An automobile is a radio station with four wheels."

I am fortunate to have had Bill as my mentor in the early days of my career in broadcasting, and later on as a friend. On December 20, 2014, just a few days before he died, I had a great conversation with him. I was able to tell him how much I loved him. There is no doubt in my mind that he had much to do with the man I am today. In our last conversation, Bill told me that he was proud of me. I let him know that I felt the same about him.

THIRTY-SEVEN

The Whizzer Wonder

Know your stuff — inside and out.

Besides writing pitches for clients, delivering donuts, performing on street corners, and observing the magic that was Bill Burton, I also spent much of my time studying the dial position and power of all the radio stations in the United States. As a salesman, it was expected that we know this information. This type of knowledge went with the territory. For example, the dial position was the station number (i.e. 650,) the power was the number of watts for that station (i.e. 50,000 watts,) and, of course, we were expected to know the call letters (i.e. WSM.) It didn't hurt to know the broadcasting format and ownership, too. It was a lot of information to commit to memory!

Knowing this information was so important to the business that The Eastman headquarters, located in New York City, designed a contest around it. The contest was called Whizzer. The objective was to test employee knowledge of station information. Considering there were thousands of radio stations around the country, retaining each of their station information was a real challenge. Personally, I found the "contest" to be invigorating and extremely competitive, which motivated me to study even harder. I put a lot of time and effort in becoming acquainted with each station until I became known as the Whizzer Wonder. Many attributed my success to a photographic memory. However, I attributed it to my competitive nature, not to mention good study habits I had picked up at Colgate. In my college days I maintained a rather vigorous study schedule and, subsequently, developed the ability to retain a lot of details, some necessary, some not. That ability to retain information was tremendously helpful when competing for radio dollars for our clients.

☙

After 90 days of hard work and training, Bill entrusted me with some assignments of my own. Eastman Radio had a special division that was called Quality Markets. Basically, this was a division made up of fine radio clients in small-to-medium size markets. For example, in the state of Michigan, Flint would be considered a Quality Market, whereas Detroit, a much larger market, would simply be labeled Eastman Radio. Obviously, the revenue potential is much higher in Detroit than it is in Flint. The same was true of the state of New York. In comparison to Albany, New York City's revenue was much higher and would be labeled

Eastman Radio. Bigger cities brought bigger dollars. Therefore, those accounts fell to bigger division heads.

While the markets were different and the dollars varied depending upon each market, the significance and intensity to garner revenue was competitive on all levels, in every market. I started at the ground floor of the radio business. And while the task load wasn't always ideal, I couldn't wait to work my way to the top. No matter what it took, delivering donuts or dribbling down the streets of Detroit, I was going to make it happen! As a salesman, I was paid a modest base salary plus commission. It was the "plus commission" that excited me. It was something I could really sink my teeth into since it meant that I could have control of my future. I was determined that the "plus commission" would be what drove the major portion of my income. I was selling air-time, a radio commodity otherwise known as "spots," and because my salary was driven by said "spots," I was motivated to sell as many as possible, regardless of station ratings. In the beginning it was a matter of survival more than anything. I had a family to support. I had rent to pay and food to put on the table. But as time went on it became a self-imposed contest to outdo myself each pay period. With each paycheck, I could see that my performance was being financially rewarded — the bigger my sales performance, the better my wages and the better my family's lifestyle. In comparison to the NBA in those days, a player's salary was based on a fixed income. A player's wages didn't fluctuate based on performance, endorsement deals and monies made off of product sales in the 60s. It was a set salary that rivaled a teacher's wage in today's market. Even as a head coach in college sports, my salary was fixed and not nearly as promising as that of a salesman in the radio business. For the first time in my life, I was setting high financial goals that were actually attainable. And I went for it!

Month after month I was making more money, far surpassing my paychecks in professional sports. To say I was motivated would have been an understatement. In addition to my own personal motivation, my boss and mentor, Bill Burton, was right behind me all the way, encouraging my success. I wasn't about to let him down.

Before I knew it, it was fall. The leaves were changing, as were my assignments. Bill was feeling more confident in my ability. He was giving me larger markets to work with, including New York, Boston, Chicago, Los Angeles, San Francisco and Dallas. Selling to these larger markets took no less effort than selling to the smaller markets. However, the commission checks were a whole lot bigger. This only fueled my desire to make good in the radio business! It was fun and I got hooked on the satisfaction of meeting and exceeding my weekly goals. I was on my way, and determined to achieve at a higher level!

THIRTY-EIGHT

For Whom the Bells Toll

Don't take yourself or life too seriously.

By the time 1968 rolled around, my skills had vastly improved and my confidence, in myself and in my new career was resurrected. Along with Bill's best in class training, I began accumulating a number of books focused on the topic of sales. I became a voracious reader. I was determined to enhance my ability to achieve a bigger paycheck and a better lifestyle. In sales, not unlike sports, statistics tell the story. For example, in basketball, one of the main indicators of a player's success is how many points he scores per game. As a coach you are only as good as your win-to-loss ratio. The same is true in sales. One of the key indicators of a salesman's success is the commission earned. For a manager, it is the profits gained.

Professional basketball taught me a great deal about

myself, about people, and about being an overall professional. Mostly, it taught me how to overcome obstacles and achieve great things. Basketball, for me, was always about setting records. Business, although a completely different beast, was no different. My performance in business was based on my ability to make money and to improve profits. Much like basketball, business is a numbers game. Having made that association, I realized that my experience, at all levels, in basketball and in business, was going to serve me well. From the time I was in Miss Costello's classroom until that particular point in my business career, I had been groomed to achieve at a high level. Whatever it was that success demanded, including a good sense of humor, I had been equipped. I had learned early on not to take life so seriously, to look at the lighter side of life, which brings me to a funny story.

୧୨

Sandy and the girls were settling in to life in Detroit. Our apartment was small, but comfortable for a young family. Because of my success at Eastman Radio, Sandy and I had begun talking about buying a bigger house. The girls were growing like weeds. They needed a home they could grow into. Kim was on the verge of turning four and Julie two. Providing for my family was something I took great pride in, but the better part of fatherhood came in the small stuff.

One night I came home from work, and just as soon as I walked through the front door, Sandy informed me that Julie had not been feeling well all day. She was worried. The moment I laid eyes on our little girl, I could see she was not herself. I stayed home with Kim while Sandy took Julie to the doctor.

She was diagnosed with an ear infection, and was given a prescription. Sandy headed straight for the pharmacy. As she was checking out at the cash register, Sandy made an impulse purchase. She bought a small, plastic toy that had little silver bells on one end and a suction cup to use as a stand on the other end. The bells would ring when you shook it. Sandy thought the toy might lift Julie's spirits, so she bought it.

When they got home, I sat Julie on my lap. I shook the toy, hoping the jingling bells would make her smile. Despite my best effort, she wasn't amused. Determined to cheer her up, I licked the bottom of the suction cup and smashed it hard against my forehead. Julie's expression went sideways as she tried to figure out what I was doing. I shook my head until the bells jingled. Julie erupted into a fit of giggles. Before I knew it we were both laughing out loud and each time I shook my head, Julie would laugh even harder. Soon Sandy and Kim joined in on the folly. No achievement in the world, whether in basketball or business, felt quite as powerful as simply making a sick, little girl smile.

My girls were happy.

I was happy.

Life in that moment was good, that is until playtime was over and I realized the suction toy wasn't coming off. The darn thing was immovable, permanently affixed to my forehead. I didn't panic right away because the girls were still joyfully amused by my performance, now turned predicament. While Sandy herded the girls off to bed, I struggled to separate the toy from my skull. For a guy who was "making it happen" at Eastman Radio, breaking sales records from week to week in Detroit, I sure didn't feel like the sharpest tool in the shed.

After more than an hour, I realized that I might actually be in trouble. Sandy and I laughed at first, but with each passing minute we grew more concerned that my gag might actually create more serious repercussions, such as a blood clot. So I jumped into the car and headed to Beaumont Hospital with bells tolling at every bump in the road. While stopped at a red light on Woodward Avenue, a driver in the car next to me was staring. I must have looked ridiculous. It was embarrassing. The only thing keeping me from taking the situation too serious was the fact that from this minor disaster stemmed my daughter's happiness!

Walking into the emergency room, the bells jingled, attracting the attention of doctors, nurses and patients alike. When I told them what had happened, they broke into laughter. I was happy to entertain, but I no longer found the situation amusing. Personally, I was more concerned with the medical implications. Fortunately for me, the doctor on call was able to perform a technique using ice cream to remove the suction toy from the middle of my forehead. While it was a huge relief to lose that plastic appendage, it was a bit of a disappointment to have a giant red welt left in its place. It was a small price to pay, I suppose.

The next morning I had an early appointment with a very

important client. Sandy was able to minimize the super-sized splotch on my forehead using some of her makeup. It didn't rid me of the blemish completely, but it helped to draw less attention to my face. When I explained to my colleagues, and even some of my clients, what had happened, I incited a roar of laughter. For weeks the story of my trip to the emergency room kept people in stitches. It may have even helped me to close a sales deal or two. When the hospital bill arrived in our mailbox, Sandy and I got a good laugh. It read: "Fee for removal of rattle from forehead."

Life is full of setbacks and stupid mistakes. What separates the successful person is the ability to own up to them, shrug off the humiliation, and laugh. Being able to laugh at your blunders, and we all have them, is a great prescription for happiness and success. It's moments like these, in life, just as in fatherhood or in business, that keep you grounded. You never want to take yourself or your life too seriously! A child's play toy taught me that!

THIRTY-NINE

Promotion requires Motion

Keep moving, even if it's uncomfortable.

Within six months I was progressing as a sales rep in the radio business. With the weight of Bill Burton's experience and coaching behind me, and the numerous books I studied on the art of selling, I was experiencing unusual success at a very young age. My income had grown exponentially. Bill would often refer to me as a rookie performing like an all-star. For the first time in a long time I was in total control of my future. My confidence grew over the next 18 months and, ultimately, beyond. One day while I was walking to an ad agency in downtown Detroit, mentally preparing for my meeting, I heard a familiar voice call out my name. When I turned to see who it was, I found Dave Debusschere crossing the street in my direction. A smile washed over my face. I hadn't seen Dave since I had left the Pistons. It was good to see him. His career had really taken off, and not just with the Pistons. Dave found much success performing as a pitcher for the Chicago White Sox. He was the consummate athlete, as well as gentleman.

"What are you up to these days, Bob?" he asked.

I grinned and, with a genuine measure of enthusiasm, updated Dave on the broken road that led me to that particular street in Detroit. As I shared with him the highlights of my transition from basketball to business, I knew right then and there that despite my disappointment with the NBA, I had finally found some absolution. I had, at long last, come to grips with the loss of my boyhood dream. I had moved on to the next phase of my professional life and couldn't have been happier.

Dave and I spent no more than a handful of minutes catching up. Seeing him after all those years brought back a flood of memories from my days in the NBA, things I hadn't given much thought to since I started at Eastman Radio. Business was the dream now. Basketball was a distant memory.

CB

Later that afternoon, Bill Burton called me into his office. He was sitting behind his desk wearing a colossal grin on his face. Before I had a chance to sit down he said, "You're being promoted to headquarters. We're sending you to New York."

I sank into the deep, leather chair across from Bill's large oak desk. I was thunderstruck. Bill went on to tell me how happy and proud he was of me. Coming from him, that was a compliment! However, it wasn't what I wanted to hear. I didn't want to leave Detroit. I was comfortable there, and I was happy working for Bill. He was a great mentor to me.

"If it's all the same, I'd like to stay in Detroit," I replied. "Sandy and I have been talking about buying a house."

Bill seemed surprised by my emotional reaction. I think I even surprised myself.

"This is a golden opportunity, Bob," Bill said. "New York is the mecca of advertising."

"I can appreciate that, Bill. However, I'd like to continue working with you."

Bill smiled, and as he stood to his feet, he said, "Son, you owe it to yourself and to your career to make this move. This is your chance to compete at the highest level in the world."

Even though I didn't want to hear it, I knew he was right. I owed it to myself, to my career, and to my family to take this next step. If I could make it into the NBA, I could certainly make it in business. Of course, it would mean going back to New York, and taking yet another incredible risk. I chewed on it for about 20 seconds.

"Okay," I said, finding my feet and shaking Bill's hand.

As I walked out of Bill's office, I was humming Frank Sinatra's "New York, New York." Smiling to myself, I said, "If I can make it there, I'll make it anywhere!"

FORTY

Do More Than What's Expected

Always do your best; you never know who is watching.

In March 1969, we packed up our things, and said goodbye to Detroit. The four of us were headed back to New York. Sandy and I agreed that this road trip would be a great opportunity for us to spend some quality time together as a family, and perhaps, visit extended family along the way. We drove up to Canada and back down again, popping in on my aunt and uncle in Buffalo. From there we headed southeast, landing in White Plains, New York. It felt good to be back in familiar territory again. Although this promotion put me back into "rookie status," so to speak, I felt as though I was being given the chance to prove myself, a feeling that had escaped me in the NBA.

Sandy and I found a nice little apartment complex located near a railroad station. A train ride into the city was an advantage, buying me time on my commute to prepare, seeing as I had been promoted and was raring to succeed in my new position. Waiting for me was an impressive team of salesmen at The Eastman Company headquarters. These men and women were established and experienced, and I, the rookie, had never felt more self-assured in my ability to achieve. Bill Burton's mentorship gave me the shot in the arm that I needed, and my rookie days with the Hawks, a period in my life when most of my confidence had been lost, was now my motivation!

ೞ

First thing every morning the sales and research staff at The Eastman Company met to discuss and set goals. These meetings were led by Executive Vice President Joe Cuff. Joe was a great guy and an even better leader. He was always looking for ways to improve and grow his staff. For example, Joe would often invite staff members to run morning meetings. This was a great opportunity for anyone who wanted to stretch his or her marketability. While many of the staff members found this task to be more of a chore, I saw it as a golden opportunity to rise to the occasion. Therefore, I volunteered as often as I could. I came each and every morning prepared to make the meetings fun and invigorating. After all, Bill Burton had taught me how to perform at a much higher level, in ways that drove positive results. Those days spent dribbling on street corners wearing Piston swag — as mortified as I was at the time — had robbed me of any nervousness or apprehension I may have had. Bill showed me how to stand out, and, going forward, I learned to adapt that lesson into my own brand of business.

When it comes to leading a team, whether it is in basketball or business, it's almost always about organizing and motivating people, something for which I had both the experience and a knack for! As Colgate's former head basketball coach, I knew what it took to groom a team and to take that organization to the next level. I had done it with the Raiders and I was prepared to do it with The Eastman Company. Joe Cuff was watching, and it didn't take long for him to notice and acknowledge my capacity for leadership. Because I showed initiative and ownership of any given situation, he immediately assigned me as the lead of all company meetings on a permanent basis, an incredible achievement after only a few months on the job.

I liked that — a lot!

And because the head sales manager at the time didn't seem to mind, I was able to step in without creating too many waves. I was happy about that because this new role allowed me even more opportunity to grow, as well as the chance to establish myself as a leader in a business that all but demanded assertiveness. These are the opportunities you don't want to miss, the kind that aren't so obvious as to grab you by the scruff and throw you into the ring. Sometimes you have to summon the courage and take the initiative, hunt for those opportunities in your professional life that give you certain experience and get you seen. Believe me when I say, management is watching and it could make a world of difference in your career.

Come spring of 1970, it was clear I had, indeed, acclimated to the heat of competition that is the radio rep business. My base salary, alone, was proof that I was onto something. And my "plus commission" far exceeded even my own expectations. Of course, with the high cost of living in New York, I had no choice but to compete at the highest level possible.

It was do, or die hungry.

Keeping affordability at the forefront of my mind, I moved my family out of the nice apartment in White Plains and into a brand-new home in Valhalla, New York. Sandy and the girls were giddy with excitement. We were moving up in the world. By 1971 I was appointed sales manager of The Eastman Company by Bob Eastman himself. He made the comment that my promotion was due, in large part, to my proven sales ability, my leadership skills demonstrated in morning meetings, and the favorable feedback coming from our clients. He seemed especially impressed that I utilized the company's private dining room to generate business far more than the other salesman combined.

"That demonstrates initiative and the desire to succeed," he exclaimed, patting me on the back. I was blown away. Bob Eastman was, above all things, an entrepreneur. He was a man of charisma and character. He had a definite presence about him. You knew when he was in the room. I wanted what Bob Eastman had, beginning with my own radio rep company.

My horizon was quickly expanding and there was no doubt

in my mind that my experience in the sports world, at every level, positive and negative, had much to do with my early success in business. Everything we do in life counts toward the future. Even the disappointments we feel weigh heavily in our overall success … *if* we maintain the right attitude. In a sense, even Harry Gallatin contributed to my business success. If not for him, I might not have been prepared for those like him, and I certainly would not have known how to deal with some of life's setbacks and disappointments. In that respect, I have Coach Gallatin to thank.

Knowing people, really understanding them and what makes them tick, is the key to good salesmanship and, ultimately, good business. It's not about pushing people to buy what you're selling. It's about understanding and anticipating their needs, even before they, themselves, know what those needs are. And it's about taking initiative and satisfying those needs. In sales, as in any business, no opportunity should be taken lightly. You have to be ready for anything! Circumstances are often random in nature and can construct obstacles that can be difficult to overcome. Bear in mind, however, the bigger the obstacle, the bigger the win! The trick is to dream big, exceed expectations, and, above all things, don't ever give up!

FORTY-ONE

Stay Hungry

Complacency leads to mediocrity.

In 1972, I bought a house on the hard, fast greens of Westchester Country Club in Harrison, New York — host to many memorable events over the course of its history — including the Thunderbird Classic that began in 1963. Pros like Arnold Palmer, Jack Nicklaus, and Ben Hogan played a round or two in its tight fairways and high rough. Kim and Julie, both golf prospects in their own right, still talk about growing up at the Westchester Country Club and what a magical childhood it was. Sandy and I were just as charmed by its rolling green hills and amenities. We were all quite content with our new homestead. We lived on Griswold Road. It was but a five minute walk from our house to The Club which had been built as a huge resort hotel in the 1920s, otherwise known as the Westchester Biltmore. There were two large restaurants onsite — a Men's Grill with outdoor patio dining and a large ballroom meant for large-scale events such as weddings and corporate gatherings. As residents, we were party to a lovely indoor pool, a large saltwater pool and, of course, the many guest rooms that were available to us and our out-of-town guests at the hotel. One of the perks of country club living was the two spectacular golf courses just a stone's throw away from our residence, one of which hosted the Westchester Golf Classic every year. That tournament attracted the best golfers in the world, as well as a par three course and an impressive golf driving range that was almost smack-dab in our backyard. That was where the four of us, in different stages of our life, developed a love for golf. Westchester Country Club was also host to 20 tennis courts, including five gorgeous, well-manicured grass courts.

Every year the best tennis players in the world stayed at The Club and practice on our grass courts the week before the U.S. Open. We watched Rod Laver, the first tennis player to win the Grand Slam twice, practice as well as Roy Emerson, Chris Everett, Jimmy Connors, and so many others. This may be the reason golf and tennis continues to be a big part of my children's lives. Personally, I never took any of these amenities for granted! Growing up with little-to-nothing, I appreciated everything I had in my life, including my girls. Everything I had, I had earned through hard work and success in sales. And while it was a dream come true, and so much more than I could have ever attained while playing in the NBA, I wasn't satisfied. I wanted more!

FORTY-TWO

Envision Your Success

You've got to be able to see it.

Before I knew it, I was promoted to vice president of sales at The Eastman Company. With the new title came a substantial raise and an impressive office that was situated on the second floor overlooking the skating rink at Rockefeller Center. I was quickly moving up the chain of command and while that was an extraordinary accomplishment, the office itself held no allure for me, other than it impressed clients.

In the business of advertising, image is everything! Heck, in any business, image counts for more than you'd think. Perception is everything, which leads me to the first time Bob Eastman invited me up to his farm in Vermont.

I clearly remember driving onto Mr. Eastman's enormous country estate. You don't forget something like that. I don't believe I had ever seen grass so green, not even at the Westchester Country Club. Eastman's estate was made up of rolling pastures for as far as the eye could see and grazing on its cool, sweet turf was a remarkable collection of Arabian horses. The afternoon sun warmed their glossy coats as they traipsed elegantly within the bounds of what seemed to be an endless enclosure. Mr. Eastman's property was, indeed, impressive, reminding me of those days I spent on Rockefeller's estate as a boy. I had come a long way since my days apprenticing for Grandpa Duffy. However, as I stood at the front doorstep of Mr. Eastman's home, a part of me still felt like that impressionable adolescent apprentice. I was in awe of Mr. Eastman's success, just as I had been of Mr. Rockefeller's. Both men inspired me to dream big!

I rang the doorbell. I could hear it chime like a church organ in the foyer. I cleared my throat and straightened my spine. I waited a moment. There was no answer, and so I rang the doorbell a second time. I waited another moment. Just as I was considering my next move, Mr. Eastman's voice greeted me from behind. He was trotting toward me on a stunning white Arabian horse, looking rather regal in his riding attire.

It was a hell of an entrance!

I spent the afternoon with Mr. Eastman on his lavish estate. He shared with me valuable nuances of the radio rep business, some of which was privileged information. I felt fortunate to be in the company of his brand of success.

Mr. Eastman invited me to lunch a few months later at the

University Club in New York City. He proceeded to discuss his short-term plans for his company. I held fast to every word. Mr. Eastman told me of his intention to replace The Eastman Company's existing president, Frank Boyle, with Bill Burton. It seemed the logical choice. Bill was the best! He was a first-rate salesman and I couldn't think of a better man for the job. Still, I couldn't figure out why Mr. Eastman would confide in me this information. It was a little puzzling, but I kept his confidence.

A few days later Bill Burton called me up to share with me Mr. Eastman's plan to promote him to president. I couldn't have been happier! It meant that Bill would be moving to New York. I knew he wasn't too keen about leaving Detroit. He and his wife had built a comfortable life there. However, he accepted Mr. Eastman's offer, on the condition that it would only be for a few years.

"Ultimately, Bob, we would like to groom you for president," Bill said.

Not only was I pleased to hear that Bill was moving to New York, but I was pleased to hear that I was being positioned to move up to president. Mr. Eastman's "plan" was evidence to me that I might actually have a shot at achieving my own dream, a bona fide future in the radio business. The perception was that The Eastman Company was looking to introduce new blood. I couldn't have been more thrilled, not to mention more ready. However, as I would soon learn, it wasn't meant to be.

Later that same week Bill shared with me the disappointing

news. A man named Stan Kaplan, a manager of a small market radio station out of Charlotte, North Carolina, had talked Mr. Eastman out of replacing Frank Boyle with Bill Burton. Apparently, while Mr. Kaplan didn't hold a big share of the market's interest, he did have a fair share of Mr. Eastman's attention. My name, nor my future with the company, was never mentioned. Bill was surprised at Mr. Eastman's change of heart, although I can't say he was disappointed. If anything, he seemed relieved to remain in Detroit. As for me, I was no longer feeling confident in my future with the company. The incident took me back to my rookie season with the Hawks. I didn't like how it made me feel, as though I had no control over my own future.

"Mr. Eastman is still very much committed to grooming you for president," Bill offered reassuringly. "However, now is not the time."

At the end of the day, I accepted Mr. Eastman's decision. What choice did I have? The whole situation demonstrated how quickly circumstances change in business, affecting people's lives — my life. In effect, it only reinforced my desire to maintain control of my own future.

FORTY-THREE

When Opportunity Calls

Take the calculated risk.

As the summer of '73 rolled around, I took a couple weeks of vacation. I needed it! Working tirelessly, I had experienced some emotional highs and lows. I wanted to spend some much-needed time at home with my family, enjoy some of the perks of Westchester Country Club living. While I was off, I received an unexpected telephone call, one that had the potential to change mine and my family's life — forever! The call came from Al Masini, the founder of Telerep. Where Eastman Radio represented national sales for radio stations, Telerep represented the television equivalent.

Mr. Masini was a big name in the television business. Besides having created the number one ranking television rep company, he had established himself as a pioneer of movies made for television, and ground-breaking shows like *The Lifestyles of the Rich and Famous* and *Star Search*. Mr. Masini sold Telerep to Cox Broadcasting in 1968. However, he worked out a deal that allowed him to stay on as president for the sole reason that he loved the business. I admired him for a lot of reasons, mostly because he had exactly what I wanted, the ability to determine his own future.

Mr. Masini had my attention.

In the breadth of that initial phone call, Mr. Masini shared with me a business deal that had just transpired with Cox Broadcasting. It involved another of his business interests, the Christal Company. From what I could gather, Cox had recently purchased Christal, a radio rep firm that was going to hell on a fast horse. Because I had established a good reputation in the business, Mr. Masini had recommended me to Cox as the man to turn the Christal Company around. This was an enormous compliment, not to mention a real boost to my confidence! It meant that I was doing what I had set out to do, which was to make a name for myself in the business world.

"Cox wants to move fast," Mr. Masini remarked. "So, if you're interested, I'd like to meet with you to discuss the opportunity."

The Universe was working in my favor. Therefore, I had no choice. I had to meet with him. I owed it to myself and to my future to hear him out. It wasn't a direction I had intended on going, but with my new goal at the forefront of my ambition, owning my own rep company, I figured it couldn't hurt. I was young and eager to glean as much as I could from those who had succeeded in this business before me. Moreover, declining a meeting with a man like Al Masini is just not something you do. I don't care who you are. Looking back, this phone call was pivotal to my overall success, and while it was unexpected and off the beaten path, it led me into a direction that became quite profitable.

CB

I met with the television mogul in New York City. From the moment I shook his hand I was impressed by him. His energy and creative vision was invigorating and quite contagious. He wasted no time expressing his confidence in me as *the* man to turn the Christal Company around. To find myself sitting across the table from the man who single-handedly created the concept for syndicated television was, indeed, a professional triumph. I was beside myself! More than anything, I was curious to see what made this man tick.

"I'm formally offering you the job," Mr. Masini smiled.

Even though I would have been hard-pressed to find a reason not to accept his offer on the spot, I agreed to sleep on it. After all, I was happy at Eastman Radio, not to mention comfortable with my earning power.

"I'll give you my answer first thing in the morning," I replied.

"I look forward to hearing from you," Mr. Masini said, as he shook my hand.

As we parted ways, I was in a state of disbelief. I hadn't anticipated this unexpected job offer from a guy like Masini. If I were to give my notice at The Eastman Company, an established organization in the radio industry, not to mention extremely profitable, I would be risking everything I had worked so hard for, including the pending possibility of taking over the position of president. Mr. Masini's offer, while potentially ground-breaking, was an incredible risk. He said it himself. The Christal Company was in trouble. On the other hand, Eastman Radio was doing very well for itself. The decision seemed like a no-brainer — stick with what's working. However, I couldn't shake the fact that this television mogul sought me out. He saw something in both me and Christal. As precarious as Mr. Masini's offer was, he was no dummy. He knew what he was doing, and if he thought for one minute that Christal was worth saving, there could very well be a big reward in it for me, perhaps bigger than even The Eastman Company.

I couldn't ignore that.

The more I thought about it, the more I realized it might be a much bigger risk to turn Mr. Masini down. Either way it felt like a crapshoot. It was like changing horses in the middle of a race I was already winning. Clearly, The Eastman Company was the safer bet. And then it occurred to me, Eastman wasn't a sure thing. There is no such thing as a "sure thing," not in basketball and certainly not in business. There are too many variables involved, too many fingers in the pie and, of course, too many obstacles to let that happen. My rookie season in the NBA taught me that.

As both a businessman and a family man I had to consider what was best for me and mine. And because it was my dream to move up the ladder at a purposeful pace, and to ultimately forge my own path in the radio business, I needed to consider the very real possibility that I wouldn't have the opportunity to move up at The Eastman Company. The truth was, while he was at the helm, Bob Eastman was not actively engaged in the everyday decision-making of his company. In fact, he was leaving much of those daily decisions up to his president, Frank Boyle, a guy whom, quite frankly, I never felt comfortable around.

Frank Boyle, in my mind, was another Harry Gallatin — an obstacle. Perhaps it was his indifference toward me or the fact that he was never agreeable with my being hired at Eastman Radio. Whatever it was, my gut instinct was telling me that I needed to pay attention to the negative vibe that he was giving off. After all, Frank Boyle was the key decision-maker at Eastman Radio at the time, which meant that he would have a hand in my future. I wasn't willing to settle for that. And so I listened to my gut and, with 100-percent certainty, I resigned my station, as well as my future with The Eastman Company. This decision freed me to accept both the job and the enormous risk that was being offered at the Christal Company. I figured I was still young and eager enough to bounce back if it didn't work out. What I certainly wouldn't recover from was an opportunity lost for fear of failure. I never wanted to ask myself the question, "What if?" Life is too short to harbor that brand of regret.

The moment I resigned I couldn't help but to think back to that terrific afternoon spent on Mr. Eastman's lovely Vermont estate. It was not hard to distinguish the disparities between the successes of Eastman Radio and the Christal Company. The Eastman Company was much more established — the seemingly safer bet. Christal was the long shot, the dark horse, but in my mind the better bet. Taking on Christal could end in one of two ways — losing a lot of money or becoming a lucrative transaction that had the potential to make me a very wealthy man. I was willing to bet on the latter, not because I'm a betting man, but because I was confident that I had it in me to turn Christal around, and as a result pave the way to starting my own company.

FORTY-FOUR

Starting from Scratch

Don't be afraid to start over — more than once.

My first day on the job with the Christal Company started at 7:30 a.m. Monday morning. I was brought on as vice-president and general manager. While I was eager to get started, I found myself face-to-face with a startling reality. I had gone from a plush second story office in Rockefeller Center overlooking the skating rink to an old, dilapidated building situated off a random side street in Manhattan. It was a grim introduction to the next chapter of my career, causing me to break out into a cold sweat. Tugging at the knot in my tie, I stepped off the elevator into a dingy hallway. Sitting on the floor of that corridor was Bella Werner. Bella was recruited by Al Masini to run the research division of Christal. She started one week before I had even been approached. Neither one of us was aware of the other … that is, until that morning when we met in the hallway. Bella was well-put- together, smartly dressed. This was a good sign. Like me, she was prepared to make a good impression. I was a little confused as to why she was sitting on the floor of that musty, old hallway. As I reached for the door knob of Christal, I was soon to find out.

"The door is locked," Bella smiled, glibly.

It was obvious by our uneasy expressions that we were both mildly alarmed by the fact that the New York business market had been open for nearly an hour and Christal's doors were closed for business, and it didn't seem there was any priority to fix that. This was a terrible business philosophy, one that could prove fatal to Christal and, incidentally, to my career. It was becoming abundantly clear why Mr. Masini recommended me to Cox. Christal was, indeed, in trouble! Technically, the company was bankrupt. For me, it was a challenge. I liked to take things that were sick and make them well again. Bella would prove to be a big part of that healing. She was a fierce competitor, hired by Cox as a research director. She would prove to be a key asset to Christal's success, as well as my own success down the road. However, at that point in time, it was her confident smile that helped me to focus on the challenge ahead.

I joined Bella on the musty floor and sat for a good long hour before the rest of Christal's staff dragged in. The difference in energy-level between Eastman Radio and Christal Company was like night and day. The Eastman Company was a take command kind of organization, whereas Christal was impotent at best. The half-hearted approach to business was disappointing to say the least and I got the feeling that I had made a terrible mistake. However, as the day progressed, I began reasoning with myself. It was the only way I could regain control of the situation and my future. Looking through a much more optimistic lens, I could see that this could be an enormous opportunity for me to prove myself. But before I could do that, I was going to have to access the damage and stop the bleeding. Triage would be the first step in rebuilding Christal.

The next order of business would involve cultural housekeeping. Christal was not running on all cylinders. I would need to recreate a much more preemptive business ethos from scratch. In effect, I would have to reinvent the wheel. With my sleeves rolled up and my attitude properly adjusted, I delved into Christal with everything I had. I recognized distinct advantages to incorporating both entrepreneurial and corporate tactics in my approach to the broadcasting business. In effect, my vision and intense motivation scared three of my sales employees away. They were not comfortable with fresh, more ambitious standards. I can't say I was disappointed. I was relieved, and, therefore, able to fill those positions with more driven people. My first hire was John Comenos, the first of many great, young talents. Then there was Paddy Ramsey, one of many superstars. As I began to see results, my own personal goals expanded. I envisioned owning my own broadcasting business. With each brick that I laid for Christal, I mentally laid one for my own brand. A new dream was emerging!

FORTY-FIVE

Teambuilding

Surround yourself with talented, motivated people.

The Christal Company was founded as a radio rep firm by Henry J. Christal. He carved out a clear niche for his business, representing a short list of very successful and powerful radio stations. His clients had strong signals, and an even stronger listener-base. In an era of AM radio, Christal dominated the ratings. However, as the world turns, technology evolves and circumstances change. AM radio was on its way out and FM radio was born. All of a sudden, there was an additional medium for the music-lover. This new technology had an incredible impact on the sound quality produced by radio stations, as well as Christal's ratings that took a massive dip. In effect, AM music radio was dying. By the time I came on board, serving as vice-president and sales manager, Christal was down to only six clients and the company was losing money. Before Cox got involved, Henry Christal had sold his company to a bright, personable, and competent gentleman named Phil Flanagan. As part of the deal with Cox Broadcasting, Phil agreed to stay on as president. I appreciated that. It was my job to build a productive and reputable rep firm around him. This new arrangement was uncomfortable for the both of us. However, we handled the transition like consummate professionals. Phil took a humble step back as I made the necessary changes to put Christal back on the map, once again making it a motivating force in the rep business.

A big part of changing Christal's culture was arranging daily sales meetings. These meetings were scheduled promptly at 8:30 a.m. (sharp) and lasted until 9:00 a.m. I was always in the office by 7:30 a.m. It was difficult to get in any earlier, especially since I was relying on New York City transit.

I was hoping to inspire the sales team, get them out from behind their desks and into the ad agencies as early as possible so to drum up business. I spent the greater part of my day recruiting new sales talent. Reminiscent to my days as head coach at Colgate, it was my objective to attract the best players. A good strategy will only take you so far. You need the talent to win games! That philosophy is as true for business as it was for basketball. The only difference between Colgate and Christal was that I had nothing holding me back, no restrictions that I knew of to keep me from succeeding. Those constraints that I did have were easily overcome with sheer determination.

Over the years, I developed an affinity for recruiting talent. I enjoyed inspiring others to be their best! I still do. One of my key responsibilities (and ultimate thrills) was tapping into the talent we already had in place. Bella Werner, for instance, was already a proven and talented researcher. Her work in statistics proved to be invaluable to Christal. Then there was John Fouts, a gentleman who ran Christal's Detroit office. John had tremendous people skills. He was a proven leader in managing our clients. And who could forget my right arm, Mildred Strom? Mildred was an incredible resource. She demonstrated an outstanding work ethic. With Mildred's help, Bella, John, Phil, and I were able to recruit scores of new clients in a short period of time. In a sense, these four talents were like my assistant coaches. As head coach, it was my job to ensure they had the tools they needed to do their job. After that, I stepped out of their way.

FORTY-SIX

Overcoming Setbacks

We become the choices we make.

Turning Christal around was not without its challenges that first year. It was a delicate balance between recruiting the kind of sales team that could attract new clients, and keeping our current clients happy. It took everything we had just to keep hold of the six clients we were representing. Some of those clients included WSM, owners of the "Grand Ole Opry" in Nashville, WGY, a powerhouse station owned by General Electric out of Albany, New York, and WTMJ, a giant out of Milwaukee who was simultaneously being wooed by other successful radio rep firms. The broadcasting business is fiercely competitive.

That being said, Christal was finally at a point where we could determine the damage and stop the bleeding. The good news was we were no longer at a loss. We were finally in the black, in thanks to an impressive sales team.

Turning Christal around was a big job on many fronts, one that required patience, perseverance, passion, and a team of people who weren't easily daunted by the competitive nature of the business. This was a once in a lifetime opportunity for me, a brand-new dream to achieve! I was confident with the odds of turning that dream into a bona fide business plan. Of course, as on any given road to success, you can always count on the usual obstacles. In this case, *that* obstacle was Bill Viands, director of radio sales at WIOD, a Cox Broadcasting station out of Miami, Florida. Although it may not have been his intent, Viands became a real thorn in my side, putting himself in the way of Christal's progress.

Viands had his own unique view of Cox's acquisition of the Christal Company. From what I could tell, he wanted our business plan to mirror that of the CBS rep firm which focused primarily on their own radio stations. While it may have been fine for the CBS rep firm, this philosophy would have kept Christal's clients at a short list, limiting profitability and possibly affecting sales of Cox Broadcasting's own stations. In an attempt to maintain his vision, Viands began micromanaging my staff, as well as challenging my every decision.

Successful rep firms like The Eastman Company were owned and operated by entrepreneurs, grass roots businessmen who were enthusiastic about their work and who demonstrated equal parts passion and performance. Industrialists like Robert

Eastman had large lists of clients and, subsequently, delivered very attractive profits. After all, growth in performance is the natural progression of any business. Viands didn't see it that way. In fact, he did everything he could to get in my way. He vehemently opposed my vision of taking Christal from number 20 in the rep business to number one, from millions of dollars in losses to a highly profitable company. I had met with this kind of resistance before. It was Gallatin all over again. The only difference between the two obstacles, Gallatin and Viands, was that I had grown exponentially, both personally and professionally, and I wasn't about to take this sort of resistance lying down. There was a lot at stake for me. When someone hits you in the chops, you fight back.

Cliff Kirtland was CEO of Cox Broadcasting at the time. He was very personable and competent — a great leader. However, it was Jim Rupp, President of Cox, who I approached on the issue of Viands. Jim was considered the "go-to executive," the guy you turned to in situations like these. I knew going to Jim was a risk, and could have easily been grounds for *my* dismissal. However, I trusted my gut. Viands had to go. There was no other way around it. I informed Jim that Viands' behavior was hurting business. Because Jim was a realist, as well as a wizard with analytics, I knew that if I presented him with the facts, he would see the bigger picture. I trusted that he, and the Cox leadership team, would do the right thing. Mr. Masini was the first to get behind me.

"Duffy has it right!" he said.

In that moment, I knew that I was on the right track. Sometimes, in order to do the right thing, you have to stand up to what's wrong in an organization. That's never easy. And depending upon the quality of its leadership, an organization can either congratulate you or crush you for taking that risk. Either way, it takes a whole lot of guts to hold fast to what you believe is right. Lucky for me, and the future of Christal, Cox's leadership team got behind me and removed Viands. I had come a long way since my rookie days in the NBA. I had learned to take risks, to stand up to guys like Gallatin and Viands. Fortunately, it paid off.

With Viands out of the way and the company's sudden growth, Christal moved out of the dilapidated building and into a brand-new high-rise situated on 56th Street and Third Avenue. My office was located on the 38th floor, overlooking an exquisite view of New York City. Teleprep was just four floors above me. Cox had me interact with Pat Gamiter, the director of television sales for Cox. Things were beginning to happen.

Leaving Eastman Radio for Christal was an enormous risk. It was one of the hardest, most significant decisions I've ever made. The business being bankrupt was the least of my concerns. I wanted control of my future — period. Life is about the choices we make, and the risks we are willing to take. Decisions determine the future, so calculate your options carefully. Know what's at stake! I always took risks that were in my favor, but not without first investing a lot of thought. It's made all the difference!

FORTY-SEVEN

Road Warriors

In order to be big, you have to think BIG!

Thanks to Cox Broadcasting, and the herculean efforts of my team, we finally had an office worthy of our hard work, one that would articulate to our employees and to our clients that Christal was, indeed, a force to be reckoned with. Getting there was no easy feat! In fact, it required all of my attention and the talent to multi-task. My hands were full and my desire to achieve was at a zenith. As focused as I was, I was careful to balance my efforts. On one hand, I was determined to build a winning team. On the other hand, I was doubling my efforts to maintain the loyalty of our most profitable clients. In order to stay afloat, I needed them to stick around. I still had a lot to learn about business, but I knew that there were other successful rep firms anxiously waiting in the wings, banking on Christal to fail, so that they could swoop in and snag our short list of clients. I wasn't about to let that happen!

On top of that was the pressure to progress. As in any competition, there is always a ranking, an order in which you're compared to other related businesses. Out of 20 rep firms in the United States, Christal was at the bottom rung. Naturally, Cox managers were concerned by this unflattering position and how it would impact their investment. They had every reason to be concerned. Christal had a lot of ground to cover if it was going to pull itself up the ranks. It was my job to alleviate Cox's concerns. I wasn't worried. I had plans for Christal — big plans!

It took about one full year to build a robust management and sales team. Coast-to-coast our sales staff was located in nine major cities in the United States, adding revenue that, within a year, benefited a growing list of 23 clients. In order to be profitable, however, we needed to double that number. I was confident that we could do it. It was time to transfer my energy from recruiting employees to recruiting clients.

It was do-or-die!

With one goal in mind, Bella Werner, John Fouts, and I hit the road. The odds were very much against us, since the top radio stations in the country had already established long-term business relationships with some of the best radio rep firms around. The job was not going to be easy. However, we were prepared. While on the road, each of us had a different role. I saw myself as the head coach. I created our story. Just as a coach uses a large whiteboard to sketch out plays with "Xs" and "Os," I was sketching out key points as to how Christal was prepared to make a positive impact on our future clients' bottom-line.

Bella spoke to the topic of research and data, and the overall evolution of the broadcasting business. She worked her magic while presenting the numbers, demonstrating how Christal could add new ways to build client revenue. John, our front man, was ingenious. Besides making a lot of phone calls, John kept the three of us organized and on point. Phil Flanagan, former owner of Christal, often joined us on the road. His presence, and ability to speak in public, added a lot to our repertoire. With each passing week and with every mile travelled, our little sales team was gaining ground. Before long, Cox-owned radio stations were leaving established rep firms, companies they had developed strong business relationships with to join Christal.

Within two short years the three of us had attracted 50 new clients. While our numbers were still relatively small in comparison to the top five rep firms, we were profitable, growing fast, and gaining on the competition. The thing that gave us a lot of traction was that our little team thought big! After all, when you go fishing, you don't aspire to catch the smallest fish in the pond. You bait your hook for the big one! We had no choice but to compete for the largest markets in each city. That's where the audiences were and, of course, the revenue that followed.

Our game plan was simple: Win the loyalty of prospective clients by offering new services that our competition hadn't considered, that the business, itself, hadn't considered. You'd think this approach would have provoked competing rep firms to throw down the gauntlet, to fight for their clients' loyalty. However, it had the opposite effect, making our job of acquiring new clients easier. Christal's approach to outshine the competition only made our competitors more apathetic. When our prospective clients took our ideas back to their respected rep firms, asking that they meet or exceed the level of customer care that we at Christal were offering, the competition flat-out refused. They were stuck in the past, holding on to the old way of doing things. In business, just as in life, you have to be free to change things up, meet the rising market. Whether basketball or business, you can't get too complacent or the competition will pull off the upset.

By the end of 1977, the Christal Company had achieved 100 clients, all of whom were highly recognizable in the business. I took full advantage of this opportunity because, as any good entrepreneur knows, shameless promotion is just one way to thrust you ahead of your competition. In an effort to create a sense of pride and a spirit of customer and employee satisfaction, I purchased full-page ads in *Broadcast Magazine*. These ads would scream Christal's success in acquiring new clients. It was a big deal and a clever use of company money, as it generated, in living color, a shining image of our success. The ads stirred public response. It was very positive and effective!

After every pitch we made to prospective clients, word got around. People started taking bets as to how long it would take before another full-page ad hit newsstands. We at Christal were having a great time! Even the top dogs of Cox Broadcasting were lapping it up, expressing their excitement with our impressive growth in profits. While this accomplishment was extremely satisfying for everyone involved, it was especially fulfilling for me. It confirmed what I had always suspected, which was that I could, in fact, build a radio rep firm of my own.

FORTY-EIGHT

First Class Frame of Mind

Focus on what you want your life to look like.

By the summer of 1978, I had been out of the business of basketball and in the business of broadcasting for 10 years. I had worked my way up from a rookie sales prospect in Detroit, delivering donuts and bouncing basketballs on street corners, to president of a successful radio rep firm in New York City — the mecca of the advertising business. My income had improved so dramatically that I was earning more in the business of broadcasting than the combined effort of the top earners in the NBA. Of course, professional basketball, sports in general, wasn't the mega-industry it is today. Sports superstars didn't earn six to seven figures in the 70s. It was unheard of, and, as I mentioned before, their incomes weren't supplemented with million-dollar commercial endorsement deals. That would come later.

Growing up, I always thought basketball was the dream. In reality, basketball was the means. And despite all of the disappointment and drama I experienced, I considered myself a very fortunate man. Had I continued on as a professional basketball player or a college coach, my life would look so different. Not only would I have been in a whole other tax-bracket, but my family would not have had luxuries and the comfortable life they had. One of the luxuries that I, personally, enjoyed most was paying for my own parking space in New York City. Normally, one wouldn't consider a personal parking space a luxury, but in the Big Apple it most certainly is. The monthly price tag for the average parking space in Manhattan rivaled a monthly mortgage payment in a modest home. It was outrageous, and if I hadn't been so discouraged with public transportation, I might have been offended by what I was being asked to pay every month. However, I had the money and I wasn't afraid to use it, if only to prevent some minor inconveniences.

I loved working in Manhattan. What I didn't love was traveling back and forth to and from the suburbs via train. The trains were often crowded and, depending upon the time of year, it could get quite miserable. Parking in the city was as much an investment as it was a luxury. The time I had in my car, alone and at a comfortable temperature, allowed me to think more clearly. And because I parked directly across the street from the entrance of my office building at 56th Street and Third Avenue, I was actually more productive.

Life was good. I was 37 years old. My daughters, Kim and Julie, were 13 and 11 — respectively. We were all having the time of our lives. When I wasn't working, Sandy and I spent a lot of our time on the golf course. In the summer months, when daylight lingered, we could be found on one of two golf courses at Westchester Country Club or hitting balls on the giant driving range near the clubhouse. I never took for granted my leisure time.

 C3

The thought of leaving Christal to start my own business made me a little nervous. I knew that I would be risking everything, including my family's comfort, for the shot of recreating a brand-new business from scratch. It would be ground-zero. I was no stranger to starting over, but letting go of what I felt was certain, in exchange for the uncertain, was a tough call.

A small part of me still mourned the loss of my professional basketball career. I think that's why I worked so hard in business. I was always trying to overcome that disappointment by maintaining control of my future. I knew that I could achieve that on my own as an entrepreneur. Working for someone else, no matter how impressive the company or how well I performed, would always leave me vulnerable to the unpredictability of someone else's business.

As I approached midlife, I felt even more vulnerable, less able to take the necessary risks I needed to take. It was time to act. I was determined to take aggressive action. At 37 years old, there was still some room to come back if I failed. It was time to start my own radio rep firm. This would be the most important decision I would ever make!

While continuing to build the Christal Company, I had plenty of time to build my own business plan. Whether I was flying across country to visit clients, making pitches to prospective clients, or playing golf with friends at Westchester Country Club, I was mentally formulating my own business. I traveled a lot that summer, mostly by plane. The time I spent in the air was some of the most creative use of my time. Whether it was for Christal or for the future of my own company, I made the most of it. It was easy to do when flying first class. Chateaubriand was served, sliced to my preference on a rolling table. Champagne was chilled in silver ice buckets. People dressed in their Sunday best for a plane ride. I enjoyed the luxury of first class air travel in those days. It was that first class mindset that motivated me.

FORTY-NINE

Power Breakfast

Know what your worth.

In June of 1978, I flew to Atlanta for three important business meetings. I was scheduled to meet with the Christal staff in the Atlanta office, then Cox-owned radio client WSB-AM/FM, and finally Stan Mouse, the new president of Cox Broadcasting. It was my meeting with Stan, the last meeting of the day that had my heart racing. This was the meeting that would change the trajectory of my career, not to mention my life, as I was prepared to submit my six months notice. This was the first necessary step to starting my own rep firm. I was nervous, mostly because I was relinquishing my position with Christal and all the spoils that went with it.

The moment I said the words out loud, acknowledging my intentions to leave Christal and open the Robert J. Duffy Rep Firm in January of 1979, it became real.

"Your future with Cox could be of far greater benefit to your future, not to mention far less a risk than your own start-up," Stan said, his expression growing pensive.

Logically-speaking, he was right. He made several good points to that end, including the issue of funding a brand-new business. However, I was firm in my resolve. Starting my own rep firm was something I wanted to do. It was something I had to do.

I wasn't budging.

"I'll get back to you soon," Stan said.

Our meeting was cut short. That afternoon, I boarded a plane headed for home. I celebrated with a scotch on the rocks before dinner. Despite the pressure I was feeling, I knew that I had done the right thing. Stan Mouse called me later in the week. He informed me that Cox Broadcasting was going to announce a merger with the industrial giant General Electric. He asked me to meet with GE's new CEO, Jack Welch, for breakfast at the Pierre Hotel in New York City. Stan said nothing of our last meeting or my resignation, which made me curious as to what was going on.

"Keep this merger under wraps until the story breaks to the New York media in a couple of days," he said.

I was intrigued, and so I agreed to keep quiet.

The Pierre Hotel was an impressive edifice located on Fifth Avenue, across the street from Central Park. Along with a few other notable New York buildings strung along Park Avenue, the hotel had a reputation for hosting "power breakfasts." These breakfasts were host to some of the biggest decision-makers in the business world, leaders from around the globe who conducted million-dollar deals over eggs, crepes and coffee. So to find myself sitting in *that* particular hotel restaurant, situated across the table from General Electric's new CEO, was a big deal.

Christal represented two of its radio markets, Albany, New York's WGY/WGFM and Boston, Massachusetts' WJIB. Jack Welch, not being big on small talk, cut right to the chase.

"Christal is small compared to GE," he said.

Jack thought that the company should be dominant in every aspect of its business, so rather than sell the small broadcasting branch, he wanted the merger with Cox. It was an opportunity to make GE number one in both television and radio. Cable television, at that point, was in its infancy stage. It was nothing more than a broadcasting brainchild. It was an idea that Jack believed had the tremendous potential to throw Cox into the stratosphere.

"There's a bright future for you as a young executive at Cox," Jack said with a knowing grin. As he leaned in toward me, I got the impression he was appealing to my common sense, as much as to my ambition as a businessman.

"I can appreciate that, Jack. I have a lot of respect for General Electric, and judging by your reputation, I have no doubt you'll take the company to an even higher level, but my heart is set on creating my own radio rep firm. I hope you can appreciate that."

After a short and somewhat uncomfortable silence, Jack

Welch looked me square in the eye. He shook my hand, and with a smart smile on his face he said, "Young man, I can see you are committed. I wish you all the best!"

And just like that, the meeting was over, as was my future with Cox. I walked out of the Pierre Hotel feeling empowered. With my hands dug deep in my pants pockets, I strolled down Fifth Avenue, headed back to the Christal office at 56th Street and Third Avenue. I took my time. I needed to process what had just happened. I had walked away from a sweet deal, one that had the potential to put me in bed with one of the most prestigious and respected companies in the world. However, in that moment, a sense of peace washed over me. I was confident in myself and in my decision. For better or for worse, I was already in control of my own future.

A few weeks later, I received a phone call from Cox headquarters in Atlanta. They seemed anxious to meet with me to discuss my plan. We agreed to meet after the Fourth of July holiday. This bought me some time to investigate my options as a new business owner. While I continued to build up Christal, I met with my banker, Alan Griffin at the Bank of New York. I was seeking advice on how to raise the capital needed to start the Robert J. Duffy Rep Firm. Alan advised me that the Bank of New York did not have a venture capital division that could effectively service my business proposal. He did, however, take the time to enlighten me on the role of venture capital, suggesting I contact John Canning of the First Chicago Corporation in Illinois. I appreciated that. Alan became a good friend of mine, and later became the President of the Bank of New York.

After the Fourth of July holiday, I flew back to Atlanta. I had no idea what to expect or how Cox would react to my resignation. Mentally, I was prepared for Cox president, Stan Mouse, to extend my time schedule, so to ensure a smooth transition. I knew it might take time to replace me. I was even prepared for him to ask me to leave much sooner. What I wasn't prepared for was Cox's proposal to sell Christal Company to me in a scheduled form of "Sweat Equity." I would earn the company without putting up one red cent, so long as I provided Cox with reasonable growth profits over a five year period, starting in January 1979 and ending in December 1983. Jack Welch of General Electric agreed to the proposal as part of a merger that was expected to close in 1979. I was given two weeks to review the financial agreement and render my decision.

That afternoon I left for the airport in a state of shock. In the course of one meeting, I had received my answer to the venture capital needed to start my own business. Call it random circumstance, but this pending merger between Cox and General Electric was a ripe opportunity for everyone involved, including me. However, this deal could not have happened had I not taken the calculated risk, stuck to my guns, and resigned from Cox.

FIFTY

Whole New Ballgame

Unless you ask, the answer will always be no.

By 1979, Christal had grown exponentially, as had my overall vision for the company and its employees. As exciting as those two developments were, there was still a measurable amount of work to be done, beginning with the monumental task of building our client roster. This was paramount to our success. We had to be relentless!

Bella, John, and I continued to pound the pavement, only harder than before. We took to the streets each and every week, wooing prospective clients with our new services. There continued to be a huge disparity in what rep firms were offering their clients and what we at Christal were offering. In other words, where the traditional rep firms held fast to the "old way of doing business," we were revolutionizing the radio rep business. We were literally turning the business on its ear with new and exciting approaches to how we served our clients. We understood that there was a high degree of risk in this approach. After all, uncharted water scares people. However, if we were successful, the result would blow our competition out of said water!

The trick was to convince prospective clients that change *was* necessary. Not only was it necessary, but it was of vital importance to their business. The "old way of doing things" was no longer viable. The three of us made it our job to inspire such forward-thinking. One of our best ideas, something that was unheard of at that time, was dual representation, representing two different clients in a market and combining ratings. Traditional rep firms tried to poke holes in that approach. They thought the idea was outrageous! Prospective clients, however, saw the merit in the idea and it made us a lot of money down the road. Revolutionizing business is no easy feat, especially since people are not inherently a big fan of change. We had plenty of naysayers, some of whom seemed quite incensed by our new vision of representing radio. What those cynics didn't realize was that this was a crucial time for the broadcasting business, an age where if you didn't jump onto the FM bandwagon, and all that it entailed, there was the risk of being left behind in a cloud of data transmission dust. With so much at stake, I couldn't let that happen. And so I became even more passionate and persistent.

This new approach quickly caught fire, arousing a movement for change in the radio business. One by one radio stations began to jump ship from traditional rep firms onto the starboard bow of Christal. And in return for our new clients' confidence, we protected our performance, upholding those high expectations for growth that we had set for ourselves and for those who trusted us to represent them. It was a promise we took seriously and we had nowhere to go but up!

Just five years earlier, Christal had ranked last out of 20 rep firms, which is why I went to great lengths to hand-pick a sales team that could stomach the business and effectively compete for revenue. Vying for advertising dollars in the broadcasting business is an aggressive market, a real shark tank. As a young head coach at Colgate I learned that effective recruiting, along with training was the difference between winning and losing games. A coach, or a businessman for that matter, can be bright and knowledgeable about the fundamentals of his job, but in the real world, when he's up against the competition, if he doesn't have the talent on his team that it takes to win games, he'll never win games, much less make a name for himself. In fact, he may even find himself out of a job. Therefore, I made sure that Christal had the talent! Together we set a goal of becoming number one in the business. We gave ourselves five years to make it happen. It would take us about that much time.

As we began to make headway, I pushed harder than ever. Christal was my baby, and about to be my own business. That fueled me to work harder. I was continually looking for ways to raise the stakes. I flew to Chicago to meet with the representatives of First Chicago Equity Group, a division of the First Chicago

Investment Corporation. It was one of the most respected banks in the United States at the time. The equity group was a venture capital division that invested money and took strong equity ownership in brand-new and/or upcoming companies who were seeking capital to successfully build their business. I had taken Alan Griffith's advice and scheduled a meeting with John Canning, bank president, along with Carl Thoma, vice president and Art Delvesco, an up-and-coming venture capital talent.

I shared with these men, and all three of the equity groups, my plan for building a broadcasting company from the ground floor. I utilized my relationships with clients, as well as prospective clients to identify opportunities to purchase radio stations, one at a time, over a five to seven year period. I came to the meeting with an impressive target list of markets west of the Mississippi. I honed in on the growth potential in those markets. K101 in San Francisco, for example, was for sale. I suggested we pursue the opportunity together, if for no other reason than to learn from it. You have no idea how happy and relieved I was when I received a call from Carl Thoma the following week.

"Let's give San Fran a try!" he exclaimed.

Unless you ask, the answer will always be no. With First Chicago's support and guidance we were able to get additional funds for leverage of nine million dollars from Aetna Business Credit and a commitment from the Blackburn Company to make a 12-million-dollar offer for K101 pretty quickly. Other, more established companies were in the hunt as well and, ultimately, we were outbid. Going forward my life was changed significantly. I became educated in the world of high finance, so it wasn't a total loss. The experience, itself, was quite valuable.

ↂ

When Carl, Art, and I met in January of 1980, I had prepared another impressive list of 10 stations in five different markets that I felt were prospects for acquisition. The signal strengths were superb and the growth of the markets was exciting. Those markets were Denver, Colorado; Sacramento, California; San Antonio, Texas; Orlando, Florida; and Portland, Oregon. All were clients of Christal. And all, but Sacramento, were turnaround situations, either due to loss or the need for format change. It was decided that I would meet with each of these station owners by the end of April to present compelling reasons as to why selling to a new company, Duffy Broadcasting, made sense. It would be a challenge. In fact, each group of stations was owned by "traditional" broadcasters. Change was going to be a hard sell. I had to convince these guys that rather than competing in a changing market, a time when the AM signal was on its way out, turning their asset into cash for their estate would be most attractive. To my delight, each of the gentlemen agreed over a five-year period to cash in, making their worries no longer applicable to the changing tide. And, so, Duffy Broadcasting was born.

FIFTY-ONE

A Gentleman's Agreement

Get it down in writing.

Initially, in the summer of 1980, I presented a compelling argument to Wally Rossman that it was in his best interest to sell. He was the owner of KPAM—FM in Portland, Oregon. Mr. Rossman was an 80-year-old man in the broadcasting business, and like all broadcasters of his generation, he was struggling to adjust to the unexpected growth of FM radio. AM radio was what guys like Mr. Rossman grew up listening to. It's where guys like him made their money. KPAM had lost much of its audience as a rock station to the new FM competition in Portland just like the rest of the markets in the United States. The losses were picking up, and the businessmen who had made their money in AM couldn't wrap their head around the sudden plunge.

I will never forget our conversation that day in Mr. Rossman's living room. Sitting by his side was a big, beautiful

Dalmatian. That spotted dog was with him 24 hours a day. After three long hours of analyzing changes in the radio business, Mr. Rossman finally conceded. It was with a heavy heart that he agreed to sell me KPAM—FM. My instinct told me not to leave that living room without some sort of a written agreement. So we drafted the terms onto a yellow legal pad and signed at the bottom. In Mr. Rossman's day, men conducted business with a handshake. And while that was a wildly romantic gesture, even for a businessman like me, I was wise enough to leave with something more binding since I knew this deal would be a hard one for Mr. Rossman to make, let alone keep. There were still a lot of questions looming, as well as some sentimental value. I could see the worry welling up in his eyes. I was glad I got his offer down in writing because 90 days later, when Mr. Rossman tried to back out of the deal, I was able to remind him of the agreement we had both signed, and even though it wasn't legally binding, it reminded him of why he was selling in the first place. After taking a deep breath, Mr. Rossman stood by his original agreement and sold me his AM/FM stations. And, to keep with the spirit of good business, we sealed the deal with a handshake — a gentleman's agreement.

That year proved to be pivotal for both Duffy Broadcasting and the Christal Company. This was the year I prove that I could take a deteriorating radio station and successfully turn it around. With KPAM—FM as my primary focus, I hired Harold Hinson, a gentleman who had a successful track record in the radio business, as the general manager to help me alter the format to a soft contemporary station. Together he and I changed KPAM-FM to KCNR Stereo 97 — "the center of everything." We had our hands full that year, not only because the market was very competitive, but because KPAM—FM was ranked pretty low in the Portland ratings, 20 of 26. We had a steep mountain to climb in order to boost both our ratings and our revenue. Despite the odds, we went right to work!

Step-by-step KCNR made inroads and our steady progress was obvious in the ratings. We could see the market was listening, as our advertising revenue was growing at breakneck speed, thanks to local advertisers. The pressure to succeed was at a pinnacle. And even though our losses were lessening month-by-month, I could see that we were set to run out of money by early fall. Investors let me sweat it out a bit, but when I needed them, they were there. KCNR eventually became quite profitable. In the Portland market, we were ranked in the top four. I was humbled by the whole experience, as well as by the people who helped Duffy Broadcasting along the way.

We hired Tom Farley as the general manager of KPAM—AM. Our AM station was not likely to chip into our overall financial success because of its limited signal. However, with Tom at the helm, nursing back to health a Christian contemporary radio station, KPAM—AM was no longer bleeding the company of money. That was a good thing! Tom was a good man. He had left the priesthood just before signing on to help support Duffy Broadcasting as the GM. He was able to do it on a shoestring budget with very little fanfare, and with the help of his wife Cheryl and his daughter Paige. Tom was a rookie, but learned my system and did a fine job.

FIFTY-TWO

Strong Suit

Be the most determined person in the room.

September came in with a bang! I was determined to see both Duffy Broadcasting and Christal become wildly successful. While I was building one brand from the bottom up, I was jockeying for position with the other. I had my hands full, but I loved the rush it gave me. That fall I uncovered an incredible business opportunity for Christal, one that could thrust us into the market's lead. It involved WGN Radio and Television in Chicago. WGN's radio station dominated the market at that time. It was the number one billing radio station in the United States and I wanted it. I knew the odds were against me in acquiring such a giant. However, I was dauntless and determined to work for the best!

WGN was owned by the Chicago Tribune Newspaper company. The station was a massive and mounting conglomerate that was, and still is, the Goliath of its time. Much of what the station aired was of interest to sports fans, spotlighting the Chicago Cubs and Wrigley Field. So, of course, I had WGN Radio in my crosshairs. I wanted to be David to WGN's Goliath. I wanted the giant's attention. I wanted to show that radio giant what Christal was made of. However, the word on the street was that WGN would never change rep firms. They already had a long-standing relationship with a small firm and because WGN had such a chokehold on the market, it wasn't likely another firm could step in off the street and do any better since the station's revenue was all but guaranteed due to their considerable audience. In short, success was thought to be a given no matter who was representing them. That was the myth I wanted to disprove.

While I was on the road pitching for Christal the year before, I bumped heads with that same antiquated philosophy — over and over again. In my dealings, most business managers had a tough time seeing past the "traditional" way of doing business. What I was offering was different. On the surface it may have seemed far-fetched and improbable. Hell, it may have even seemed like a threat to their business and, ultimately, to their livelihood. However, because I was a man with vision, it was my job to challenge the status quo, to kick through those closed doors, and to deliver a brand-new way of doing business. I knew my odds weren't good with WGN, but I owed it to myself and to Christal to give it a whirl. However, I would need to switch up the presentation a bit.

Just as Bill Burton had taught me in Detroit, I went straight to the top. I invited WGN's new CEO, Jim Dowdle to view my presentation. I was relieved when he accepted, along with his leadership team. At that point, you could say, the ball was in my court. The good news was that I had their attention. The bad news, if you could call it that, was that I had to find a way to keep it.

One of the reasons I invited Jim Dowdle to the presentation was because he had just come from Hubbard Broadcasting in Minneapolis. Incidentally, Hubbard was a client of Christal's. We attracted its business just two years earlier, which goes to show that everything you do leads to something bigger down the road. Although I had never met him in person, I thought having Jim at the table might give us an advantage, seeing as he had an idea of what Christal was capable of. In any case, I was ready. I had been trained by the best, taught to sell only to the person who had the authority to say, "Yes!"

Jim Dowdle was that guy!

The station's leadership team was polite, though a bit standoffish. John Suder, Jim's appointed radio and television sales vice-president, was outgoing, friendly and, moreover, interested in what I had to say. He asked a lot of good questions, as did the rest of the team. Like me, Suder played college basketball. He played for Syracuse. Although my college basketball career was much earlier than his, he was familiar with my career in both college and the NBA. This, no doubt, gave me the edge that I needed.

While my presentation was the same as it had been for

other prospective clients, I was sure to emphasize the improvement of revenue for the Chicago Cubs, since that team had just been purchased by the Tribune Company. I had done my homework and felt strongly that we could significantly improve WGN's revenue. I also proposed that WGN Radio assume a new pricing system, converting the antiquated system that had existed in the radio business since the beginning of time to a much more profitable system that had been designed for television. I was, of course, referring to the Grid Pricing System. It was a whole new approach to an old way of doing business, but the idea was intriguing. Television had done very well with this pricing system, why shouldn't radio get in on the same action? It was at that point of the presentation that I could see confusion collecting on the faces around the table.

What this would mean for WGN Radio was that the cost per commercial would increase as the spots available to purchase would decrease. In other words, the price would go up based on demand vs. sticking at a fixed price. It was just better business, especially for a station like WGN who had the greatest demand for advertising in the country. Al Masini of Telerep introduced me to the revenue potential of this concept.

At the close of my presentation, I shook hands with the leadership team. As one of the WGN managers was leaving, he turned to me and asked, "Are you playing golf this weekend at Westchester Country Club?"

Before I could respond, he finished. "Rick Buckley was

here in Chicago yesterday and just headed back to the Winged Foot Golf Club in New York to play in a tournament."

It was a simple question, but it got my head spinning. Rick Buckley was the guy who owned the Buckley Rep Company, *the* rep firm that represented WGN at the time. The fact that Rick had been in Chicago the day before, had me convinced that I might have a better shot at this opportunity than I originally thought. It couldn't have been a coincidence that he had come into town the day before I was scheduled to present. Surely, he had shown up to protect his interest. Buckley was a smart man for taking the time to do so, but I can't say it was a smart move to leave town so soon, especially for a golf game.

"I have golf games scheduled for Saturday and Sunday in New York at Westchester Country Club just five miles from Winged Foot, but I am so convinced that Christal can exponentially increase your revenue that I am not leaving Chicago until I earn the privilege of your business. I want to represent you. It is Labor Day weekend. Rick Buckley chose to leave town to play golf, but I'm here. My priority is WGN and, if you have any questions, I will be available to you all weekend long. You can find me at my hotel until Monday morning."

I strode out of that room feeling like a million bucks. That's not to say that my stomach wasn't tied up in knots. It was. Nevertheless, that's the high price one pays for taking control of one's own future. It is equal parts confidence and chance, and if you calculate the risk, the odds can weigh heavily in your favor. I had calculated this risk front to back, and even though I was nervous for the outcome, I was confident I had done my best. I left nothing on the court! After extending my hotel stay through Monday morning, I called my wife to let her know that I would not be making it home for the long weekend. She was disappointed, but she understood.

❧

It had been a long night and by the time mid-Saturday morning rolled around I was questioning my decision to stick around for the three-day weekend. I stared blankly at the coffee and donuts that had been delivered to my suite, wondering what I had committed to. With doubt kicking in, I didn't have much of an appetite. It only got worse with each passing minute. The telephone wasn't ringing. The silence was hurting my ears. I replayed my presentation over and over again in my head. I analyzed each question that had been asked, each statement that had been spoken. And just as I was about to medicate my anxiety with a big glazed donut, the telephone rang. It was Jim Dowdle.

"I'm in the lobby," he said. "I brought some of my team along. Can we come up?"

I had just enough time to wash the sticky glaze from my fingers, straighten my tie and smooth back my hair before there was a hard knock at the door. My heart pounded as I greeted the men. I invited them in. In a matter of minutes we were celebrating the partnership of WGN and the Christal Company. I was ecstatic. My plan worked. It was my push for change in an archaic business that changed Jim's mind. He liked my vision for the future of radio and wanted WGN to be a part of it. That afternoon I boarded a plane and flew home. I couldn't wait to see my family. It was one of the most memorable Labor Day weekends of my life. I had achieved the impossible! I had fought for and won WGN, the highest billing radio station in America!

FIFTY-THREE

Give and Take

Great success comes at great cost.

In March of 1981, a banner first quarter for both Duffy Broadcasting and the Christal Company, I was able to negotiate a deal for Duffy Broadcasting to buy KLIR—FM in Denver, Colorado. KLIR was a well-run FM station that was producing a reasonable profit. Duffy Broadcasting invested five million dollars toward this purchase, a 43-percent increase of what Christal paid for KPAM—FM in Portland, Oregon. The deal just made good business sense.

Denver had a larger market and the advertising revenue available reflected a stronger opportunity. Roger Anderson was the principal owner of a group of stations located in mid-sized markets, most of which were located in Kansas. We closed on July 1, 1981. I still have a copy of the check I signed to Anderson for two million four hundred thousand dollars as a down payment. Like Portland, where we put down one million five hundred thousand dollars, the balance was to be paid over the course of the next few years. I was getting good at negotiating my own deals. I had learned a lot from First Chicago Bank and Frontenac, my first two venture capital partners, on how to invest money in order to get the best return. I liked working with numbers, almost as much as I liked working with people. Even now, as I manage my own money, the experience of those negotiations resonates with me. Business had become my new sport. Like basketball, I had to work my tail off in order to be better than the other guy.

That fall, Lew Campbell, a gentleman who served as the GM of KLIR, and I evaluated the business. KLIR had a great sound. It was all thanks to a guy by the name of Jim Schulke. Jim was known nationally as the "guru of the beautiful music format." The problem with this particular station was that it was sharing the audience with KOSL, also a "beautiful music" station. Unfortunately, the size of the market at the time simply wasn't big enough for both stations.

The following year I made the decision to change KLIR's format to adult contemporary. It was a risk that would prove to be quite successful. Within one year of the change we had fine-tuned the "New FM 100" with the vision of "soft rock with less talk." This was all accomplished with KLIR's original staff and program director Mike Anthony. Within a couple of years, we had proven Duffy Broadcasting could, indeed, turnaround radio stations that were losing audiences and achieve success where it was measured — in profits! Both Portland and Denver had become increasingly profitable, and ranked in the top five stations in their market. This was a wonderful time in my life! I had successfully grown two companies, coast-to-coast, with a single vision that was driven by determination and developed by past experience. Both Duffy Broadcasting and the Christal Company were picking up momentum. My employees were happy and each was invested in the business. We were all at our best and the sudden growth in profits provided an amazing energy within the office. Compared to the money I made in the NBA, I was able to earn financial success at an incredible level in the broadcasting business.

☙

In January of 1983 I realized that with the rapid growth of Duffy Broadcasting and my pending ownership of the Christal Company, I needed to relocate to New York City. There was little choice in the matter. I had to relocate or lose one or both of my companies. I needed to be on the job both day and night in order to keep up this incredible pace. It was the only way to fully achieve my progressing goals.

Unfortunately, with the growing demand on my time, my family was feeling the strain. And while I knew it would cause a terrible rift, I moved out of the Westchester Country Club in February and into an apartment conveniently located across the street from my office on 56th Street and Third Avenue. By March of that same year, Sandy and I were legally separated.

Looking back, it was a high price to pay for success, but it was necessary, in my opinion. I made the decision to separate, knowing that I would always take care of Sandy and the girls.

They remained at Westchester.

I moved to the city.

I cried like a baby that first night in New York.

The divorce was final one year later.

While I wasn't able to keep our family intact, I always made sure that they had what they needed, and that I spent weekends with my girls. It was a traumatic time in all of our lives, so much so that I wondered if I had it in me to keep up such an incredible pace. Only time would tell. I will say that I loved living in the city. If I had to do it again, I would have raised my girls in Manhattan. I always thought suburbia was the place to be, but coming down the elevator from my penthouse and stepping out onto the streets of New York, I found the accessibility an incredible rush. There were 20 restaurants within my reach, some with some of the best Italian food in New York City.

I can tell you this much, living in the city saved me a miserable commute, particularly in the wintertime. It's no fun waking up to frigid temperatures, scraping ice off the car windows and then rushing back inside to warm up with a cup of coffee before driving to the train station. It beat bracing against the cold as I stood at the station waiting for a train that may or may not have had a working heater, to say nothing of the views I had from my penthouse. New York City was an amazing place to live.

CB

I was in bed one night listening to KCNR in Portland, 3,000 miles away. I dialed in by telephone, occasionally, to stay in touch with our format. That night I fell asleep with the telephone receiver pressed to my ear as I listened. I was physically, mentally and emotionally drained. I woke up the next morning, close to eight hours later, with the telephone still pressed to my ear and KCNR still playing into my pillow. Mind you, it was a long-distance phone call, a hefty expense for a good night's sleep. I got a good laugh when I thought about how much that call would cost me. I was a hands-on kind of leader. I had a responsibility to my employees and to my investors. I had a lot of people counting on me, including Sandy and my girls. I was not about to let them down, even if that meant working in my sleep!

FIFTY-FOUR

A Tough Call

Trust your instincts.

It was the middle of summer in 1983. I was attempting to purchase yet another rep firm, one that was owned by RKO. It was a small rep firm that, like CBS, focused primarily on its own highly-rated stations. I was attracted to the powerful station, more so than the rep firm, itself. I knew that it was a market that could offer Christal substantial growth. The whole process to compete for that business lasted just a few weeks. Unfortunately, RKO ended up selling to Katz Communications. Though Christal's bid was competitive, it was Katz's reputation that had us beat. Katz was considered number one in the rep firm business at the time, both in radio and television.

I was disappointed. I was also more determined than ever. I became relentless in my pursuit for creative growth opportunities for Christal. By the middle of August a group of my venture capital shareholders from Duffy Broadcasting approached me with an interesting strategy — merging the Christal Company with Duffy Broadcasting. Of course, this seemed like the natural progression of things since the revenue and impressive profit growth of the Christal Company would only add to Duffy Broadcasting's growth, subsequently, increasing the ability to catch Wall Street's eye. The combination of the two companies could raise larger sums of money — fast!

However, without a merger, my investors would find it difficult to raise additional venture capital since my upcoming ownership of Christal could possibly be considered a conflict of interest. In that regard, Duffy Broadcasting would need an operating president, a COO, whereas I would be CEO and Chairman. Honestly, the thought had never occurred to me, and because I respected their concern and expertise, I agreed to consider the deal and give my venture capital shareholders an answer by the end of the month.

Over the course of the next several days I wrestled with the decision of merging the Christal Company with Duffy Broadcasting. On one hand, I was about to own 100-percent of the Christal Company, which was to be very profitable. To merge too soon could affect my future. On the other hand, even though it was still too soon to tell, Duffy Broadcasting had the potential to make me a lot more money. It was a tough call.

Within a week I knew what I had to do. However, I needed

a sounding board, a trusted ear to bend. So I turned to nationally-respected broadcaster and president of the National Radio Broadcast Association Bill Clark. At the time Bill was also president of Shamrock Broadcasting, owned by Roy Disney — brother to Walt Disney. I looked to Bill because he was smart, experienced and he knew Duffy Broadcasting from the inside out. In fact, he had just agreed to serve on Duffy Broadcasting's board of directors.

Over the years Bill had become a friend of mine and had been since my early days with Christal when he hired us to represent the station KABL—FM in San Francisco where he lived. He was managing the station for Roy Disney. We had spent a great deal of time together, mostly while serving on the NRBA board. Bill was running Shamrock's broadcast facilities, including the television division, when I approached him about my decision.

I shared with Bill my decision to retain 100-percent ownership of Christal at the end of 1983. And although I would not be responsible for the day-to-day management of Duffy Broadcasting, as founder and chairman of the board, I could continue to impact its future by acquisition and leadership to aid in the growth and financial success of the company. Bill agreed it was the right thing to do. Within 24 hours, I notified my investors and promptly (and temporarily) moved into my new role of CEO and Chairman of the Duffy Broadcasting Company. That was a good day. However, there wasn't much room for ceremony, as there was too much work to be done, especially when I had reason to believe that within 30 days, or by October 1, 1983, Duffy Broadcasting was going to purchase KIXI—AM/FM in Seattle and/or KGMS/KSFM in Sacramento. Without the merger, I could see that the future of both the Christal Company and Duffy Broadcasting, though separate, was very bright!

FIFTY-FIVE

Breaking New Ground

It is always best to face the music.

On January 1, 1984 I was set to become the owner of the Christal Company. As the transition approached, I arranged for my employees to have the option to invest in Christal's future, a modest investment opportunity that would help take employees beyond taxable income. They earned it, and their response to the investment option was outstanding! Employees were excited about becoming Christal investors. This made me happy because I had never seen them more motivated. Cox had a hand in helping me design the employee investment program, and I was very appreciative of that. I wanted those who had a hand in our success to benefit. At the same time I was considering the possibility of buying yet another rep firm. I wanted to maintain momentum and gain a larger share of the rep firm business — a bigger piece of the pie. I was setting a precedent, as this had never been done before.

I liked that!

I had proven to myself, to our clients, and to the competition that change was, in fact, necessary and that dual representation, representing two separately owned stations at the same time, was possible! With that in mind, I flew to San Diego to persuade our client, Force Communications, to allow Christal to pair its adult contemporary FM station with an older beautiful music FM station, so that the combined audience would be more attractive to advertisers and, in effect, increase revenue for both stations. Norm Feuer, a partner at Force Communications and manager of the stations, agreed to give it a shot. Shortly after, Bill Clark, president of Shamrock Broadcasting and manager of the giant beautiful music station, KABL (Cable) in San Francisco agreed to the same, coupling with a rock station. We were breaking new ground!

Ironically, what made my job easier was my competitions' stronghold on the "traditional" way of doing business. The relics of radio had a vice-grip on their laurels. They weren't about to let go of their antiquated ways, not even for the sake of better business. Competing rep firms were so focused on how radio operated in decades past, they failed to recognize how radio could operate more profitably, by combining station audiences and targeting higher revenue levels. That's where I came in! Christal cornered the market on new and innovative ideas. So in that respect, we had a monopoly on the future of radio at the national level. My team and I were beating a new path through an old business. Consequently, like all new approaches, we became the butt of broadcasting jokes. Most people are afraid of the unknown, and so they make fun.

One of the big rep firms, The Blair Company, had been number one in the radio rep business for decades. Its management team tried to poke holes in the ideas we pitched to prospective clients. When I introduced our new grid card pricing to Blair's number one news client, KTRH, as well as its growing FM rock station in Houston, Blair Company countered. "That's okay for television, but it'll never work for radio."

Two months later that same AM/FM station combo in Houston took its business from Blair Company and gave it to Christal. We were only too happy to oblige! That's the nature of any business, proactively anticipating your clients' needs and meeting them before they even know (or appreciate) what their needs are. The radio business was changing fast and Christal was already ten miles up the road waiting for it to happen, and we were prepared to acquire those businesses that hadn't seen it coming. Every good salesman knows that the art of selling has more to do with anticipating, than it does surprise. Know your clients' needs before they do — period.

As Christal began dual representation of two separately owned radio stations at one rep firm, competing firms chimed in. "It's not loyal to your clients" and "It'll never work," they said. Meanwhile, as the competition was reacting to the sudden change in market, Christal was busy picking off three more of their clients. When it comes right down to it, particularly in the business world, that old-fashioned sentimentality goes out the window. Bottom line: It's about making money, increasing profits. In sports, the bottom line is winning games. As a coach, if your team isn't winning, you're out of a job. In business, if you're not making money, you're going out of business. Whether you're a coach or a businessman, if you have the opportunity to make your team or your business more effective, you take it.

A few years earlier, while I was dreaming up new ways to increase revenue for the Christal Company, I took a shot at buying the Alan Torbet Rep Company. Torbet had been bought by Bonneville Broadcasting in the early 80s. Bonneville was owned by the Mormon Church in Salt Lake City. At the time I believed a merger with Torbet and Christal could mutually benefit all parties involved. It would also solidify Christal as the number one rep firm in the country, not only in revenue, but in public perception. Bonneville Broadcasting showed interest in my proposal. Therefore, we immediately began exploring a merger. I presented my idea to Arch L. Madsen, CEO of Bonneville in Salt Lake City. Mr. Madsen seemed intrigued. He put me in touch with Joe Dorton, a member of his leadership team who, incidentally, was located in New York City. While this was much more convenient for me, the New York media got wind of our merger talks and caused a professional rift between Bonneville and Christal. Mr. Madsen was extremely upset. He summoned Joe Dorton and me to

Salt Lake City to discuss the situation. Needless to say, I was also extremely upset.

While boarding a plane to Salt Lake City, I bumped into Alan Torbet. Alan had sold the Torbet Rep Firm to Bonneville, although he was still involved in the company. I was quite surprised at his attitude toward me. For some reason he was under the impression that I had leaked the Bonneville/Christal conversation to Broadcast Magazine and Inside Radio. Caught off guard, I simply replied, "We will see."

Later that day in an impressive corporate conference room, Mr. Madsen asked me directly if I had leaked the "merger" to the press. He was running the show and wasted no time on formality.

"No," I replied calmly. "I did not."

You could cut the tension in that room with a knife. Joe Dorton, Bonneville's New York executive, my contact in the deal, was asked the same question, to which he replied, "No."

If you ask me, his response sounded a little too rehearsed, if not overly emphatic. I could see Mr. Madsen was growing flustered, and perhaps siding with his employee. I was the odd man out, but I had been here before. I was no stranger to this situation. The only difference between now and when I was a younger man was that I had more confidence in myself and in the direction I was moving. That's when I spoke up.

"Why don't we get the owner of *Broadcast Magazine*, Sol Taishoff, on the phone? Let's get it from the horse's mouth who leaked the story."

This was the only card I had. It was the only reasonable way to reveal the truth. My reputation was at stake. I wasn't about to sit back and do nothing. And so without a word, Mr. Madsen reached for the telephone sitting in the middle of the long conference table. I leaned in, maintaining eye contact with Mr. Madsen. The telephone began to ring. On the second ring, Mr. Taishoff picked up. Mr. Madsen cut right to the chase. I watched him closely, reading his severe expression as he spoke to the magazine executive. Even though I knew that it would not be my name that was given by Mr. Taishoff, my heart was racing. When Mr. Madsen hung up the phone, he looked in Joe Dorton's direction. That was a huge relief. The meeting was summarily adjourned. I stood up, smoothed my tie, buttoned my coat, and left with my integrity intact. Unfortunately, the damage had already been done. The hope for a merger was DOA — dead on arrival. Circumstance, outside of my control, set me back, but it also set me up for something bigger. This experience, as difficult as it was, was going to help me make a major decision that would change my life very soon!

FIFTY-SIX

The Road to Number One

Put your faith in your people.

As I began hiring executives to run the day-to-day business of both Christal and Duffy Broadcasting, I realized I was opening up a new door, a passageway into something extraordinary. After considering a number of possible radio people to assume the role of president of Duffy Broadcasting, my investors and I decided to hire a gentleman who had just resigned as the head of Belo Broadcasting in Dallas, Texas. His name was Marty Greenberg. Marty was a consummate professional, a man who had a fine career with ABC Radio, and whose experience included managing stations like WLS—AM/FM in Chicago. With his background in corporate radio, I had every reason to believe that Marty could be a real asset to Duffy Broadcasting, especially as we prepared to go public and grow the business to an operating maximum of seven

AMs and seven FMs, as was allowed by the FCC at that time. Because Marty was based out of Dallas, it made sense to establish our headquarters right there in the middle of that large metropolis. Not only did it seem unnecessary for Marty and his wife to pull up roots, but the location was conveniently close to the markets we were planning to acquire in combination with Denver and Portland, stations that we had already changed and made profitable. In that sense, Dallas was ideal!

Late in the month of October, Christal's managers gathered in Houston for a few days. It was a great opportunity for the leadership team to meet and to brainstorm, as well as to learn of the growth strategy for Christal's future. One of the key agenda items was to share with managers the results of a recent study that had been conducted over the summer by a research group.

The motive for the study was to generate ideas that could take the Christal Company to the number one position in the radio rep business. Christal had overcome great odds and not only had we built from scratch a great list of clients in a short period of time, but we were also perceived by people in the radio business as being one of the top three rep firms in the country.

That particular research group had a great reputation in the radio business for gathering pertinent information that could help benefit business. Without going into too much detail, their findings were very complimentary of the Christal Company. However, there was one caveat. Because Christal had suffered a very public decline in the early 1970s, the research group felt Christal's name could get in the way of future growth, and so they made a strong recommendation to change our name from Christal to Duffy. This was not something I had planned on doing, and so the response from our managers was important. Each of the men and women who had been hand-picked, and who had helped to resurrect the Christal name, were proud of what we had achieved. Therefore, not one of them wanted to change it. They identified with Christal. I respected their loyalty, and so I agreed to keep Christal's name. I knew we could get to the number one spot with it. I was so proud of my team for sticking with it. No coach or any other type of leader can succeed without committed and talented players. That meeting reassured me that I had all the right people on board.

That day still brings a smile to my face!

With Duffy Broadcasting gaining momentum, a new president in place and its headquarters in Dallas, and the Christal managers highly motivated to get to the number one position by 1984, I was encouraged and confident that both companies were going to continue to achieve great things, albeit separately. My role in Duffy Broadcasting was no longer operational. However, it was still significant to our growth. In the first quarter, I would become the owner of the Christal Company. Everything seemed to be progressing according to plan. However, that was all about to change in an amazing way!

FIFTY-SEVEN

Taking Care of Business

Confidence is your best asset.

One morning while working in my New York office, my executive assistant, Mildred Strom, poked her head in to let me know that Jim Schulke was on the telephone. Jim Schulke created the format that, for decades, dominated major FM radio stations from coast-to-coast. He was a true entrepreneur. After a bit of small talk, Jim invited me to meet with Katz Communications to discuss their interest in acquiring the Christal Company. Although I was surprised, I agreed to meet with Katz. After all, Katz Communications was known for being number one in both the radio and television rep business. I had no reason not to take the meeting. Any businessman worth his salt will keep an open mind when opportunity knocks, if for no other reason than he might learn something.

The first meeting I took with Katz happened at the famous Bull and Bear Prime Steakhouse at the Waldorf Astoria Hotel on Park Avenue in New York City. I met with Katz Communications' president Jim Greenwald, and Ken Swetz, head of Katz' radio rep firm. Both gentlemen got right down to business.

"Would you be interested in selling Christal to Katz?"

They had my attention.

I listened as they shared their ideas as to how the Katz radio rep firm, combined with the strength of the Christal radio rep firm, could create a dominant number one in the business. Both Jim and Ken were fishing for a deal. I could see they were serious, so I assured them that I would take a few days to consider it. After a few sleepless nights, I realized that selling the Christal Company to Katz Communications was the best decision for everyone involved, including its employees.

As a stand-alone company, it was going to be difficult for Christal to continue growing unless we could buy another rep firm. I had done everything that I could with the company. I was ahead of the game, and I figured that was the best time to get out. Despite the difficult economic times, I brought Christal from the verge of bankruptcy to the number three biggest radio rep firm in the business. The hard part would be determining Christal's market value. How does one put a price on the blood, sweat and tears invested in one's business? Christal had a great deal of sentimental value, and its people, most of whom were a big part of the firm's success, meant the world to me. Nevertheless, a second meeting with Jim and Ken, and the Katz's attorney was scheduled in November.

I expressed mixed feelings about selling Christal, telling all three men that a sale would all depend on what I thought the company was worth. I prepared a value-based spreadsheet on multiple earnings over the previous 12 months. Though rep firms did not have the same assets as radio stations, my proposal reflected how broadcast facilities, radio and television, were sold. That simplified the process. I also added that I would have to be paid in cash, and that the transaction would have to be completed before the first week in January. I made it absolutely clear that after New Year's Eve Christal was no longer for sale. Rumors of this sale, should the story break to the broadcast press, could damage Christal. In short, we had to make this deal right away or not at all. All three men at the table sitting opposite me agreed.

My eyes were fixed on Christal's future, and so there was an issue that had to be immediately addressed with Cox's CEO Bill Swartz. Since the middle of 1983, I had put a lot of thought into what needed to be done about Cox Broadcasting stations when the ownership of the Christal Company transferred to me. When I decided not to sell Christal back to Cox halfway through our five-year agreement, Bill Swartz, who had just become president of Cox told me that he would switch their stations to another rep firm if I did not sell. I took that as a direct threat. I scheduled a meeting with Bill the first week in December of 1983. Whether I sold Christal to Katz or not, it was essential, in my mind, to face this situation head on.

When I sat down with Swartz, he was in a good mood. He even complimented me on the job Christal was doing for the Cox stations. Though the pleasantries were appreciated, I cut right to the chase, reminding him of his "statement" that he would remove the Cox radio stations from the Christal Company after I took ownership, an event that was about to take place in less than a month. Swartz got real quiet.

Taking the offense, I informed Swartz that I had made an executive decision to drop Cox Broadcasting from Christal's client list, just as soon as he was able to find another rep firm. I had to protect Christal and its employees. I already had all but one of Cox's markets covered — Dayton, Ohio. Swartz looked shocked.

Once he realized the seriousness of the situation, and the reasons why I had to protect Christal, he assured me that Cox Broadcasting was happy as a client and that they wanted to stay on with Christal. At that point, I saw an opportunity. It was time to close the deal, and so I reached into my briefcase and pulled out a stack of new contracts for all of the Cox stations. Each would require a long-term agreement signed by both parties. When I placed the contracts in front of Swartz, along with a fountain pen, I suggested that we get down to business. Time was of the essence.

"I can't sign these until the next board meeting, and that's not for 90 days," he said.

"If this deal is going to happen, it needs to happen now."

There was an uncomfortable silence.

"I have a flight to catch later this afternoon. If these contracts are not signed and in my briefcase when I board that plane, we will no longer be in business together," I replied, firmly.

I didn't have 90 days. I had to respond to potential clients, particularly in Atlanta, Miami, and Los Angeles. There was a lot riding on this transaction, though you would never have known it. I remained calm, cool, and collected. Despite Christal's recent growth, Cox Broadcasting was still 15-percent of its business. When you crunch the numbers, that's a big chunk! However, I had reason to believe I could quickly cover 80-percent of the potential revenue lost should Swartz decline to sign these contracts. Nevertheless, it was a risk, albeit a calculated one. Whatever happened, Christal Company and its employees were counting on me and I was not about to let them down. Fortunately, for everyone involved, I boarded my flight later that afternoon *with* Cox's signed contracts in hand.

FIFTY-EIGHT

Raising the Stakes

Consider the alternatives.

I returned to my office in New York City the next morning feeling even more invigorated. Christal had a very bright future ahead. Duffy Broadcasting, on the other hand, ran into its first major setback. Marty Greenberg called with the news that Walt Nelskog, owner of KIXI—AM/FM in Seattle, Washington had opted not to sell us his radio station. Like Portland and Denver, KIXI in Seattle was a client of the Christal Company. I had initiated this deal, but it was Marty who had been working to close it for three months. This was a devastating update! While Mr. Nelskog remained a client at Christal, he never did open up as to why he decided not to sell. Even though we had invested a lot of time and effort into the acquisition of KIXI—AM/FM, the only thing one can do in a situation like that is to accept it and move on.

Meanwhile, Katz Communications was calling, literally chomping at the bit. I scheduled another meeting for the week before Christmas. Going into that meeting, I decided that I would *not* negotiate the asking price or any other major point for that matter, regarding the sale of Christal. If that was not acceptable to Katz, then I was not going to sell. This was a calculated risk!

Since joining The Eastman Company, having my own rep firm was always *the* goal. Though I knew it would be a much bigger risk to keep Christal, I felt strongly that the odds were in my favor to get a premium value for it. I was getting rather good at calculating my odds. In every risk I had taken since high school, I carefully weighed the odds, considering the alternatives should I encounter an unexpected obstacle. One should always consider the alternatives when taking risks. Like my meeting with Bill Swartz the week before, I committed myself to a goal of achieving the "win-win" situation with Katz Communications. It was that brand of confidence that made the difference. Katz graciously accepted my offer and agreed to sign a contract before the first of January 1984. I was a few weeks away from closing the deal of a lifetime!

One of the caveats to the agreement was that I stay on as chairman of Christal until December 1984. At the time, I understood why this was important to the acquisition. Katz was supportive of my commitment to Duffy Broadcasting and the time that would require of me, but they were also willing to pay me a sizable income in an effort to keep Christal's clients happy over the course of the next year.

I agreed.

The closing of the Christal sale did not take place until March 1984. We had to wait until the transfer of Christal's ownership from Cox to me was complete. When that happened, I met with Katz in a high-rise building on Park Avenue, directly across the street from the Waldorf Astoria Hotel. Each party was represented. I had no reason to be nervous, but my adrenaline was through the roof. In a little more than 90 minutes, the deal was complete. In that time Cox transferred Christal's ownership to me and I, in turn, sold Christal to Katz Communications. I actually owned Christal for less than 30 minutes. The meeting ended when Colleen Frey, vice-president of The Bank of New York, confirmed that the large sum of cash from Katz had arrived in my bank account. Summarily, everyone involved shook hands and parted ways.

I tried to remain calm as I walked out of the conference room. In just 16 years, March of 1967 to March of 1984, I had gone from a sales trainee delivering donuts in Detroit to a financially independent businessman in New York City. I was not quite 43 years old. That same day, I crossed Park Avenue and stood in front of the Waldorf Astoria Hotel for a few minutes, digesting what had just happened. I had successfully become a wealthy man! I was free to do whatever I wanted. With a smart smile on my face, and the future of Duffy Broadcasting on my mind, I ambled north on Park Avenue to the tune of Frank Sinatra's "New York, New York." Again, I said to myself, "If I can make it there, I'll make it anywhere!"

This deal raised the stakes for me. All I could think about going forward was how I could take Duffy Broadcasting to that next level for my investors and for my employees. I had a great feeling of independence!

FIFTY-NINE

Fastest Growing Company

Don't look back.

It's been 30 years since that day in New York City, and my reasons for selling Christal still hold true. Katz, along with Christal went on to dominate the radio rep business. As for me, I was not quite 43 years old when the deal closed. The path my life has taken since that day has been quite special. I had no idea that I would achieve financial independence by selling Christal. If I had, instead, merged Christal and Duffy Broadcasting, that same opportunity would not have happened. Inside Radio called me the "industry darling" who built the firm into a twenty-four million dollar payoff. This was confirmation to me that I had made the right decision to keep the two independent. My only regret, if you can call it that, is that the merger might have made a lot more money, and it would have allowed me to continue operating the combined companies. In business, timing is not always everything, but it can make a considerable difference when making deals. And once a deal is made, you've got to stick with it. Don't look back or second-guess yourself, regardless of what occurs. Just keep moving forward, even if it's uncomfortable at first.

Christal kept me around as a part-time chairman from March until the end of December 1984. That was a bit of an adjustment. At that point, Katz had total control of Christal. It was my job to simply remain visible, if for no other reason than to keep our clients comfortable. The transition had to look seamless. I was a figurehead, powerless in nature. While it was a little awkward, it gave me time to recalibrate, refocus my energy on Duffy Broadcasting.

With the Seattle acquisition of KIXI—AM/FM having just fallen through, it became necessary for Duffy Broadcasting to purchase another market. Marty Greenberg had just closed a million dollar deal in March of 1984 with KRZN, an AM station in Denver, Colorado. In all, we owned KCNR—AM/FM in Portland, Oregon and KMJI/KRZN in Denver, Colorado. Both markets were very profitable. I was also looking to acquire another market, a client of Christal — KGMS/KSFM in Sacramento, California. Following numerous meetings that summer, Duffy Broadcasting, operated under Marty Greenberg, purchased the two properties in Sacramento for 10 million dollar. Unlike Portland and Denver, Sacramento was already a profitable operation. After closing the Sacramento deal in September of 1984, our company's balance sheet was looking very attractive and our investors were pleased. Marty handled the operational details and our new Dallas headquarters was running on all cylinders. With business going well, it was time to target yet another special acquisition, something much more personal to me — Bella Werner!

CS

Bella and I were married in October of 1984 at the Saint Regis Hotel off Fifth Avenue in New York City. Over the years I had grown quite fond of her. One day, in the middle of all of my business negotiations, I realized I had fallen in love with this wonderful woman. She was bright and accomplished and she managed to make a successful career in a man's world. Our personal "merger" made perfect sense. Bella's experience and success in the rep business was very helpful to me, particularly in the fall of 1983 when I had to decide whether to keep or sell Christal. She had become a very important part of my life. Together we purchased a brand new home in Manhattan, a two-story penthouse in a condominium called The Kingsley on 70th Street and First Avenue. It was an amazing property. It had two patios, one that overlooked the East River and the other Central Park. I was a very fortunate man!

In 1985 I was relieved of my responsibility as part-time chairman at the Christal Company, now owned by Katz Communications — "relieved" being the operative word. I was finally free to focus all of my energy on Duffy Broadcasting. As chairman of the organization, I began to think bigger, beyond growing the business one market at a time. I started looking into purchasing multiple markets at one time. The press jumped all over this.

In January of 1986, Duffy Broadcasting agreed to purchase San Antonio's KONO—AM and KITY—FM from Mission Broadcasting for 11 million dollars. Our company's growth strategy was to own radio stations in growth markets. Therefore, I continued to approach broadcasters nearing retirement, guys who had been in the business most of their lives, offering them a chance to sell and get out of the business while the getting was good. I found this approach to be most productive. Like Portland, Denver, Sacramento, and Orlando, each station was a client of the Christal Company. Because I had established a business relationship with these stations while with Christal, it made my job easier.

The plan was working!

Since Duffy Broadcasting's preference was to buy radio stations that had strong signals and, preferably, were not making money, I zeroed in on Phoenix's KLZI-FM and KSUN-AM. Both stations were owned by Transcom Limited Partnership. President Bob Herpe and his partner, Eric Hauenstein, decided to sell. I offered seven-and-a-half million for both stations. This was a fair market value in the fall of 1986 for stations losing millions. This was the most money any company had paid for an AM/FM combo in the market. I had gotten to know Mr. Herpe relatively well since we both served the industry as board members of the National Radio Broadcasting Association (NRBA.) I believe it was that relationship that closed the deal. Duffy Broadcasting was quickly working its way toward the FCC threshold of owning seven AM radio stations and seven FM radio stations. The press ate it up!

Inside Radio reported, "Duffy sells KCNR—AM/FM Portland for about seven million. Buyer is Fort Vancouver Broadcasting's Bill Failing who owns KKSN-AM there. Failing will keep his AM and spin off Duffy's day timer. Duffy purchased the duo five years ago for about three million. Duffy was a top bidder for the Gulf/Taft spinoffs that eventually went to CBS for $107 million. Duffy's last bid was near $100 million, which makes that group a contender for future radio buys."

The sale of Portland's KCNR was designed to secure the capital needed to purchase WORZ—FM in Daytona Beach/Orlando Florida. We bought the station for eight million dollars a week later. Incidentally, WORZ—FM was also a client of Christal's. The Orlando market was just starting to grow and, as part of the sun-belt, made more sense for the other markets we were keeping — Denver, Sacramento, San Antonio and Phoenix. We went on to buy yet another market. According to Inside Radio, Duffy Broadcasting was known as the "fast-growing company" when we purchased an AM/FM stations in Austin, Texas. Business was looking pretty good!

SIXTY

The Top Ten

Always keep your end-game in sight.

1987 began with a bang! A very flattering piece was published in the annual edition of a national periodical called American Radio, ranking the most admired radio stations in the country. The magazine polled radio broadcasters throughout the country each year, soliciting station managers for their feedback on who they felt were the most admired stations in the business. Out of 157 stations, KVIL—FM Dallas was ranked number one and KDKA Pittsburgh was ranked number 10. There was another poll in the same issue that focused on America's most admired radio organizations as selected by said organization CEOs. Out of the top 20 that were ranked, Capital City's ABC being number one, Duffy Broadcasting was ranked number 10 as the most admired company in all of the radio business! I couldn't have been more proud! In addition to the national recognition we received in American Radio magazine, Duffy Broadcasting was simultaneously being courted by Wall Street. Financial services corporations, including First Boston, Morgan Stanley, Drexel Burnham Lambert, and Kidder Peabody were interested in helping Duffy Broadcasting to go public. This would allow the general population the chance to buy shares in our growing company.

This was a big deal!

If anybody could take Duffy Broadcasting to its zenith, it would be Wall Street. Not only would going public put Duffy Broadcasting within arm's reach of a lot more capital, but it would also reward its current investors with a profitable exit strategy. The latter is what made it interesting. I wanted that kind of an end-game for my investors, those who had stood by me.

At the time, investors liked to achieve their return in seven to 10 years after their initial investment. And since 1987 would mark Duffy Broadcasting's seventh year in business, we were all looking for a good exit point. It was time for our board to consider its future. No one was more aware of this fact than me.

As an entrepreneur, I was blessed to have been put in the company of some very bright, bold and wonderful people. Smart businessmen like Paul Finnegan of First Chicago, Dave Dullum of Frontenac, Jeff Garvey of Austin Investments, Copey Coppedge of Boston Ventures and another gentleman associated with Fleet Bank Venture whose name, I regret to say, escapes me made me a better businessman. As I recall, all were educated at Harvard and

Stanford, and they were all just as invested as I was in the success of Duffy Broadcasting.

The process of hiring one of the aforementioned Wall Street giants to take Duffy Broadcasting to the next level was eye-opening! I learned a lot that year, especially from my shareholders. However, it wasn't until I found myself having a one-on-one conversation with Fred Joseph, president and chief executive officer of Drexel Burnham Lambert, that I realized how far I had come in such a short time. Drexel Burnham Lambert was a financial institution that had grown to become the fifth-largest investment bank in the nation. Sitting in Mr. Joseph's office, discussing the future of my company was huge! After several meetings with a handful of impressive financial service corporations, we narrowed our search down to two finalists — Drexel Burnham Lambert and Kidder Peabody. I was competing at the highest level of my game.

It felt good!

After much deliberation, we decided to go with Kidder Peabody. Personally, I felt more comfortable with their approach to our future. While Drexel Burnham Lambert was a hot and exciting prospect on Wall Street at the time, they came off a little too aggressive for my taste.

Kidder Peabody was the best choice. They hit the ground running with Duffy Broadcasting's campaign and began preparing us for what was known as "the road show." This would mean traveling from coast-to-coast in the spring with key investors to prepare them for our debut as a publicly-traded company. While the "road show" was taking place, a board meeting was scheduled at the Hilton Hotel located at Chicago's O'Hare International Airport. It was time to get down to business. We had come a long way in a short period of time and we all felt it was necessary to discuss next steps. Operationally, as a group, we recognized the great assets we had acquired. Our balance sheet was also looking impressive with profits that were twice our debt. That was an incredible feat for such a young company!

At the same time, we also recognized that a couple of our radio stations had a sudden drop in audience ratings, including Denver. This was surprising news, and it made me wonder how Duffy Broadcasting was going to face these potential bumps in the road. As chairman and CEO of the organization, I was confident that a drop in audience ratings could and would have a negative effect on our revenue, as well as our profits. I expressed my concerns to the board. Our Chief Operating Officer, Marty Greenberg, who was responsible for managing each of our radio stations, felt otherwise. He contradicted my estimation and articulated to the team that despite lower audience ratings, he believed the revenues would continue to increase that year. Marty and I had opposing viewpoints. I think it had to do with the fact that our backgrounds in the radio business were quite different. And while those differences in experience were considerable, it led us to a healthy discussion on the topic of Duffy Broadcasting's future, which, in turn, gave us all pause — something I believe we may have needed.

Suddenly it became clear that going public might not be the best option. Perhaps the best option would be to wait, take some time to recover our audience ratings and then revisit the idea of becoming a publicly-traded company down the road. Since it was my name that was being represented, I felt that holding off a year or so would be a much more effective strategy. We could go public the following year — 1988. After all, we had just bought markets in Austin, Texas and Phoenix, Arizona. Both were financial turnarounds. Waiting to go public would buy us time to turn those stations around. I knew that we could make it happen within the year. And I was confident that buying time would make Duffy Broadcasting more attractive to Wall Street. This suggestion led to a whole new discussion — our investors' future commitment to Duffy Broadcasting.

If we were to put this plan into effect, wait another year to go public, investors would have to commit to at least another five years before seeing a return on their investment. That's when it became clear that selling Duffy Broadcasting was the better option, since there were already interested buyers. Personally, I didn't like the idea of selling. I would have much rather gone public, but I knew that selling the company was worth exploring. Each of my investors had joined the cause at different stages of the game, making their stakes vastly different. Naturally, each would have a different perspective on the matter of selling versus going public.

My lead investor, Paul Finnegan of First Chicago

Corporation, had already put in seven years. He was a terrific partner whose interest came early on in the game. I was fortunate for his counsel. Carl Thoma and Art Delvesco supported me in founding Duffy Broadcasting. They were immediately joined by Frontenac and Mike Koldyke and Dave Dullum. I still appreciate their confidence in me. Copey Coppedge of Boston Ventures came onboard in the late summer of 1983. And while he did a fine job supporting our mission, Copey had at least another four years to go before seeing a return on his investment. When discussing the possibility of selling Duffy Broadcasting, my investors were all over the board, based upon their own entry into the organization. I must acknowledge, however, that all of Duffy Broadcasting's investors worked closely together, despite any differing opinions and interests. They were all professional and completely focused on one thing, the best interest of the organization.

Just before we adjourned the meeting, the board discussed the limitations for growth of Duffy Broadcasting. Because of an FCC rule that limited a company's ownership of radio stations to no more than seven AM stations and seven FM stations at any given time, we opened up the conversation on how to successfully grow our business. I knew that we could buy into larger markets like Taft Broadcasting and Capital City, but again, that would take a long time and a lot of money, more than one hundred million dollars per sale. At that point we didn't have much more to prove. We were already ahead of the game, purchasing and operating nine stations in six markets. It came down to this: "Does Duffy

Broadcasting focus on today versus a possible forward balance sheet pressure?"

It didn't take the board long to agree that the situation called for us to sell and take the gain today. The truth was we had great assets and the decision was to make, what Paul Finnegan referred to as, "a successful exit."

SIXTY-ONE

Know When to Leave

Get out when the getting's good.

The national press is a perceptive animal. In just a little over 30 days since our last board meeting, *Broadcasting Magazine* called me at my home in Carefree, Arizona. To this day, I have no idea how the sale of Duffy Broadcasting leaked to the press. However, I could tell by the reporter's inquisition that he was well-informed of the pending transaction. Our investment bank, Kidder Peabody, had not yet finalized its strategy for the potential sale of Duffy Broadcasting. In any case, I cooperated with the reporter, giving him just enough information to make the pending article a fair and positive piece. When the piece was published in March, I was disappointed to find that the statement I made regarding the sale had been omitted. In that statement, I clearly specified that Duffy Broadcasting had not planned on selling, and unless we were offered fair market value for our property, a sale would no longer be an option. What the article did state was this: "Duffy told BROADCASTING that his decision to sell the company follows a number of acquisition inquiries, particularly in the past two months, from radio executives, brokers, and investment bankers, an interest he attributes to a 'lack of exciting inventory' [available radio stations in growth markets] in the marketplace. We did not have a plan in 1987 to sell the group. But whether you're a private or public firm, you have a responsibility to your shareholders to evaluate any interest in your company and to determine if it's real. Thus far, I believe the interest is real."

Not long after Broadcast Magazine's article was released in March, Radio News followed up. "Long time broadcaster Bob Duffy has put his radio group up for sale. The bidding will begin at $110 million, even though some feel the group is worth only $85 million. Duffy is in excellent markets ... Owner Bob Duffy could make his lifelong dream come true: owning a professional sports franchise. Duffy lives in Phoenix, which has been mentioned as getting pro baseball and/or football in the future. Remember Duffy made out like a bandit when he sold his Christal rep firm in March '84." The reference to Phoenix sports was a surprise, not to mention premature. At 46 years old, purchasing a sports team in Phoenix wasn't really on my agenda. That's not to say that I didn't dream of owning my own team one day. I did! In fact just six months previous to Radio News' article being published, I partnered with E.F. Hutton in hopes of purchasing a sports franchise back East or in the Midwest. I had a lot of fun doing the homework, researching the financials of those professional sports teams that were for sale. Together E.F. Hutton and I reviewed the books for the Tampa Bay Bandits and the Washington Generals, both teams were a part of the new AFL football league. I also reviewed the books for a few Major League Baseball teams, including the Cleveland Indians, the New York Mets, and the Minnesota Twins. I even ventured into the NBA. If I couldn't play professional ball, perhaps I could own my own team. My adrenaline was high when I got to review the books for the Chicago Bulls. That particular franchise included debt liability in connection to the Chicago Stadium. I didn't know a lot about owning sports teams, but what I did know was that their value had come a long way since the 1960s. Still, due to the astounding multi-millions that were being lost to operations in that business, and the amount of financing it would take to function going forward, I came to the conclusion that owning a professional franchise at that time was not a profitable business. It was more of a hobby for your average billionaire. E.F. Hutton was as disappointed as I was with my decision, but the reality was pro sports was not a safe bet in those days.

As we neared the sale of Duffy Broadcasting, the board decided that since we had only owned our Phoenix property for seven months, we could not get fair market value for it. There was not enough time to make a losing station profitable, so we agreed to hold onto it a little longer and make it profitable.

SIXTY-TWO

Life Goes On

All greatness must pass through adversity.

In the fall of 1987, five of the six markets that made up Duffy Broadcasting had been sold for the price tag of eighty-four million dollars. Though it was an incredible achievement, the sale was awfully hard for me to digest. While I understood the financial reasoning behind our decision to sell, I couldn't wrap my heart around it. Letting go of those stations that made up Duffy Broadcasting was tough, one of the toughest things I've ever had to do. The vision, energy and commitment it took to create that company was an emotional experience, like raising a child. It's still very emotional for me to talk about almost three decades later. My partners and shareholders were terrific people and I miss their camaraderie. A lot of heart and soul went into building that organization and I owe a lot of my success to those wonderful people! So many of Duffy's employees, from our headquarters to each radio station that we owned, were fantastic talents and I treasure the time we had together. Unfortunately, random circumstances necessitated an early sale. And while the sale itself was an incredible achievement for a guy my age, it was hard to let go.

Not long after the sale, I was presented with yet another incredible entrepreneurial challenge, one that left me with an even greater feeling of achievement. As it stood, Duffy Broadcasting still owned one radio station — KLZI—FM in Phoenix. Because we only had this station for a little more than seven months, and it was still losing money, my investors asked me to make it profitable. I was delighted to take on the challenge.

I wasted no time sinking my teeth into the business. Marty Greenberg, our COO, was responsible for all of the station operations, just as he had been for all of our other markets. It was no secret that he had been struggling with KLZI—FM. The decks were stacked against us. When Duffy Broadcasting purchased the station in November of 1986, it was one of three adult contemporary radio stations in the Phoenix market. It was also ranked at the bottom of the three, where KKLT—FM (otherwise known as K-LITE) dominated the top. I wasn't threatened by the fact that we were at the bottom of the list. I had been there before, and so rather than stew in the minutiae, I instantly began gunning for the top spot. After all, the uphill struggle is the *real* expedition of life, and I had been conditioned for the challenge.

KLZI—FM had one thing going for it, one rising star who

was an indication to me that we could turn things around. His name was Jerry Ryan. He was the general manager. He was an impressive broadcast talent with an incredible instinct. He had a way of making our staff feel important ... needed. That was his greatest contribution to our achievement at KLZI—FM. Jerry was creative. He thought big, and he was not afraid to take risks. I worked closely with Jerry, and I believe he was vital to Duffy Broadcasting's success in the Phoenix market. Together, he and I took on multiple adult contemporary competitors who, on paper, had incredible advantages.

As Duffy Broadcasting planned for KLZI—FM's next steps, Marty Greenberg hired a research group to suggest ways in which to increase audience ratings. After studying the market, the research group recommended we introduce a "ten-in-a-row" music format as a way to get noticed. Marty had confidence in the research group's findings, and so we immediately put the "ten-in-a-row" format into action.

Jerry Ryan, on the other hand, focused his energy on creating an amazing morning show. He felt it would set us apart from our competition. Meanwhile, his idea for a morning show was not well-received, and in its first year, the new KLZI—FM continued to hold steady at number three in the adult contemporary (AC) competition in the Phoenix market. We continued losing money. This was not a good sign. Rumor had it I was gearing up to sell the station to Viacom which, in turn, would switch the format to country. Nothing could have been farther from the truth. I hadn't given up on successfully turning this station around, nor had Jerry.

In early 1988, Jerry and I decided to change the call letters of our station from KLZI—FM to KESZ 99.9. This was a radical result of our commitment to climb the ranks. In order to get out of a rut, sometimes you've got to do something fundamentally different. Sometimes you've got to get off the beaten path, so to create a whole new brand. Changing the call letters provided us a fresh start, not to mention a better signal as we introduced a whole new mix of music. Essentially we gave ourselves a new identity. Our new label was EZ-ROCK. We deliberately narrowed our target audience to 25-34 year olds, compared to KLZI's 25-49 year olds. KKLT, at that time, dominated the 35-49 year old market. The truth was we needed our own position as a base from which to grow, and so we focused on those consumers who, according to a study by Viacom Brand Solutions International, were considered the Golden Age of Youth. I believe it was this change in direction that really set the pace and gave our employees a new vision and hope for the future. We were committed to making the station a winner and providing my partners a good payday!

As we continued to hone in on this "winning formula", Jerry recognized the outstanding talent of two radio personnel who he thought could put his morning show on the map. The best part about it was that they were already on the payroll. Beth McDonald and Marty Manning co-hosted KESZ's new morning show, becoming daybreak's drive-time from 6 a.m. to 10 a.m. This was the start of something big, a significant step toward establishing our own unique image in the battle for the adult contemporary audience in the Phoenix market. Jerry's strategy was working!

By the end of 1988, KESZ reached the number two spot in the adult contemporary ratings. We were finally turning a profit, as well moving up the chart to the number one spot. In December of 1989 we hired Steve LeBeau as our program director. At that point, he and Beth McDonald co-hosted the morning show, and Marty Manning became our traffic man.

The research group Marty Greenberg hired suggested that we not focus on the morning show, but rather focus on the music itself. However, because Jerry's morning show was taking off, we chose to forego the suggestion, and the research group left KESZ the following year. Steve Lebeau also left to pursue another opportunity.

The following summer Jerry Ryan hired T.V. weatherman Bill Austin to replace Lebeau, and on June 1, 1990, KEZ's radio morning team of Beth and Bill was born. It was a match made in broadcasting heaven! According to an Arbitron survey in 1991, "KESZ's morning show made the biggest leap, climbing two full rating points, from a 2.9 audience share three months earlier to a 4.9 share. The program finished fifth overall among all morning shows, pushing past typical Valley favorites such as The Morning Guys on KDKB (93.3 FM), Kelly and Co. on Y-95 (KOY 95.5 FM), Barry Young on KFYI (910 AM), and even Jones and Boze on KSLX (100.7 FM)."

From start to finish, the process of successfully flipping KESZ in Phoenix was a wonderful way to end my career in business. Partnering with Jerry Ryan was one of the highlights of my career! The guy had raw talent. Not only did he establish one of the greatest morning shows in the United States, but he also originated the first All Christmas Music promotion that has been highly praised by the radio industry, and has had a lasting impact on our audience. It was this type of originality and innovation that reminded me of the early days, when as the founder of Duffy Broadcasting, I had no corporate office or staff. However, what I did have was ingenuity and enthusiasm. I was both the COO and the CEO. When you are fighting for your place in the world, particularly from the bottom of the heap, you are often at your most creative and resourceful. You almost have to be in order to survive in life ... and in business!

I cherish all those who contributed to our success at KESZ, including Beth McDonald, the late Bill Austin, Marty Manning, Perry Dimone and Carla Foxx — each one a superstar in their own right. And then there was Patty Graham, Christine Tondelli, and Lynn Wasieko, to name a few of our incredible sales staff who set records selling airtime and boosting profits. These ladies were dynamos and, combined with the talent of our on-air personalities, established a fabulous station that is still successful today. It was a great station to be a part of. Duffy Broadcasting sold KESZ 99.9 in May of 1991 to Arizona Television Corporation for eleven million dollars, which meant the company, in totality, was sold for ninety-five million dollars.

On February 8, 1996 President Bill Clinton signed a bill, the 1996 Telecommunications Act, eliminating the cap on the number of radio stations that companies could own nationally. This was a game-changer! Subsequently, Arizona Television Corporation sold KESZ, along with their partner KNIX in 1998 for approximately one hundred million dollars to Clear Channel Broadcasting, which became the largest radio company in the world. Clinton's bill got the attention of Wall Street, and so the competitive value of top radio stations sky-rocketed from 1995 to 2000, including all the other radio stations that Duffy Broadcasting had once owned between the years of 1980 and 1987. Realistically, with this new rule in effect, these assets would have easily been worth between four hundred fifty and five hundred million dollars. Hindsight is 20/20 and, if back in 1987, the shareholders and I had any indication that the US government would consider such a dramatic change in the FCC rules, we never would have sold. Those are the types of random circumstances that keep life interesting! I'm proud of my achievements in the broadcasting business, but when I think of the money I might have made, had I held onto Duffy Broadcasting until 1996, I shudder to think what that could have done for my end-game.

CB

Ironically, around that same time, I had yet another opportunity to invest in a major sports team. Out of the blue, I received a phone call from Dick Van Arsdale of the Phoenix Suns.

Dick had a great career in the NBA as a player. In 1968, in the expansion draft, when Phoenix and Milwaukee got teams, Jerry Colangelo took Dick first. After 12 seasons in the sport, nine of which were spent with Phoenix, the Suns retired his number.

Dick was calling that day to see if I was interested in investing in the Phoenix Suns. Jerry Colangelo, president of the team, was about to buy the franchise from its original owners.

I was definitely interested!

The next day, I met with Jerry Colangelo and Dick Van Arsdale in their office on Thomas and Central Avenue. Cotton Fitzsimmons, the Suns' head coach, and Paul Westphal, his key assistant, stopped by to say hello. Overall, I was very impressed, though not excited about investing in a limited partnership. I worked hard to control my own future. Being in a "limited partnership" made me uncomfortable, and so I turned the offer down.

A few weeks later, Jerry Colangelo called me to discuss another investment opportunity, requiring a much larger sum of money. I agreed to hear him out. I even took a night (with very little sleep) to consider it. However, I wound up passing on the opportunity. I thought it best that I stay in control of my own financial destiny. It was no reflection on Jerry, since I respected his reputation and achievements in the sports world.

The Phoenix Suns went on to achieve great things when he became owner. And Colangelo didn't stop there. He went on to found the Arizona Diamondbacks baseball franchise, winning a

World Series and resurrecting the USA Basketball Team. Years later he became a legend, and was selected to be in the Basketball Hall of Fame. To this day, he has my utmost respect.

Like any good businessman, I am always looking for the positive angle in any given situation. It's not about how personable you are, how handsome you are or how well-dressed. It has more to do with what is inside of you. It is the art of persuasion, motivation, and human behavior. Achievement is about knowing exactly what you want. It is about recognizing and managing life's circumstances, good and bad, and finding the opportunities in both. It is about anticipating needs, yours and those to whom you are providing a service or product. Don't get stuck in your past failures. My career in sports taught me that. From my days in the NBA, and on into my business career, I developed a knack for recognizing and managing life's random circumstances, and the obstacles that follow. I got good at finding my way around those obstacles using good decision-making skills and taking calculated risks, and I've enjoyed an incredible life of financial independence because of it. I have lived a life in which I have control of my own future. I get to choose. Above all else, that was the dream!

Christal Company Manager's Meeting 1983

Duffy Broadcasting Manager's Meeting 1986

PHILANTHROPY

"Giving is the best part of success."

Bob Duffy, Chairman of Foundation Board, Scottsdale Healthcare
(© Brad Reed)

SIXTY-THREE

The Good Life

Work hard so that you can play hard.

At the age of 43, I was retired. While I was still operating on a part-time basis as chairman of The Christal Company for Katz Communications, as well as maintaining my responsibilities to my Duffy broadcasting employees and shareholders out of my New York City penthouse, I had reached a time in my life when I could relax a little. It was a long time coming — sort of!

At the time, the word "retirement," didn't sit well with me. After all, I was a 40-something year old man with a lot of miles left to go, not to mention a lot of ambition. In a sense, I was just getting started. The word retirement implied that I was done making a difference. Images of old age consumed me, feeding false notions that in order to be retired one had to be incapacitated and bored. Personally, I preferred to think of my "retirement" as financial independence, the freedom to spend the remainder of my life doing exactly what I wanted to do, when I wanted to do it.

This was a lot to process, especially since my commitment to Katz Communications was coming to an end. It was time to consider my next professional endeavor, and there were a lot of opportunities to take into account. The one opportunity I no longer wanted to pursue was purchasing a professional sports franchise. While I had a strong partner in E.F. Hutton, not to mention the means and experience to move forward in that particular pursuit, professional sports teams, in general, weren't a smart business move in the early 80s, if we wanted to make a profit. They had limited access to revenue and they certainly weren't the booming institutions they are today. All of the teams I looked at, from the Washington Generals and the Tampa Bay Bandits, to the Cleveland Indians and the New York Mets, to name a few, were deep in the red. I had no way of knowing that with the advent of cable television, and the financial backing of big corporations, that the potential for revenue in that market would skyrocket a decade or so later. While it may have proven to be a financial windfall, for those who could afford losses, I was comfortable with my decision not to invest in a sports team at that time.

In the spring of 1985, Bella reached her own professional crossroads. She was ready to resign as the director of research at the Christal Company. Katz Communications, of course, wanted her to stay onboard. However, because we were married, she no longer felt comfortable working for a company that we, with the help of our fantastic employees, had resurrected, yet no longer owned. Her leaving was no reflection on Katz. It was a personal decision, one that she had given a lot of thought to. When she came to me for my opinion on the matter, she barely got the words out of her mouth.

"I'm thinking of resigning from Christal."

"Yes!" I said, leaping out of my chair with delight and taking her into my arms.

My response startled her. I just couldn't hold it in. That's all I ever wanted. It's all I ever worked for — to be in control of my own future, now *our* own life! As it turned out, this would be the most fun chapter! There was no pressure to achieve, and I would soon discover that there were other important ways that I could now contribute my time, talent and experience. It was this spirit of freedom and giving that ultimately gave me the most satisfaction in my life.

Soon after Bella submitted her resignation to Katz, I started planning our summer vacation in the Hamptons. This retreat would symbolize a fresh start, a chance to exhale and begin again. Along with our summer rental, Bella and I were officially in the market for a winter home. We dreamed of a warm place to hole up in during the cold winter months. That March, we took a trip to our favorite vacation spot in sunny Scottsdale, Arizona. We were excited about house shopping. Initially we were considering condominiums. However, one night over dinner I made the random suggestion that we take a drive up to the charming, little town of Carefree. I had given a speech up there six months earlier at the Carefree Inn. While it rained the entire visit, there was something special about that little town that stuck with me. The name, itself, seemed fitting for this next chapter of our life.

It was Easter Sunday when I returned to Carefree with Bella, a 25-minute drive north of Scottsdale. We weren't there for more than 15 minutes when Bella leaned into me and whispered, "I think this is where we should be."

She felt it, too. Almost immediately, we fell in love with the mountain vistas, the wide open spaces, and the boulders that were as big as buildings. We had never experienced anything so unaffected and beautiful back East. After driving around for a short while, looking at homes in the area, we decided to park the car and amble around on foot. We felt a connection the minute we planted our feet on the firm desert soil. Walking through the small town felt so different from the city life we had grown accustomed to. While passing the local post office, a voice called out to me.

"Duffy! What are you doing here?"

Surprised to hear my name, I swung around to find Ward Quaal, Chairman of the Board of the Tribune Company, headquartered in Chicago. Ward was an American broadcasting giant. He was also the man who turned the call letters WGN into a nationally recognized and respected radio and television institution. I was convinced that running into this man was providence, one of those random circumstances that happen for a reason. It had taken everything that had occurred in my life up until that point, and all the people in it, to get me to that very sidewalk in front of that particular post office in Carefree, Arizona. It took Mom, Dad, Grandpa Duffy, Miss Costello, Mr. Lazarro, Bill Burton and even Coach Gallatin to prepare me for this. It brought it all back, my struggle to achieve as an NBA player, and as a young coach at Colgate. It evoked the reality of my success in the world of business. All of it, every step of the way, required decision-making, calculated risk, overcoming obstacles, and determination to get me there. It took all of that, just so that someone of Ward Quaal's caliber could stop me in my tracks in a town whose total population at that time was somewhere in the ballpark of 1,500. Talk about randomness! My life was about to change in a big way — once again!

When Ward learned that we were in the market for a winter home, he couldn't wait to tell us about a new spec home that had just been built high atop Black Mountain. He lived in the foothills below and loved the lifestyle.

The next morning Bella and I met with a real estate agent. We took a tour of the place. We were inspired, falling in love with the vast number of saguaro and giant boulders on the 10 acre property. It was so far removed from New York City and the hustle and bustle of metropolis life. Even more impressive than the surrounding landscape were the views from the patio that stretched out no less than 50 miles in any given direction. The Valley of the Sun was a dream come true, and contrary to our life in New York.

From the top of our Kingsley penthouse, 40 floors up, we

could see Central Park, the Empire State Building, the George Washington Bridge, the Hudson River, the East River, and most of Manhattan. While those landmarks were spectacular, the Arizona desert gave us a whole other perspective. On that calm, clear day we could see the Four Peaks on the eastern skyline of Scottsdale, Camelback Mountain, Pinnacle Peak, the McDowell Mountains, the Superstition Mountains, South Mountain, Moon Valley, downtown Phoenix and all that lay in between Scottsdale and Tempe. It was breathtaking! It was also too good a deal to pass up. We knew that we had to move quickly, lest it be scooped up from under us. Therefore, we wasted no time negotiating a fair deal. In comparison to the New York City housing market, it was a steal! Within 24 hours, the Bank of New York wired me the cash from my bank account, and the house was officially ours. Handing over the keys, the real estate agent gushed at how quickly the sale went through. I reassured him, as a businessman, that I knew a good deal when I saw one. Two days later we hired Warner Interiors to assist us in designing and furnishing our new home.

Cß

That summer we rented a beach house nestled on Dune Road in Southampton, New York. It was a beautiful home on the shining south shore of Long Island. The house was neatly sandwiched between the Atlantic Ocean and the Shinnecock Bay. From our front door, and just across the road, we had the most exquisite view of the ocean and from our backdoor the bay. It was peaceful and quiet. Life moved at a relaxed pace in Southampton, much slower than what I was used to. It had a calming effect on me, which was a good thing. While I still had high hopes for Duffy Broadcasting, my involvement as chairman was non-operational. And because I still had a strong desire to achieve, I began to casually contemplate resurrecting another business or, perhaps, tackling another startup. However, that summer, I settled into my new skin, and the great and tough task of starting a life with the onset of early retirement.

SIXTY-FOUR

A Carefree Life

Create a life you don't want to retire from.

In late October of 1985, life in Carefree changed dramatically. Bella and I settled into to our new home in Arizona, adapting almost immediately to the warm weather. I spent my days working on my golf game on magnificent golf courses, while operating as chairman at Duffy Broadcasting. Bella played tennis at the Boulders Golf Club, which, combined with her love of reading, brought her peace of mind. Together we were living a great and privileged life, and we didn't take that for granted.

Even though we were considered young, our neighbors welcomed us with open arms. Bella and I were in our early 40s, relative youngsters, compared to our neighbors who were 10 to 20 years older. Most were former CEOs of big corporations or retired entrepreneurs. I was amazed by the level of professional success in our neighbors' collective resume. What was even more amazing was their level of goodness. We had never met a warmer, more humble bunch of people. We were often invited to fun social gatherings. These events took me back to the days I spent on the Rockefeller estate as a boy, apprenticing for Grandpa Duffy. I carried the image of that wealthy estate around with me my whole life, through the highs, the lows, and everything in between. A young man or woman with a dream in their heart, and the stomach to pursue it has the power to wield their own future.

I believe that!

Bella and I talked about traveling, wandering around the world while we were still young enough to do it. There was nothing stopping us. She and I traveled to Japan and China. We, along with other broadcasters and spouses affiliated with the National Radio Broadcasters Association (NRBA,) had been asked to represent the United States as a guest of Radio Beijing. Traveling within the confines of a communist regime was a unique experience. It sparked our youthful curiosity. And so, over a period of time, we traveled to different parts of the world, like England, Germany, Ireland, Scotland, and Italy to name a few. Friends of ours who were decades away from retirement didn't get it. They would often ask, "What do you do with your free time?"

Initially, I found that question hard to answer, but then it occurred to me. There was only one way to respond without over-complicating it or trying to convince them that I was as busy as I had ever been. So I would politely respond, "Whatever I want."

The conversation usually ended there. If I learned nothing else, I learned that life, itself, will always fill the vacuum of going to work every day. In fact if one has a purpose, one never stops working, not even after retirement. Find a reason to get up every morning, even if you are no longer working to earn a living. No matter how old you are or what stage of life you are in, your life will be fulfilling.

I was fortunate in that I never had to wake up and worry about money ever again. I could do anything and go anywhere without *that* concern. There is a great deal of peace that is born with financial independence. I say that with gratitude. I don't take any part of my wealth and success for granted. I worked hard for everything I have, which is why this next platform in my story is so important. I was at a point in my life where I began to seek ways to return the favor.

SIXTY-FIVE

Giving Back

Real wealth is not what you have, but what you give.

While it was great to achieve financial freedom, and to have the means to purchase new and expensive homes and cars for myself and my wife, nothing compared to giving back to the people who supported me along the way. One of my next big "projects" was to make life a little easier for Mom and Dad. They both had a hand in my achievement. As it happened, Dad was retiring from the Bedford Police Department. It was the perfect opportunity for me to provide my parents peace of mind as they entered into their own retirement. They had recently visited a development in Southbury, Connecticut called Heritage Village. It was an hour's drive outside of Katonah. They were wild about it. However, the mortgage for a new house in that development was well-beyond their means. Knowing that they came from a long line of proud people, not to mention a generation that worked hard for what they had, I realized buying them a house would not be an easy sell. It took me a good month to construct a convincing argument.

One day I suggested that I purchase their dream home in Heritage Village, assuming all financial responsibility, allowing them to live out the rest of their days rent-free. After a fun conversation, wherein I had to assure them that it would not be a financial burden on me, they both agreed. It gave me great happiness to do this for them. I had never felt more alive! It sparked something in me, a desire to give in other ways. It was that spark that ultimately set me on a path to philanthropy.

My parents had a great time moving into their new home. Dad played golf all day. Mom continued to work at the telephone company just across the state line in Carmel, New York, a half-hour away from home. Bella and I would visit them once a month. When temperatures dropped, Mom and Dad became snowbirds and flew to Arizona for the winter. We set them up in a nice apartment in our home in Carefree. Wintertime in Arizona is ideal, particularly for the retiree whose bones ache in cold weather. Dad and I golfed. Mom enjoyed shopping and the sunshine. The time we spent together was priceless! I was always looking for ways to repay Mom and Dad for their endless supply of love and support, careful not to step on their delicate sensibilities.

One summer Bella and I unexpectedly visited Mom and Dad. After some small talk, I invited my parents to join me outside in the visitor's parking lot to see the new car we had recently purchased. It was hard to keep a straight face. As we approached the shiny, new Cadillac, I could see Dad's face light up. The Cadillac was his dream car. I invited Dad to get behind the wheel. I was barely able to contain my enthusiasm, as I hopped into the passenger seat. He looked like a teenage boy, as he slid into the driver's seat, gently caressing the steering wheel. He flirted with the Cadillac, appreciating each and every luxurious detail. Dad was in love. That was obvious. He fell hard and he fell fast. Unable to keep it to myself any longer, I handed him the keys.

"She's all yours," I said, the words catching in my throat.

Dad looked at me, his forehead crinkling in confusion.

"Thank you for everything, Dad," I smiled.

Growing up I rarely saw Dad cry. When he did cry, it was a big deal. That day in the parking lot, behind the wheel of his brand new Cadillac, was a big deal. Dad cried like a baby. We all knew what this gift meant to him; it was written all over his face. I will never forget that day, and it didn't end there. I invited Mom to sit in the passenger seat next to Dad.

"Take a peek inside the glove box, Mom."

Mom had a puzzled look, but didn't waste a moment. Waiting for her in the glove box was a long, thin box. It was Tiffany blue with a white satin ribbon neatly tied around it. Mom put her hand to her lips and gasped. With trembling fingers, and tears streaming down her cheeks, she opened the box to find a lovely strand of pearls.

"Thank you, Mom."

I was barely able to get the words out. Mom looked at me, in a way only a mother can. She smiled through tears. Hers was the smile I had come to count on through everything. It was as consistent as the sun, in parent-teacher conferences, in the high school bleachers, at my college graduation, at the front door when I was cut from the NBA, and even in that moment, I looked for that smile. I could see she and Dad were both overwhelmed, but there was one more surprise.

"Pop the trunk, Dad."

The four of us gathered around the backside of the car. Folded neatly in the trunk of his new Cadillac was a new mink coat for Mom. Her initials were embroidered on the inside. Mom threw her arms around my neck. It was the greatest feeling in the world. I didn't want it to end. That experience led me to want to give again.

SIXTY-SIX

Charitable Contributions

Make life a little easier for others when you can.

Not long after I surprised Dad with the Cadillac, Colgate University invited me to The Cornell Club in midtown Manhattan. At the time, Colgate made use of the club's lavish meeting and event space to host and entertain its alumni. Not only were these events memorable, but they were also a great way to raise money for the school. Incidentally, The Cornell Club was a stone's throw from my old stomping grounds at The Eastman Company, near Grand Central Terminal, and Rockefeller Center.

Bob Tyburski, a development officer for Colgate, and a gentleman who has since become a special friend of mine, was the first man to formally introduce me to philanthropy. Tyburski or "Tybo," also played for the Raiders varsity basketball team in the mid-70s. He was captain of the team, and the last guy to wear my number — 24, which was eventually retired. He invited me into

345

the world of charitable giving, revealing the path in which I could contribute toward improving the student experience at Colgate and, ultimately, giving student-athletes the financial assistance they needed. This appealed to me on a profoundly personal level. That kid whose dream of achieving a college education depended upon scholarships and the goodness of others was now in a position to give back. I didn't take that for granted, so I handed Bob a check, a substantial endowment that would serve as the Robert J. Duffy Scholarship. This scholarship was designed to provide a male or female student-athlete the financial assistance needed to attend Colgate. I couldn't think of a better gift or a more important purpose for this next chapter of my life! This was my first real taste of philanthropy, as well as the gateway to many more charitable contributions to come, including recently helping to send Colgate's 2015-2016 men's varsity basketball team to Spain for some summer competition and a chance to bond. Tybo also contributed, along with Dennis Cronin who I coached at Colgate. I had gone from a kid needing financial assistance to a philanthropist providing it. It sure felt good!

ભ્ય

Among the many friends Bella and I made in Carefree, Doug and Esther Williams were among the best! We met the couple at one of the many parties we attended. It was Doug who introduced me to my next big philanthropic venture. One day he invited me to his private office in downtown Carefree, situated on a road cleverly named Easy Street. Doug was a former CEO of his own consulting company in Connecticut. Even though he was retired, he stayed on top of what was happening in the business world. Renting in that same office building was Lou Menk, former CEO of Burlington Northern Railway, and Jack Parker, former vice-chairman of General Electric. All were active philanthropists, and all three men became good friends of mine.

Doug told me about two charitable organizations that were near and dear to his heart: The Heard Museum and Scottsdale Memorial Hospitals. Doug was a benevolent man and spoke passionately about each organization. He stressed the significance of their respective boards, underlining the contributions that were needed to make an impact on the community.

"I'd like to recommend you as a board member for both organizations," he said.

I had just sold Phoenix radio station KESZ 99.9, and had begun to settle into my retirement, albeit early, so I wasn't sure I was ready to commit to serving on a board. Writing checks to charitable causes was one thing. Committing my time and energy was another. Deep down, I knew it was a chance to do something special. After all, it was never my intention to retire in typical fashion. In some capacity, I wanted to keep some skin in the game, and so I agreed to both recommendations. Within two weeks, Doug introduced me to Jim Schamadan, CEO of Scottsdale Memorial Health System, and Tom Hudak, board member of the Heard Museum. Impressed by both men, I couldn't wait to jump on board.

SIXTY-SEVEN

Suit Yourself

The opinions of others aren't your problem.

Life, as I learned at a young age, provides many opportunities to do great things. The only trouble is, those opportunities aren't always obvious in their presentation because they are clothed as obstacles. They also come at great cost, often requiring hard work, determination and a certain degree of personal growth. Over time, I began to recognize recurring obstacles in my life — different situations, same problem. I got good at seeing those obstacles coming at me a mile away, improving my ability to strategize.

Upon my entry into the wonderful world of philanthropy, I was unsure what to expect. However, I was confident that I knew a thing or two about business, not to mention how to find my niche. I figured my business experience would prove to be an asset, and whatever I didn't know about philanthropy, I would learn along the way. I wanted to make a difference in my community, and the thought of serving on the boards for The Heard Museum and Scottsdale Memorial Health System was enticing. The following week I met with Doug Williams at his office.

"My recommendation to get you on the board at Scottsdale Memorial Health System was met with some resistance. A fellow board member rejected the motion," Doug said. "He's concerned you don't have experience serving on a board."

I sensed Doug's uneasiness delivering this news, considering he was the one to rally my confidence in the first place. While I didn't want to put Doug in an uncomfortable position, I was heated, and it showed. I didn't respond right away, as I had been up against this sort of resistance before. I wanted to take a beat before I said something I might regret. Just as the silence was about to get uncomfortable, I responded.

"Doug, I am a businessman, an entrepreneur who has successfully turned more than one failing business into millions of dollars. One does not accomplish this sort of thing in the short span of 16 years, retiring at the age of 43, from having spent his professional career sitting in a board room. I'll make it easy for you. I'm no longer interested in Scottsdale Memorial Hospitals."

Doug was a gentleman, so he didn't press me on the issue that day. However, he hadn't given up on the idea. One week later, in hopes of opening up a dialogue, he invited me to sit down with both him and Jim Schamadan, CEO of Scottsdale Memorial Health

System. At that point, even though my temper had cooled, my cage had already been rattled. I meant what I said. I was no longer interested in serving on their board. Because I respected him, I didn't make a big deal of it. I did, however, assure Doug that I was not going to change my mind. Doug seemed surprised by my response, insisting that I at least hear them out. Out of respect, I agreed.

In that meeting, Mr. Schamadan reassured me that the majority of Scottsdale Memorial Health System's operational board was for me joining. He graciously asked that I reconsider my position. Not wanting to deal with yet another Harry Gallatin at that particular juncture in my career, or ever again for that matter, I politely declined. And with that I thanked them both for the opportunity, shook their hands, and parted ways. Mr. Schamadan understood and was a real gentleman. I could not have known that just a few years down the road the Scottsdale Hospital System would become a wonderful part of my life.

SIXTY-EIGHT

The Heard Museum

Celebrate your successes, but stay focused.

Meanwhile, I accepted Doug Williams and Tom Hudak's invitation to join the Heard Museum's board of trustees. It was 1994, and as in other areas of my life, I rolled up my sleeves and went straight to work. I served on a number of committees, as well as attended monthly board meetings. I had a lot to learn, but I was a quick study. I was motivated, and impressed by my fellow board members and the museum employees. Their enthusiasm, expertise, and commitment to the cause was contagious. I was primed, focused and determined to help and make a difference. I worked hard that first year. Mentally, I was as involved as I had been in my sports and business careers. It didn't matter that I wasn't personally profiting from this venture. I knew going in that there would be no compensation, no financial return on my investment. Except for the satisfaction I got from seeing good things happening

351

for the Heard, and the mental and emotional rush I got in the process, I was putting in my own time and money to serve in this capacity. It was my first stab at it, but philanthropy felt like the natural progression to my journey. I never wanted my retirement to get stale, especially not at such a young age.

For more than 86 years the museum has served the metropolitan Phoenix community, committing its every breath to the arts and culture of American Indians of the Southwest. With much thanks to the generosity of donors, volunteers, and staff members, this museum has made an incredible difference to the past, present, and future of the Phoenix community. From the moment Doug told me about it, I knew it was special. I knew it was something I wanted to be a part of.

The idea for the Heard Museum was inspired in 1895 by two people who had just moved to Phoenix. Dwight and Marie Bartlett Heard had much influence on the small township of about 4,000 people. In 1912, Heard purchased and published the *Arizona Republican*, a newspaper now known as the *Arizona Republic*. The Heards had a mutual interest in the Arizona Native American culture. Their collection of Indian art began with a Pima basket and grew into a world-renowned museum that was opened to the public on December 26, 1929 — mere months after Dwight Heard died of a heart attack. There was history in this project, something I could relate to.

During my first year as a trustee, I found the Heard Museum to be a very exciting opportunity. It had a great story behind it. The Heards began the museum out of their home. Over the years, additions were made to grow their collections, and years later, it was still growing. Fortunately, for me, after I arrived, there was a plan in place to add 70-percent more square footage, creating a campus feel for the museum. Being on the committee to help contribute ideas and raise the money needed was a lot of fun. The results were spectacular! Besides personally making a major donation, I was able to recruit nine other donors from the town of Carefree. All who donated, including me, have our names inscribed on a plaque next to the water feature that leads visitors to the front door. It was a great feeling to be involved. The little, old Heard Museum that began out of the Heard home grew into a much larger campus! It had the feeling of a small college. It was a real eye-catcher.

In 1995, the board discussed the possibility of expanding the museum's presence in the Phoenix area in the form of a satellite location. The dialogue got heated. Board President, Dan Albrecht, and a number of trustees, believed the expansion would be a big mistake, arguing that similar museums in the country, specifically in Chicago, had attempted this and failed. As the board debated, I could visualize it. I was confident that a satellite facility could be a tremendous success if planted in an affluent neighborhood like North Scottsdale or Carefree. Lou Menk, a fellow board member and Carefree resident, believed it, too. He and I discussed our options and decided that, together, we could raise the capital needed to rent a satellite facility 26 miles north of its sister museum. I knew that between Lou and I, we were resourceful enough to get it done.

After presenting our idea at the following board meeting, the project was voted on and approved, on the contingency that construction costs were covered. That's when the real work began! Wasting no time, Lou and I got down to business, splitting a short list of 10 potential donors in the Carefree area. We were motivated! In the short span of just four days, Lou and I acquired nearly all of the funds needed to build the satellite facility. I paid a visit to Herb Drinkwater, former mayor of Scottsdale. Within minutes, he made a significant donation. The balance of which was covered by Rusty Lyon, owner of Westcor and the Boulders Resort. He and his wonderful wife, Rosie, dedicated their donation in memory of their late son Roy Dennis Lyon. And with that, we were able to see the project through to its completion. It was quite an accomplishment!

We had a grand opening in 1995. The residents of North Scottsdale and Carefree loved the new satellite facility. It was called "Heard North." The celebration was beautifully organized by Patsy Stewart of the Heard and Marcia Berman, along with a committee of donors. The building was originally located at El Pedregal Festival Marketplace, but was moved 12 years later two miles to The Summit in Scottsdale in 2007. It included two exhibit galleries, a café, and a museum shop.

One year after the Heard North's opening, Dan Albrecht, stood up at a board meeting and personally apologized to me for having been against the idea. That was a very classy move and I told him so. In addition to Dan's apology, other trustees of the board demonstrated their support and leadership by attending important Heard North events. This meant a lot to me and to the museum, itself, which became profitable quickly.

♋

Wanting to raise more money, I continued to look for ways to "make it happen" where it mattered. Out of nowhere came an epiphany, a fundraising idea that could potentially attract big donors to the Heard Museum's cause — a golf tournament! Golf, is, after all, a wealthy man's sport. Over the years I participated in many golf tournaments. Golf is a big draw in the Phoenix and Scottsdale area. People visit from all over the world to golf and enjoy the weather.

One day while having lunch at the Phoenix Country Club, I shared my idea with Tom Hudak and Clint Magnussen. Both were golf enthusiasts, and both had similar thoughts that a golf tournament was a great fundraising idea. It didn't take us long to form a committee of go-getters, so to put this plan into action.

Denny Lyon, owner of Russ Lyon Realty, was on the Heard Museum board. He, along with Mike Messenger, who ran Russ Lyon Realty, agreed to sponsor the event that would become the Russ Lyon Realty Heard Golf Classic. Mike was especially instrumental in making it happen. The event was to be held at the Boulders, which at the time was a five-star resort.

In the 90s, the fee to participate in an Arizona golf

tournament was between $250- $500 per person. That was a lot of money, but in order for a charitable organization to cover expenses, as well as make a small margin of profit, something had to give. Any good businessman knows that in order to increase profit, you do one of two things: 1.) Increase participation or 2.) Increase the entry fee. It was an easy call. We went with option number two — increase the entry fee to $1,250 or $5,000 per foursome. The last thing you want to do is increase the number of participants on a limited playing field. Increasing participation would create a logjam on the golf course, thus creating disgruntled golfers. It was our goal to keep everyone happy, offering participants — individuals and corporations — a special experience. Displeased participants were *not* an option. And so with a fee increase, we were able to maintain a positive experience, as well as boost our annual net profit up to one hundred five thousand.

In its first 10 years the Golf Classic netted one million fifty thousand dollars. It's thanks to the committee! Close to 90-percent of the participants supported the Heard year-after-year at the Boulders Resort. I retired as chairman, and for the next six years, Chip Weil, CEO of the Arizona Republic newspaper, and Bill Nassikas, a hotel entrepreneur, served consecutively as chairman, and did a terrific job keeping the golf tournament alive at a first-class level. Considering the shrinking economy in 2008 onward, this was an incredible feat. In all, the committee did a great job! Everyone involved has a right to be proud of what was achieved.

In 2002, the Heard Museum nominated me for an award at the 18th Annual Philanthropic Leadership Awards Dinner that was held at the Camelback Inn in Scottsdale, Arizona. I'll never forget the letter Frank H. Goodyear, Jr., director of the Heard, wrote. "Your role in fundraising for the then Heard Museum North gallery and shop, and your own generosity to it, created a facility that has become of great importance to the Heard. It anchors us in a great community. And, your continuing leadership with our golf tournament, has made that event the envy of non-profits in the community—and earned the Heard Museum over $625,000. We are proud to honor you, Bob. You represent the best of what true philanthropy is."

Frank's letter meant a lot to me. So did a letter I received from Lonnie L. Ostrom, President of the Arizona State University Foundation. After I received the 2002 Spirit of Philanthropy Award that same year, he wrote: "Through your work with the Heard Museum, you serve as an inspiration to us all, proving again the power of a single determined individual and the increased strength when that individual provides leadership for the community. On behalf of the Arizona State University Foundation, I thank you for your dynamic leadership in our community and offer you our sincere congratulations on your well-deserved 2002 Spirit of Philanthropy Award. Your life models the adage that philanthropy makes a community strong, and we are all the most fortunate beneficiaries for your generosity."

SIXTY-NINE

Scottsdale Healthcare Foundation

Focus on doing good works and recognition will follow.

A few chapters back, I shared why I made the decision to just become a trustee of the Heard Museum, while choosing not to simultaneously join Scottsdale Memorial Health System's operational board. Well, that decision didn't last long! In 1998, three impressive people got my attention: John Ferree, President of the Scottsdale Healthcare Foundation, Michael Greenbaum, one of the founding trustees, and Laura Grafman, Executive Vice-President of the Foundation. Over time, all three had done a superb job in educating me on the significance of healthcare. All three became special friends. Their passion for healthcare sparked a flame, and I joined the Foundation board, which like Scottsdale Healthcare Shea Hospital, was also founded in 1984. I was motivated to help deliver the best possible healthcare to the Valley of the Sun.

In the early 80s, Scottsdale Memorial had only one hospital located on Osborn Road in downtown Scottsdale. The board had recently raised almost six million dollars to construct a second hospital just 25 minutes north — Scottsdale Memorial Shea. At that time, it was the largest fundraising campaign the Valley of the Sun had ever seen. Exceptional leaders were revealed in that particular project, including Herb Cummings, Mike Greenbaum, George Getz, Alec Gentleman, and the man who invited me into the local philanthropic world, Doug Williams. First Lady, Nancy Reagan, cut the ribbon at the dedication on January 3, 1984.

This was a big deal!

After just a few months serving as a trustee of the Scottsdale Healthcare Foundation, it was clear to me that I was going to enjoy being a part of this incredible organization. Scottsdale Healthcare and I had one very important thing in common. We both had the drive and the desire to "make it happen" where it counted! Whether constructing buildings, fighting disease, improving patient care, and/or technology, Scottsdale Healthcare was determined to tackle the obstacles, and lead the fight in advanced healthcare in the community.

Everyone involved had big ideas! From the administration to the Foundation, from the medical staff to the community, they all strived for nothing short of the best. We were a team of positive thinkers and dreamers who weren't afraid of hard work. That mindset and work ethic excited me. Just as I had discovered in sports and business, determination is what gets the job done. Every few months a new project was being planned for and launched. During my service, the Foundation was instrumental in helping to raise money for the ground-breaking robotic surgery technology known as daVinci by Intuitive Surgical. We also helped to fund a top-level trauma center at the Osborn Hospital campus, and one of my personal favorites, the Virginia G. Piper Cancer Center at the Shea Hospital campus.

The first time I heard about the Cancer Center, I thought to myself, "Wow! Cancer is a big deal, and a treatment center like this could be a game-changer!" Cancer, next to heart disease, is a meaningful part of the healthcare system. Therefore, I knew it was going to be spectacular! Construction began with an empty lot — a fresh canvas. While the center was adjoining the Scottsdale Hospital Shea, it was also designed to be its own entity. The center was the first of its kind in the Valley of the Sun, and everything that went into its development was first-rate. I believed in the project so much that I decided to contribute a significant donation. It was a great feeling to be a part of its legacy, not to mention to contribute to the specialized care offered to patients. The ribbon-cutting ceremony was in 2001. A few hundred donors and doctors were invited to the celebration.

In 2003, another great opportunity presented itself during a meeting with the executive committee at the Scottsdale Healthcare Foundation. One of the committee's functions was to select the leadership positions of the Board of Trustees. I always enjoyed being a part of the process of filling the key positions. In that meeting Michael Greenbaum opened up the discussion as to who he thought would be the right candidate for chairman of the Foundation's board. He immediately engaged a couple of trustees in the conversation, describing in detail the qualities of what that person might look like. He never mentioned a name. However, I had a sneaky suspicion he might be talking about me. I quickly dispelled that thought, as it was too far-fetched.

And then it happened.

The committee named me as the next chairman of the board. I was speechless! I had only been a trustee for five years. It honestly never occurred to me that I would even be a candidate for the position. Regardless, the position was offered to me. In a slight daze, I accepted, thanking them for their confidence in me. I was motivated to do my best as I drove home that afternoon.

It was a big job!

The position required that I also become an ex-officio member of the Operational Board. I was provided a thorough orientation by the System CEO, Max Poll, as well as the board's chairman Bob Johnson. I realized that serving both the Institution's Operational Board and the Foundation was going to take a lot of time and effort. However, I welcomed the challenge.

One of the first big projects that crossed my path as chairman was the construction of a third hospital, the Scottsdale Healthcare Thompson Peak Medical Center. This project was especially exciting because it was located near my home in

Carefree. Of the three hospitals, it was the furthest north, which was of great convenience to those of us living in the north valley. We held our planning meetings in a modular office building on the empty lot before we broke ground. Committees were formed by donors and residents in North Scottsdale who wanted to contribute both their ideas and donations. I am in awe to look at the hospital today. The inside looks more like a five-star resort than a medical facility. I contributed another significant donation to the project, and am proud to be a part of its legacy and success. All four of these significant achievements took a lot of time and energy. We, as a committee, learned more about the care and needs of people and our healthcare system than we ever thought we could. It was productive, fun, and high energy!

My last four years as chairman of the Foundation board was one of the most special experiences of my life. Interacting with the Scottsdale Healthcare administrators, staff, doctors, nurses, donors and trustees was an education unto itself. The people who fit all those categories were totally committed to helping their fellow human beings before, during and after they needed help as a patient. More often than I realized, patients are not able to pay for the necessary services and yet, because of the work we did, they received the same first-class service as those who could. Hence, those who could afford a larger medical expense would provide care equality for those who could not. Not only was it the law, but it was the right thing to do. In short, hospitals are not greedy, just concerned for their patients in need.

As chairman of the Foundation's board of trustees, I felt it was important for me to lead the Foundation board, represent the Foundation at the System level and in the community, and encourage and inspire the staff to be their best. At the board level, we were not only successful in raising money, which was, of course, our primary purpose, but we were also able to retain and recruit a number of outstanding men and women to the board who would go on to serve long after I retired as a trustee. As the Foundation's representative on the System's board of director's, I felt a strong commitment to attend all 11 meetings each year during my five-year tenure and any other event to which I was invited to as an ex-officio member of the board. Just as I had done in business, I made it my top priority to get to know every staff member of the Foundation by name and to greet each one warmly whenever I visited the Foundation offices. I made myself part of the Foundation family and I still maintain those close relationships to this day. I strongly believe what John Ferree recently told me, which is that "fundraising is a team sport."

In February of 2007, after nine years serving as a trustee for the Scottsdale Healthcare Foundation, I retired from the wonderful world of philanthropy. It was time. I wanted to focus on the balance of my life, really breathe in the days ahead, and play more golf again.

Just before my official retirement date, I was invited to a party, an occasion I believed was meant to celebrate the great effort our staff had poured into the Foundation. I was only too happy to acknowledge their accomplishments. I had no idea what was really going on. Bella wasn't feeling well. She stayed home that night, and so I went alone. The party kicked off with cocktails, and then a sit-down dinner. It was lovely. I will never forget when John Ferree, President of the Foundation, took to the stage to do the honor of addressing the room. After which he asked the entire staff to join him on stage. Everyone but the spouses and I stood up and assembled in rows, facing the thinned out audience.

I was still clueless.

John looked directly at me. Singling me out, he thanked me for my time with the Foundation. As soon as he finished speaking, the entire staff broke into song. It was an amazing rendition of *Thanks for the Memories*, only the words were changed to personalize my service. When I realized I was the man of the hour, and the song they were singing was written with me in mind, I had a tough time holding back tears. Everyone there was special to me.

I received a letter from Jan Miller, Vice-President of Major Gifts with Scottsdale Healthcare Foundation, following the celebration. She wrote: "Thank you for the 'excellence' you have tirelessly given to Scottsdale Healthcare Foundation for the past four years as its Chairman and leader and for your previous six years as a trustee. You have given tirelessly of your time, leadership, community influence and advocacy for this organization. For this, we are extremely grateful. You have continually set an example for others to follow with your philanthropy ... You are passionate about this organization and you show it with your hard work and philanthropy! Always a smile and a high level of motivation — you have lead our board and the foundation staff to great success!"

In 2008, the Scottsdale Healthcare Foundation nominated me for an award at the 24th Annual Philanthropy Leadership Awards Dinner. It was to be held at the Arizona Biltmore Resort and Spa. John Ferree wrote me a letter, acknowledging the nomination. "All of us are very much looking forward to honoring you with the Scottsdale Healthcare Foundation 'Spirit of Philanthropy' award at the Association of Fundraising (AFP) Awards Dinner on Wednesday, November 12, 2008."

The nine years I spent with the Foundation, working with those wonderful people, were some of the best times of my life! The last four years as chairman, in particular, led to some of the best friendships I've ever known. I suppose that's why I kept in touch with the Foundation. These were quality people, so when they asked for my help, I considered it a privilege to serve. For example, on August 13, 2009, Bella and I invited 94 donors and potential donors to our summer home at Forest Highlands in Flagstaff, Arizona. We catered the event, serving cocktails and a first class sit-down dinner. Tom Sadvary, President and CEO of Scottsdale Healthcare, and a terrific leader, was our keynote speaker. He spoke about the overhaul of our nation's healthcare system. The night was a huge success!

My good friend, Executive Vice President of the Scottsdale Healthcare Foundation and board member of the Virginia G. Piper

Foundation, Laura Grafman, wrote to me later that week, affirming that the "evening was perfect," and that "everything about the evening was impressive." Even though I was technically retired, the feeling I got from helping the Foundation was rewarding.

US Senator John Kyl, who was a hard act to follow.

Right before I was to be introduced, the band opened the ceremony with a beautiful rendition of God Bless America. That was just the inspiration I needed. It took me back to my days in the NBA, a young man standing on the court as the National Anthem played. So, just as I had done all those years ago, I took a deep breath, and I said to myself, "Go get em!"

I was prepared. I had rehearsed my speech for days. My daughters found it funny because every time they'd turn around, whether I was in the kitchen making a sandwich, in the living room, or in the shower, I was rehearsing my speech. I had rehearsed it many times, but now it was game time! The whistle was about to blow, and just like on the basketball court, or in the boardroom or on a Detroit street corner in front of the General Motors building, I felt a sudden sense of calm.

John Ferree, a gifted speaker, introduced me, and as I stepped up to the podium, I was as relaxed as I had ever been. I won't ever forget that feeling, as I confidently gazed out into the audience, unable to see anything but the bright stage lights shining in my eyes. That moment, as I stood before family, friends, donors, doctors and nurses, was my happy ending in the world of philanthropy. After all, giving was the most satisfying thing I had ever been involved in. It was the first time in my life that I wasn't actually focused on achieving, and yet it became my greatest achievement.

It was a stunning evening! Nancy Hilton-Harris, who led

the Honor Ball committee, created a beautiful ambiance with her immense talent. After I finished my keynote address, Nancy looked at me and said with a big smile on her face, "Slam dunk!" I will never forget that. This was, indeed, the kid from Katonah's biggest moment!

Bob Duffy with his beautiful daughters, Julie and Kim,
at the 2013 Honor Ball.
(© Brad Reed)

EPILOGUE

Final Thoughts

You can make it happen where it counts!

Sports, business, and philanthropy — the three major careers in my life, combined into a form of education. Each platform prepared me for the next level, taking my dreams beyond my wildest imagination. My experience in the NBA provided me with an intense amount of motivation to achieve in a highly competitive environment. It also handed me some hard life lessons. Those lessons only cemented my determination, as I moved into my business career. My experience in business confirmed that I could not only succeed, but that I had the stomach to compete at a higher level, gaining financial independence at a young age. And, finally, my philanthropic experience, above all things, demonstrated to me that helping others via time, energy and financial contribution gave me a wonderful sense of satisfaction. The appreciation I have received from the charitable organizations

I was involved with is genuine, constant, and a true gift. I highly recommend to you, my reader, to join a cause. You will always get back more than you give. That, in and of itself, is its own reward.

Upon completion of this book, I am better able to wrap my arms around all that I have achieved in my life. There are days when it is still hard to believe. I spent many days, weeks, and months invested in the telling of my story. It took three-and-a-half years in total. Whether it was writing or editing or rewriting, the process was both challenging and rewarding. Now that it's done, I feel a great sense of pride, relief, and satisfaction. The catharsis I mentioned in the prologue manifested itself time and time again throughout the writing process. As I revisited old letters, photos, and news clippings organized in several of my scrapbooks that my mother, Marian, and my wife, Bella, put together for me, I was reminded of memories long forgotten.

It is my intention that all of the hard work that went into the telling of my story will serve you, the reader, as a starting place for achievement in your own life. It is possible to achieve what others consider impossible! I want you to know that. And while only you can determine the value of this book, and the message it reveals, we appreciate you picking it up and giving us the opportunity to share my own personal roadmap to success.

I would like to recognize the wonderful contributions of my co-author Natalie June Reilly. I wrote my story by hand on a ton of yellow legal notepads. Natalie would decipher my handwriting, bringing my words to life with her capacity for story-telling and the technology of the 21st Century. Not only is Natalie talented, but she is patient. She worked side-by-side with me every step of the way. She was always supportive of our mission, no matter the obstacles. Together we were a productive team!

Finally, I'd like to reemphasize the key ingredients that I believe will help you make your dreams a reality, lessons I learned along the way that helped me to control my own destiny.

Focus on your dream

Resist negativity

Think big

Be positive

Envision Success

Understand reality

Expect obstacles

Overcome setbacks

Enjoy the moment

Stay motivated

Take calculated risks

Believe and achieve

Do these things ... and you, too, can "make it happen!"

Bibliography

Archibald, J. J. (1962, November 19). More Play for Duffy Hawks Trade Mantis. *St. Louis Post-Dispatch* .

Archibald, J. J. (1963). Wilkens Injured In Pileup. *St. Louis Post-Dispatch* .

The Basketball Yearbook. (1962). Bob Cousy's All-America Preview. *The Basketball Yearbook* .

Best College Reviews. *Best College Reviews*. n.d. 27 April 2016.

Broadcasting Magazine. (1987, March 30). Riding Gain on Radio. *Broadcasting Magazine* .

Burnes, B. (1962, October 14). Can the Hawks Bounce Back? *Globe-Democrat* .

Burnes, R. L. (1962). The Bench Warmer. *St. Louis Post-Dispatch* .

Christian, B. (1991, January 12). Arbitron report shows KEZ climbing quickly. *Tribune Newspapers* .

The Colgate Maroon. (1967, January 19). Decision on University Athletic Policy Due; Duffy Scores Lack of Basketball Scholarships. *The Colgate Maroon* .

Colliano, J. D. (1985, March 18). Up-To-The-Minute Weekly Management News for Radio Executives. *Inside Radio* .

Colliano, J. D. (1986, September 29). The Latest News, Trends and Management Information. *Inside Radio* .

BIBLIOGRAPHY

Cousy, B., & Hirshberg, A. (1963). *Basketball is My Life*. J. Lowell Pratt & Company; Revised edition.

Daniels, L. A. (1992, May 8). *Albert Parry, Russian Expert, 92; Predicted Sputnik 1 Launching*. Retrieved August 17, 2016, from **http://www.nytimes.com/1992/05/08/nyregion/albert-parry-russia-expert-92-predicted-sputnik-1-launching.html**

Dell Sports Magazine: Basketball. (1962, February). Cousy Rates the Rookies. *Dell Sports Magazine: Basketball* .

Glasser, S. (1962, March 28). Duffy 2nd Draft Choice of St. Louis. *The Colgate Maroon* .

Goldpaper, S. (1983, May 21). *Clair Bee, Ex-L.I.U. Coach, Dies; Gained Basketball Hall of Fame*. Retrieved June 17, 2015, from The New York Times: **http://www.nytimes.com/1983/05/21/obituaries/clair-bee-ex-liu-coach-dies-gained-basketball-hall-of-fame.html**

Goldstein, J. (2003, November 19). *Explosion: 1951 scandals threaten college hoops*. Retrieved June 17, 2015, from ESPN Classic: **http://espn.go.com/classic/s/basketball_scandals_explosion.html**

Hirshberg, Al. (1961, January 1). *Basketball is my life*. Prentice-Hall.

Harrod, J. (1965, April 28). Crossroads. *Colgate Maroon* .

Marecek, G. (2006). *Full Court: The Untold Stories of the St. Louis Hawks*. St. Louis: Reedy Press, LLC.

The New York Times. (1962, February 8). Sherard Paces Army to 70-63 Victory Over Colgate. *The New York Times*.

BIBLIOGRAPHY

http://www.nfl.com/news/story/09000d5d80b75df1/article/ernie-davis-legacy-lives-on-long-after-his-death

Oatway, B. (1955). Looking at Sports.

Office of Communications, Institutional Advancement. (2013, December 15). *History in the Making: Lapchick Statue Coming to Campus*. Retrieved May 26, 2015, from St. John's University: http://www.stjohns.edu/about/news/2013-12-15/history-making-lapchick-statue-coming-campus

Orange Hoops. (n.d.). *#24 Ernie Davis*. Retrieved October 29, 2015, from Orange Hoops: **http://www.orangehoops.org/edavis.htm**

Patent Trader. (1959, June 14). Bob Duffy On Dean's List Varsity Cager Next Season. *Patent Trader* .

Patent Trader. (1960, January 7). Duffy Sets Records in Downeast Event. *Patent Trader* .

Patent Trader. (1962, October 4). Duffy Joins All-Stars For Game With Knicks. *Patent Trader* .

Platt, B. (2013, June 17). *Forty Years On: The Changing Face of Dartmouth*. Retrieved October 29, 2015, from Dartmouth Now: **http://now.dartmouth.edu/2013/06/forty-years-changing-face-dartmouth**

Powers, J. (1952). The Powerhouse. *The Daily News* .

Radio News. (1987, April 6). Duffy Broadcasting for Sale. *Radio News* .

Reynolds, Bill. (2006, February) *Cousy: His Life, Career, and the Birth of Big Time Basketball.* Pocket Star Books.

BIBLIOGRAPHY

Rochester Democrat and Chronicle. (1961, January 11). Colgate Five

Sports Illustrated. (1962, February 26). Faces in the Crowd. *Sports Illustrated* .

Syracuse Hall of Fame. (n.d.). *Jim Boeheim.* Retrieved December 1, 2014

Teitel, J. (2014, March 5). *He put the "Bee" in Basketball: CHD remembers Hall of Fame Coach Clair Bee.* Retrieved June 17, 2015, from College Hoops Daily: http://www.collegehoopsdaily.com/put-bee-basketball-chd-remembers-hall-fame-coach-clair-bee/

Tests UR Here Tonight. *Rochester Democrat and Chronicle* .

Watkins, M. (2002). *Dancing with Strangers.* New York: Simon & Schuster.

Wyche, S. (2008, October 8). NFL.com. Retrieved January 5, 2016, from Ernie Davis' legacy lives on long after his death

ABOUT THE CO-AUTHOR

Natalie June Reilly has a Bachelor of Arts degree in Communication. She is the author of *My Stick Family: Helping Children Cope with Divorce* and *Pax the Polar Bear: Breaking the Ice*. Natalie is a prolific writer whose work has most notably appeared in *The Arizona Republic*, *Chicken Soup for the Soul*, and *Raising Arizona's Kids*. She also founded Nothing but Love Notes in 2016, the first community-based organization to inspire handwritten love notes expressing gratitude for the everyday hero, veterans and first-responders who bravely serve their country and community. She has since been recognized for her efforts with a letter of commendation from the State of Arizona, signed by Governor Doug Ducey. Natalie was also given Special Citizen Recognition/Peoria Star Award by Peoria Mayor Cathy Carlat. You can reach Natalie at girlwriter68@hotmail.com.

Made in the USA
San Bernardino, CA
17 August 2017